Beyond Human

BUCKNELL STUDIES IN LATIN AMERICAN LITERATURE AND THEORY

Series editor: Aníbal González, Yale University

Dealing with far-reaching questions of history and modernity, language and selfhood, and power and ethics, Latin American literature sheds light on the many-faceted nature of Latin American life, as well as on the human condition as a whole. This highly successful series has published some of the best recent criticism on Latin American literature. Acknowledging the historical links and cultural affinities between Latin American and Iberian literatures, the series productively combines scholarship with theory and welcomes consideration of Spanish and Portuguese texts and topics, while also providing a space of convergence for scholars working in Romance studies, comparative literature, cultural studies, and literary theory.

Selected Titles in the Series

Rebecca E. Biron, *Elena Garro and Mexico's Modern Dreams*
Persephone Brahman, *From Amazons to Zombies: Monsters in Latin America*
Jason Cortés, *Macho Ethics: Masculinity and Self-Representation in Latino-Caribbean Narrative*
Tara Daly, *Beyond Human: Vital Materialisms in the Andean Avant-Gardes*
Earl E. Fitz, *Machado de Assis and Female Characterization: The Novels*
Thomas S. Harrington, *Public Intellectuals and Nation Building in the Iberian Peninsula, 1900-1925: The Alchemy of Identity*
David Kelman, *Counterfeit Politics: Secret Plots and Conspiracy Narratives in the Americas*
Brendan Lanctot, *Beyond Civilization and Barbarism: Culture and Politics in Postrevolutionary Argentina*
Adriana Méndez Rodenas, *Transatlantic Travels in Nineteenth-Century Latin America: European Women Pilgrims*
Andrew R. Reynolds, *The Spanish American Crónica Modernista, Temporality, and Material Culture*
Elisa Sampson Vera Tudela, *Ricardo Palma's Tradiciones: Illuminating Gender and Nation*
Mary Beth Tierney-Tello, *Mining Memory: Reimagining Self and Nation through Narratives of Childhood in Peru*

Beyond Human

Vital Materialisms in the Andean Avant-Gardes

TARA DALY

Bucknell University | Bucknell University Press

Lewisburg, Pennsylvania

Library of Congress Cataloging-in-Publication Data

Names: Daly, Tara, author.
Title: Beyond human : vital materialisms in the Andean avant-gardes / Tara Daly.
Description: Lewisburg : Bucknell University Press, [2019] | Series: Bucknell Studies in Latin American Literature and Theory | Includes bibliographical references and index.
Identifiers: LCCN 2018029490 | ISBN 9781684480685 (cloth) | ISBN 9781684480678 (paperback)
Subjects: LCSH: Literature, Experimental—Latin America—History and criticism. | Avant-garde (Aesthetics)—Latin America. | Materialism in literature.
Classification: LCC PQ7082.E97 D35 2019 | DDC 860.9/11—dc23
LC record available at https://lccn.loc.gov/2018029490

A British Cataloging-in-Publication record for this book is available from the British Library.

∞ The paper used in this publication meets the requirements of the American National Standard for Information Sciences—Permanence of Paper for Printed Library Materials, ANSI Z39.48-1992.

www.bucknell.edu/UniversityPress

Distributed worldwide by Rutgers University Press

Manufactured in the United States of America

To Laura and Jasper

Contents

Illustrations

A Note on Translations

Unless otherwise noted, translations are mine.

Beyond Human

Introduction

Revitalizing the Andean Avant-Gardes

Ernesto, the critically beloved, nearing-adolescence narrator of José María Arguedas's novel *Los ríos profundos* (*Deep Rivers*) (1958), runs his hands over the cool Incan walls that line the shadowed alleys off the Plaza de Armas in Cuzco, Peru: "El muro parecía vivo, sobre la palma de mis manos llameaba la juntura de las piedras que había tocado"[1] (The wall seemed to be alive, the joints of the stones I touched flamed in the palms of my hands).[2] Arguedas's juxtaposition of hands with stone, and his description of the fiery friction between them, provides a literary glimpse at the ways in which life is a material experience: Ernesto's hands and the stone seem to reciprocally animate each other. Arguedas emphasizes material relationality throughout his fictional corpus to make sensible, and critique, the Western tendency to consider Incan walls as "dead rock" in the hands of the living human. Later in the novel, these same rocks will seemingly speak to Ernesto, imparting memories to him that the Andean landscape holds.[3] At the base of Arguedas's novel is a multifaceted material analysis that challenges Western humanism's subject–object dualism. Arguedas disorients readers in rendering the stone alive, challenging the assumption that inert matter is inferior to the living. His literature, instead, departs from relationality among materials as its starting point and partially anticipates what is known as new materialist thinking.[4]

I focus this book on twentieth- and twenty-first-century Andean avant-garde art in Peru and Bolivia to make two central arguments. The first is that a subset of authors, visual artists, and performance activists in the Andes cultivate a life philosophy of vital materialism. By "vital materialism," I refer to the idea that animate and inanimate materials have the power to affect human life, not just the reverse. This idea manifests itself in the ways the artists of this book challenge dualisms, whether it be through blurring the parameters of the object of art and their own bodies, or their challenges to binary relationships between nature and culture or subject and object. They insert their own physical bodies directly into their creative productions, lending lifelike characteristics to the objects. Through their inventive language and forms, the artists of this project animate "life" as an affective relationship between the human body, which includes the mind, and other materials. Vital materialism is a feature of the avant-gardes of the 1920s and 1930s but continues beyond it, reemerging in the 1960s and today. By showcasing this vital materialist element, I argue that there is a consistent avant-garde orientation to life in the Andes that manifests itself as the desire to shift relationships between materials, beyond the human.

The second argument this book makes is implicit in the first: the plural concept of the "avant-gardes" in the Andes is not fixed but dynamic; it is not dead but thriving in a range of new forms.[5] It is not an institution, nor a "type" of art, but an orientation in the material world.[6] In interpreting the avant-gardes through the theoretical lens of orientation, I emphasize that art that aims to be socially transformative is contingent on the orientation of bodies among the materials of their environment. Avant-garde artists approach materials as entities to be transformed, but in the process unearth the impact the material world has directly on them, and of which they are already a part.[7] In order to make an alternative orientation in the world to that of capitalism or communism, they make sensible plural ways of being within Andean worlds, and beyond the geographic parameters of the same. They ultimately create projects that evade the capitalist desire to institute and commodify art, and the communist desire to conflate it with life-as-labor. The hierarchical relationships between labor, bodies, and values within capitalism, and captured in the absolute coincidence of the three within communism, produce risks to vital lives. Individuals, the state, institutions, global economic models, and, increasingly, unstable ecosystems, undermine the sustainability of life. But material resistance to the same prevails in nuanced ways that avant-garde art, as a moving assemblage of the past, present, and future, makes sensible.

There have been two recent trends in the humanities to which this project contributes. First, as a result of antiglobal capitalist movements and ongoing critiques of neoliberalism, there is a growing new materialist turn in multiple disciplines that builds on but revises Marxist-based materialist histories. Vital materialism fits within new materialist studies in its aim to break through the impasse of dualism, or thinking through "difference." Its desire, instead, is to think from the perspective of incremental *differings* among materials, not the binary *differences* between two (impossibly) discrete organisms or things.[8]

Second, due to challenges to global capitalist models, there has been renewed inquiry into the umbrella term "avant-garde," what exactly constitutes it, and if the movement is (or movements are) alive or "dead." This analysis is particularly relevant given the pink tide and the renewed leftist tendencies it has brought to the fore in Latin America over the last decade.[9] The first body of scholarship is relatively new territory to tread, and the second requires approaching established critical territory from a reoriented position. This book aims to bring these two lines of inquiry together in the context of the Andes, with a view to what the region's plurality of cultures and cosmovisions lends to contemporary discussions on new materialist modes of thinking as they unfold in the twenty-first century.

The two complementary lines of argument the book undertakes move us beyond established critical readings of the avant-gardes in the Andes as first, humanizing and as second, historical to show that they transcend those categories in their appeal to vitality: they lay bare the animacy of a range of materials, within and beyond the discursive category of "human." Ultimately, they are oriented toward a horizon line that recognizes the human, in its various forms, as only one species among many in the process of becoming with and within the broader material surroundings of its ecosystems.[10]

Orienting the Andes

The Andes is a terrain of physical extremes, named for the longest continental mountain corridor in the world, that stretches from the southern tip of Colombia to northern Argentina. On the most basic level, the term refers to this geographic land form.[11] "The Andes" has also, however, been used as shorthand in the twentieth century for the central countries of the region—Ecuador, Peru, and Bolivia—to capture what is culturally common to them, based on their pre-Columbian past. The attribute that these three countries share, to greater and lesser degrees, is their significant indigenous populations. Sixty-two percent of Bolivia self-identifies as indigenous, whereas in Peru 13 percent of the nation is indigenous, and in Ecuador, 7 percent of the population self-identifies as indigenous.[12] The highland Quechua and Aymara of the Andes as well as the myriad Amazonian indigenous groups of these three central Andean countries have maintained their original languages and practices since the colonial era. At the same time, none of these cultures is frozen in time, all being highly adaptive and increasingly urban.[13]

The Andean nations of Peru and Bolivia, the focus of the book, share unique external colonial histories and internal neocolonial realities, in part because of these significant indigenous populations. In the case of both countries, the indigenous populations and the region have been historically Orientalized, or perceived as other, both from within the nation and from without.[14] Late nineteenth- and early twentieth-century Orientalizing discourses tended to paint the indigenous "problem" in the Andes as one impeding its arrival to "modernity." For instance, Bolivian Alcides Arguedas's essay "Pueblo enfermo" (A sick people) (1909) presents a bleak view of the indigenous population that interprets their peonage and the harsh living conditions of the altiplano (high plateau) as causes of their alcoholism and degeneracy. Arguedas poses pedagogy, and specifically literacy, as the key to the health of the nascent Bolivian nation at the turn of the twentieth century.[15] In Peru, novels like Clorinda Matto de Turner's *Aves sin nido* (1889) presented a romantic portrayal of the indigenous cultures that became known as an example of *indigenismo,* a discourse that held indigenous persons as figures whose beneficent souls could be saved from their race via education and marriage to the *criollo* (Creole) ruling class. The discourses of indigenismo in the region, which vacillated from conceiving of the indigenous populations as either folkloric and antiquated, or "backward" and in need of cultural rehabilitation, took shape as arguably *the* defining discourse of the first half of the twentieth century.[16] Because the indigenous populations of Peru and Bolivia were framed by the literate *criollo* class as a problem to "be resolved," from colonial times until today, they have understandably been a dominant component of the definition of the Andean region. This said, multiple other orientations that form part of the cultural landscape of the Andes and that intersect, complement, and diverge from *indigenista* discourses have remained less emphasized—feminist, queer, and, more recently, urban indigenous peoples as they represent themselves—within studies of the region. Gradually over the second half of the twentieth century and the beginning of the twenty-first, these diverse groups have increasingly participated in critiques of racism, capitalism, patriarchy, and exploitative environmental practices, pointing to potential partial alliances between indigenous and nonindigenous peoples. In a nutshell, the rich cultural and geographic diversity makes the Andes a particularly compelling contributor to more global conversations occurring on new materialisms and the environment.

Indigenous peoples have recently stepped more visibly into the fore of national imaginaries, particularly in the cases of Bolivia and Ecuador, as part of the "pink tide" in the Andes region.[17] The "pink tide" refers to a diverse range of political practices that Eduardo Gudynas has referred to under the umbrella term "Los progresismos" (Progressivisms), and that began with the election of Hugo Chávez in Venezuela in 1998 (Chávez assumed the government in 1999). The pink tide reached its apogee around 2010, and is labeled "pink," as opposed to Marxism's "red," due to the socialist tendencies within these governments. As part of the pink tide, citizen sectors that had been historically marginalized became protagonists of recent presidential elections.[18] As part of these diverse movements, in the Andean region, on September 28, 2008, and January 25, 2009, respectively, Ecuador and Bolivia incorporated the rights of nature into their newly written constitutions based on the indigenous philosophy of *buen vivir* (good living), or *sumak kawsay* (living well) in Quechua.[19] These concepts as well as *plurinacionalidad* (plurinationality), partially originate in indigenous systems of thought.[20] The concept of plurality "finds its present political sense in the Andean countries based on the political growth and visibility of the organizations and peoples of the low-lying regions and the Amazon and the consequent pluriethnic image of the societies in question."[21] By proposing the term "plurinational" or "pluriethnic," indigenous peoples assert that they are living "modernity" in their own ways, and specifically, with their own orientation toward nature, social development, and governance.

The concept of *buen vivir* builds on the idea that the state control more resources and their subsequent distribution, and approaches development from a more socialist-oriented perspective, instead of the neoliberal model of global imperial "resources" of the North, or elsewhere, as the solution to the underdevelopment of the South. While the ideas behind *buen vivir* come from indigenous groups, I agree with Gudynas and Oliver Balch that "*buen vivir* owes as much to political philosophy as it does to indigenous worldviews. It is equally influenced by western critiques [of capitalism] over the last 30 years, especially from the field of feminist thought and environmentalism," and doesn't require "a return to some sort of indigenous, pre-Colombian past."[22] As an alternative to capitalism's *vivir mejor* (living better), which is based on the premise that the economy is the driving factor of development, *buen vivir* describes a way of life and a form of development that emphasizes social, cultural, environmental, and economic issues as working together and in balance, not separately and hierarchically. In the context of Peru, while the constitution does not invoke nature as actively as the cases of Bolivia and Ecuador, Marisol de la Cadena's work on cosmopolitics in and around the Cuzco region has elaborated the innovative ways in which indigenous groups incorporate nonhuman "subjects" into the political realm in ways that interrupt anthropocentric humanism.[23] These nonhuman actors are even portrayed in the Constitutions of Bolivia and Ecuador, where Pachamama, or Mother Earth, is afforded rights.[24] The incursion of Nature-as-subject into the Constitution is an indication of the plurality of belief systems within these countries and partially overlaps with new materialist arguments that see nature and culture as "always already 'naturecultures'" that are impossible to separate.[25]

I present this brief background on the changes that part of the Andes has been undergoing in recent years to situate the plural approach I take to leftist aesthetic projects in Bolivia and Peru in this book. A plurality of orientations before the material space of the Andes forms the avant-garde assemblage

I present. I draw on the present to look to the past, as well as to situate the past in relationship to the present. The Andean artists of this project are partially influenced by indigenous cultures and partially by other factors that contribute to what makes up the Andes, in its geographic, cultural, migratory, linguistic, and nuanced complexities. For instance, the bilingual José María Arguedas was informed by a Quechua cosmovision due to his deep investment in all aspects of the language and the culture, as writer, ethnographer, and Spanish and Quechua-speaker.[26] Julieta Paredes, of Aymara ancestry, works frequently with Aymara and Quechua indigenous peoples in and around La Paz and draws on Aymara terms and concepts in her work (as well as critiques them). And Alejandra Dorado, who grew up in Cochabamba (where an estimated 50 percent of the population speaks Quechua) knows some Quechua and has an intimate knowledge of community practices. Magda Portal, of the working, middle-class in Lima, was partially influenced by the Puno avant-gardes, and César Vallejo was ironically described by José Carlos Mariátegui to most authentically reflect an indigenous sensibility. While someone like Portal in Lima speaks from a different social position than Paredes of La Paz, they are partially oriented toward a common goal relative to their time and space: material transformation of society in the name of a more sustainable and just environment.

I pose plurality as my approach to the Andean avant-gardes because, unlike discourses of transculturation, hybridity, or heterogeneity, plurality is not based on twoness, nor a biological model of "mixing" genes, but rather an acceptance of coexistent differings within categories of indigenous or nonindigenous, mestizo, criollo, or otherwise. Plurality in the Andes reflects the myriad ways that subjects orient themselves before the material world and, in turn, the ways that materials orient them. In Peru and Bolivia, diverse subjects orient themselves before modernity in ways that extend beyond the difference between indigenous and nonindigenous and instead encapsulate much broader incremental differings among subjects. For instance, the feminist activist group Mujeres Creando Comunidad eschews "Western" or "North American" feminism, but is also not composed only of indigenous women, nor does it operate strictly on indigenous principles of complementarity, which members of the community openly criticize. Likewise, Vallejo, while considered by Mariátegui to capture the authentic indigenous experience through lyric form, was not indigenous, but also not "Western." His work stretches from the radically unclassifiable *Trilce*, to his committed Marxist phase, to his global solidarity with antifascist movements, particularly in 1930s Spain. His work started in Peru but is concerned with social justice issues that supersede geography. In fact, in all the chapters, the artists from the Andes inhabit multiple imagined and real spaces and temporalities: the cosmological, the global, the regional, and the local. In other words, the Andes is plural, and there are plural orientations (bodies in relationship to shared common objects or objectives) from which a politics concerned for the life of the ecosystem emerges.

In what follows, I revisit the Andean avant-gardes of the 1920s, the 1960s, and today as partially in alliance with some of the "new" political orientations of the pink tide era, particularly because they take the material relationality of life as their starting point. In the Quechua cosmovision, time is not conceived as linear as it is in the Occident, but as a spiral structure in which one can go forward or backward. Likewise, in Aymara and Quechua, the future is conceptualized as that which one cannot see because it comes from spatially behind the relative present. Josef Estermann has written in *Filosofía andina: Estudio intercultural de la sabiduría autóctona andina* (Andean philosophy: Intercultural study of autochthonous Andean knowledge)—*Pacha* is the word for time *and* space in Quechua—that the new as something absolutely unknown does not exist in Andean thinking because of the coexistence of times and spaces. As he explains, "El 'tiempo' es como la respiración, el latido cardíaco, el ir y venir de las mareas, el cambio de día y de noche. El 'tiempo' es relacionalidad cosmica, co-presente con el 'espacio,' o simplemente otra manifestación de *pacha*"[27] (Time for the Quechua is like breathing, the heartbeat, the coming and going of the tides, the change between day and night. Time is cosmic relationality, co-present with space, or simply another manifestation of space). The most important temporal modifiers, therefore, are not "ahead" or "behind," nor past and future, but "before" and "after" because they start from relationality as the principle, not duality. This approach to temporality informs my project alongside linear time due to the multiple knowledge systems that shape and influence "the Andes."

In this book, I look at the ways that the Andean avant-gardes move outward to inform the globe about vital materiality and plurality, not (only) the reverse. The vanguard interventions I undertake are plural in their orientations in the region: coming from diverse bodies but that care about and for the space that is the Andes, both as a geographic location and an imagined community. While each of the chapters presents authors born in the Andes, and whose works are informed by local conditions, the intent of their works also moves well beyond only regional concerns. Andean points of view, whether they originate in indigenous "cosmovisions," the early twentieth-century thinking of *indigenista* intellectuals, in queer movements in urban capitals today, or as they travel to other places, contain and display an interest in the material specificities within which the inhabitants of the region orient themselves and are orientated in the world. This orientation can travel to other regions, enabling others to learn from and with Andean artists.[28] The artists of the project demonstrate that partial alliances can make sensible the potential overlaps in plural points of view that could form future assemblages that work toward material changes within and with a network of overlapping ecosystems.

Revisiting the Avant-Gardes

Why revisit the avant-gardes? The avant-garde movements in Latin America, in dialogue with those of Europe, have most frequently been researched in a historical frame that focuses on the decades of the 1920s and 1930s. That body of research looks at the ways that art and politics became linked during the revolutionary socialist period in Europe and the Americas in the early twentieth century. After what seemed like the failure of communism as a universal project by midcentury, many considered *the* avant-garde as a political and artistic project as dead. This assumption was based on an interpretation of the avant-garde as a set of political and artistic practices whose success would necessarily end, at least in theory, in an international-scale revolution—one that authors like Vallejo and Portal wrote on behalf of at various points in their careers. Instead of considering avant-garde art as a linear project that was unable to meet its utopic end, I argue that it emerges and retreats as part of the spiral nature of incremental social changes that navigate between the local and the cosmos, in various geographic settings. The avant-garde is ongoing because "life" is excessive to the human's ability to ever fully represent it, causing a perpetual need for new orientations toward "life forms to come," as I develop following here.[29]

Critics have interpreted the avant-gardes in both Europe and Latin America as a diverse set of artistic and political movements that emerged in the aftermath of World War I. Concerned with all things "new," the avant-gardes consisted of innovative and ground-breaking artistic experiments aimed at dismantling the separation between art and "daily life." As a response to the devastation after World War I, as well as the rise of technology and machines at the turn of the century, artists began to radically question the role of art in an increasingly industrialized and capitalist-driven society that seemed to be careening toward self-destruction. Reflecting on these projects of the interwar period, Peter Bürger framed the avant-gardes as a comprehensive "art into life" program, sparked in reaction to the perceived autonomy and elitism of art that preceded the war in Europe. He traced what he perceived as the alienation between life-as-labor and the "world of art," the latter as it was represented through exclusive institutions to which only certain subjects had access. Writing in retrospect, however, Bürger declared the "failure" of the avant-garde because avant-garde art eventually became institutionalized, thereby reproducing the exact same gap it proposed to close. As he writes, "the failure of the avant-garde utopia of the unification of art and life coincides with the avant-garde's overwhelming success within the art institution."[30] The institutional success of art was evidence of a commodification process that reaffirmed capitalism's extractive power over materiality and squelched alternatives to the same.

However, the assumption upon which Bürger's definition of "failure" rests is that art could actually "coincide" with life. However, in my revisionist interpretation of the avant-garde, "failure" is inevitable because the absolute coincidence between art and life is impossible. "Life" as material exchange and not just labor and "life" as something immanent to the material world are always happening beyond the reach of the representation of the same in art. Therefore, the "failure for unification" that Bürger signals is the central paradox underlying the avant-garde art projects, but simultaneously, that which perpetuates their existence as ongoing challenges to one-size-fits-all models of capitalism *and* to communism. The rift between life as it is represented in art and "life itself" perpetuates the possibility of avant-garde orientations: ongoing agitations to dominant but, as Jacques Rancière argues, incomplete, forms of organizing life.[31]

A substantial amount of research on the historical discussion of the avant-gardes in Latin America and Europe has departed from the human as the center around which the movements take shape. José Ortega y Gasset's interpretation of the avant-garde in his essay "La deshumanización del arte," (The dehumanization of art) (1925) was that artists strived to create a radical separation between themselves and the practices of everyday life. In his own words, "Vida es una cosa, poesía es otra"[32] (Life is one thing, poetry is another). In Ortega y Gasset's description, avant-garde art was a revolt against previous artistic trends, particularly nineteenth-century realism and mimesis. Through its abstraction and focus on creating a "separate" world, avant-garde artists were to demonstrate that the representation of the human was secondary to their commitment to art's aesthetic function. It would follow, therefore that in order for humans to recognize this distinction, the avant-garde object should create alienation in the name of making this difference between art and human life sensible. Ortega y Gasset's precepts only reconfirmed the centrality of the human as an "aesthetic being" who could gaze, distanced from an inert artistic object, as if, as Vicente Huidobro will write in "Arte poética," "el poeta es un pequeño dios"[33] (the poet is a little god). In other words, in distancing the human, "dehumanized" art only served to reinforce the uniqueness of the superior, godlike human.

In the context of Latin America, Vicky Unruh has argued the ways in which, in intimate dialogue with the European avant-gardes, Latin American vanguardists were part of a cultural milieu marked by an interest in, as at least superficially differentiated from Ortega y Gasset, the "rehumanization of art."[34] This resulted in a poetic generation conscious of what Portal would name a "double mission in aesthetics and in life."[35] The "rehumanizing" bent in the Andes operated in contradistinction to Ortega y Gasset's descriptive notion of the avant-garde as a practice of "art for art's sake." Instead, avant-garde artists sought to create a more inclusive aesthetic that drew from the real experiences of everyday life and its laborers, and that reflected colonial legacies and neocolonial realities of Latin America.

In the Andean avant-gardes, rehumanizing efforts responded to the exclusionary nature of the national political community based on class, race, and, to a nascent degree, gender. While international communism was based on the fundamental starting point of class as the entry point to revolution, Peru, Bolivia, and Ecuador's indigenous peasants stood as a distinct population from the mestizo working classes. As Jorge Coronado's work in the context of 1920s and 1930s Lima has illuminated, "Discourses of indigenismo were always ways of figuring how the region might become more modern."[36] For this reason, Coronado explains that the leftist intellectual class in Lima associated with the avant-garde, like José Carlos Mariátegui, used "el indio" in various forms to "conjure modernity in early twentieth-century cultural production in the Andes."[37] Mariátegui (1894–1930), via his work in the journal *Amauta* (1926–1930) as well as in countless essays, would primarily argue that the way to "humanize" or "modernize" the indio was by addressing the problem of land, as elaborated most extensively in "El problema del indio" (The Indian problem).[38] In his initial presentation of *Amauta*, Peru's most well-known avant-garde journal, he goes as far as to declare that "todo lo humano es nuestro"[39] (everything human is ours), speaking to his ambitious endeavor to revolutionize, via this journal, every aspect of human life. However, there is an implicit assumption within the endeavor that humans are completely incorporable into a unified system of art or politics that will account somehow for "everything." The limits of this "everything human" are impossible to locate because "human" *is* part of nature, not the owner of it, and therefore, unable to control or direct the much broader category of life.

Within the broader rubric of indigenismo, Antonio Cornejo Polar names the conflation, at times, between "vanguardia" and "indigenismo" during the first four decades of the twentieth century: "En el área andina . . . la vanguardia social se mezclaron con frecuencia y en algunos momentos y circunstancias aparecieron prácticamente unimismadas—lo que facilita entender además las relaciones que articularon por entonces, en más de un caso, al vanguardismo con el indigenismo"[40] (In the Andean area . . . the social vanguards frequently mixed, and during some moments and in some circumstances practically seemed to be the same thing—which makes it easy to understand the relationships that were articulated then, on more than one occasion, between vanguardism and indigenism). While I am not refuting the intimate relationship between indigenismo and the avant-gardes in 1920s and 1930s Peru, simultaneously, leftist movements in my readings have also gone well beyond the "vanguardismos indigenistas" too, as they continue to (re)emerge into the twenty-first century.

Humanizing the indigenous population ultimately equated to "nationalizing" or "institutionalizing," as in, bringing the existence of subjects previously left out of the state into modernity. Behind these efforts, however, and within both capitalist and communist framings, the "humanizing" impulse, as Javier Sanjinés's work in various fora has brought into view in the case of Bolivia, primarily reinforced a neocolonial modernizing enterprise that assumed a Western concept of the (modern) human as central and exclusive reference point. To become "modern" was to become a *better* human being, translated today into the capitalist discourse of *vivir mejor* (to live better) in contrast with *vivir bien* (to live well). In Sanjinés's readings of early twentieth-century Bolivia, for instance, the lettered class of La Paz framed social progress as linked to, if not conflated with, the discourse of *mestizaje*. Franz Tamayo, the early twentieth-century philosopher and advocate for the indigenous populations, covertly held up the lettered *mestizo-criollo* as both the ineluctable teleological end of educational programs and the new face of the nation. Against such a reading, Sanjinés turns to the raw viscerality of the body to trace indigenous peoples' resistance to a disembodied "one-eyed" humanistic approach to nation-building.[41] But, if the body (the visceral) as per Sanjinés's reading, provides a "two-eyed perspective," how does the body also move us beyond the human vantage point to a different, more radical material locus for social change?

I argue that the avant-garde is not about transforming the human and materiality as separate entities but, rather, a transformation of the relationship itself among humans and their ecosystems. I take a philosophical approach to rereading authors with a new materialist lens in order to bring out what is a collective avant-garde approach to animating materiality in a way that runs counter to the subject–object divide of Western philosophy, as well as counter to the idea that we can "see" an avant-garde object or name an avant-garde product. The way a body moves toward or away from surrounding materials leads to seeing the human as embedded in a natureculture. This orientation opens or closes artists to the material objects, living or inert, around them. Vallejo and Portal, who serve as the bookends to the book, are the two authors most associated with the historical avant-garde of the 1920s–1940s, and that considered themselves as such relative to their time. But beyond the innovation and political commitments they each express vis-à-vis their work, I draw out the way that they interact with natural materials in their writings to highlight the relationship as it runs in the background to their other aims.

Unlike Portal and Vallejo, Arguedas did not want to associate with the high experimentation in art of his era, choosing to differentiate himself from those authors like Julio Cortázar or Alejo Carpentier because of the underdog status he occupied and his lack of interest in making a name for himself as part of an established literary community.[42] That said, he was influenced by the political aspects of avant-garde socialism and its potential future in the Andes. He writes in his first diary, "cuando llegue aquí un socialismo como el de Cuba, ¡se multiplicarán los árboles y los andenes que son tierra buena y paraíso!"[43] (when socialism like that of Cuba arrives here, the trees and the walkways that symbolize the good earth and paradise will multiply!). However, his work performs the social critique of the avant-gardes and opens up access to a materially animated world expressed partially in Quechua. The radical reorientating his works perform offers access to a different way of being in one's body because it breaks the duality between nature *and* culture. Their convergence in his work demonstrates the exchange between nature and the human as bidirectional, not one way. The perspective Arguedas lends to the animate nature of his ecosystem based on his set of embodied experiences is what makes him avant-garde versus the form or style of his writing alone. The access his literature provides to another way of conceiving of the natural environment is avant-garde in terms of the reciprocal relationship between humans, animals, and natural materials that it illuminates.

In the cases of Paredes and Dorado, they use their bodies as a surface for political disruption, demonstrating the way the body is not separate from nature or culture but already enmeshed in those interlinked networks. Life is not just a biological product but a culturally enhanced one too. And so, while each of the artists of the project emerged out of varying circumstances and has a distinct relationship to the term "avant-garde," I consider the polysemic nature to the term, but use it to capture the work that the artists of this book perform to reconfigure the relationship between the human and the naturalcultural environment. As Julio Premat argues in his recent revisiting of the avant-garde, one effective approach to the concept "no es buscar una definición, sino un campo de aplicaciones y simbolizaciones del término"[44] (not to look for a definition, but a field of applications and symbolizations of the term). I contribute to such an application by bringing this collection of authors together under the rubric of the avant-garde as an orientation between humans and materials. The term therefore defines not the object of art itself but rather the movement that it performs: how does it cause us to turn toward or away from each other and our ecosystems, while demonstrating that the materials of ecosystems orient us and sustain all of our relationships?

Beyond Human

I propose "beyond human" as a way of reorienting interpretations of the avant-gardes in a way that acknowledges the blind spots in reducing the avant-garde debate to an all or nothing project that ended with World War II. "Beyond" is an adverb that captures the failure of the rational Western approach to the "human," as if a universal, disembodied, or autonomous being, in accounting for the future of social change. This "failure" is made sensible in the avant-garde art I analyze in the book because materials beyond human control are made sensible as agents within the projects. By this I mean there are instabilities that infiltrate even the "most human" of technologies, language, and of nature,

DNA. Culture and nature are open systems that are defined by the transmutations that occur within them, partially outside of human control. "Beyond" human encapsulates that there is not a way to separate out the "human" as an autonomous category or as disembodied eye(s)/I(s) that stand alone, outside of natureculture. "Beyond human" is not "anti"-human or posthuman, as in "after" the human, but is a way of trying to reconceptualize human life as a form of being oriented in relationship to other matters in motion.[45] Avant-garde art, precisely because of its innovative ability to transcend the relative conventions of representing matter, gives us access to this more capacious way of conceiving of the way we as humans come to matter in and among the other materials of the world at different historical moments that intersect and overlap.

To move "beyond the human," I draw on a plurality of voices. Feminist and decolonial artists, writers, and philosophers of various orientations have named and criticized the colonial legacies of Western humanism, within and beyond studies on the avant-gardes, that contribute to my argument.[46] They have also critiqued communism in a Latin American context because of its blind spots to race. For instance, the category of "human" carries legacies intimately tied to the biopolitical hierarchies of race, class, gender, and sexuality that determined the context of the co-constituting system of coloniality/modernity, or what Aníbal Quijano defines as "the coloniality of power." For Quijano, capitalism continues to reproduce these colonial legacies, and Marxism falls short at capturing the material reality of Latin America because it does not account for the ways in which race was used to naturalize the colonial relations between Europeans and non-Europeans, leading to the development of a global economy out of the matrix of class and racial hierarchies.[47] Quijano's work points to the oversights of Marxist arguments in Latin America, relative to the colonial conditions that preceded it. As Santiago Castro-Gómez synthesizes, "For Marx, colonialism was nothing more than the past of modernity and would disappear altogether with the global crisis that would give rise to communism."[48] As history has shown, colonial legacies have not disappeared, and new forms of community that are not communist continue to form, particularly of late in the Andes. These histories defy linear progression and its accompanying myth of a universally modern teleology.[49]

Silvia Rivera Cusicanqui and María Lugones, among others, have incisively pointed out the blind spots in Quijano's critique of capital, to the extent that his position virtually ignores the ways in which gender and sexuality influence the possibilities for participation in political economies. They consequently have demanded a more nuanced inquiry into the material specificity of the formation of the Latin American subject. For instance, Rivera Cusicanqui argues in "La noción del derecho o las paradojas de la modernidad postcolonial" (The notion of rights or the paradoxes of postcolonial modernity) that the *Déclaration des droits de l'homme et du citoyen* (Declaration of the Rights of Man and of the Citizen) (1789), the basis for human rights discourse, is constructed on the discursive shoulders of Western humanism, thereby making the female subject a discursively impossible one.[50] Her decades-long work is consistently committed to demonstrating the ways in which the material realities of women are unaccounted for in the definition of "human." The chapters in this book on women and on feminisms complicate "human" as a multiplicity of beings that differ in degrees.

Likewise, Mabel Moraña incisively questions humanism and its colonial legacies, noting "podría decirse que el humanismo es parte del fenómeno de colonialidad, ya que sus principios se proyectan desde el mundo letrado colonial a nuestros días, atravesando instancias de formación, consolidación y debilitamiento de las culturas nacionales"[51] (one could say that humanism is part of the phenomenon of coloniality, given that its principles are projected from the colonial lettered city to the current day, crossing instances of formation, consolidation, and the weakening of national cultures). The women I work with in particular in this book implicitly critique Western humanism in incorporating and critiquing the (dis)embodied subject by drawing attention to their materiality as influencing their orientation toward their world. In turn, they expand the avant-garde to projects that do not originate with class concerns but rather the intersectionality of class, race, gender, and sexuality.

Due to a range of alter-globalization movements, particularly as they have manifested themselves in the last two decades, numerous critics have reopened conversations on the avant-gardes in ways that also revisit materiality as more than a class-based political topic. In a return to the topic of the avant-gardes in *The Politics of Aesthetics* (2000), Rancière spends time distinguishing the avant-garde as a political strategy developed under the communist party versus the avant-garde as an aesthetic project that "anticipate[s] life forms to come."[52] The latter continues to make sensible new orientations in and toward "life," whereas the former necessarily fails as a universalizing political model because it cannot ever account for the plurality of material variation in the realm of the real. Rancière argues that the "the arts only lend to projects of domination or emancipation what they are able to lend to them, that is to say, quite simply, what they have in common with them: bodily positions and movements, functions of speech, the parceling out of the visible and the invisible."[53] Rancière's phrase, "Projects of domination or emancipation" is purposely broad, evading reference to a universal capitalist or communist model and signaling the coexistence of often competing political projects in ongoing negotiation, rather than a binary between two neat systems. "Bodily positions and movements" are contingent on their relationship to natureculture. They therefore are an orientation, at base.

A call to revisit the avant-gardes is also echoed by critic Evan Mauro. In a recent revisiting of the historical avant-gardes, he argues that they come onto the scene first during a "nation-based articulation of biopolitics, where the nation-state's institutional expansion is posited as the solution to a growing number of deficiencies in the prior mode of social reproduction, bourgeois liberalism, whose very remoteness from 'life' was precisely the complaint of the historical avant-gardes."[54] Framing the avant-garde as not that which is gone, but that which continues, Mauro goes on to argue that "many of its forms, rhetorics, and basic gestures survive beyond its expiry date, especially in today's anti-capitalist and alter-globalization movements."[55] In a comprehensive revisiting of Bürger's and Renato Poggioli's theories, Mauro argues that "the avant-garde problematic has been prematurely laid to rest."[56] Mauro's provocation caused Bürger to revisit his own "historical" avant-garde theory, noting that "the avant-garde could gain a renewed relevance in a future that we cannot imagine," leading to "the possible realization of a utopia in which art and life are united."[57] These new returns to the avant-garde are based on a nonlinear reading of history as well, because they too would seem to see the impact of the past in the present and, in the case of Bürger, an unimagined future, speaking to their malleability in a new era.

I argue that the avant-gardes are based on a belief in a politics of nonclosure that is never to arrive. By a politics of nonclosure, I mean that "life" as oriented in avant-garde subjects is still becoming, that is, changing as the subjects move among and with the materials of the world. Simultaneously, beyond the human, other materials are changing among and within themselves. Utopia, precisely as "no place," means *not* arriving to a fixed identity but rather moving toward an always out of reach position. This is what the plural Andean avant-gardes do: make sensible the ways that materials move to insinuate forms of life beyond the human as the human looks and is oriented today.[58] However, in orienting the interpretation of the avant-gardes in such a way that I position the movements as "beyond" the human, its utopic horizon line is perpetually out of reach. I agree, and borrow, therefore, from queer scholar José Muñoz as he argues with respect to queer, that it is an "ever-moving queer horizon line."[59] It does not arrive, but is that which orients toward new material configurations for life, such as those theorized, if not realized in practice, in philosophies of *buen vivir*.[60]

Recent literary and arts scholarship in the Andes attests to renewed interest in the historical avant-gardes, in large part in light of the political orientation toward the left (again) that has taken hold in diverse and contradictory ways in the region. For instance, avant-garde production in the Puno region, led by Alejandro and Arturo Peralta, the latter who went by the pseudonym Gamaliel Churata, has recently been revisited and engaged more deeply in critical debates. Whereas Antonio Cornejo Polar observed years ago that *El pez de oro*, Churata's most substantial work, was one of the biggest challenges remaining to be taken up by Peruvian scholars, Unruh, Moraña, Elizabeth Monasterios, Helena Usandizaga, and Marco Thomas Bosshard, among others, have undertaken the challenge of interpreting this work.[61] Churata's work challenges binary thinking between indigenous knowledge systems and the West in its embrace of multiple strands of philosophy, from Catholicism, to Buddhism, to Aymara and Quechua cosmovisions, combined in a way that eschews incorporation into any "field," and that conceives the Andean from a pluralistic orientation that is not about smoothing out various systems of thought but making sensible their dense intertwinement.[62]

Yazmín López Lenci, through an analysis of magazines and manifestos of the 1920s and 1930s in Peru, has traced the transformation of the term "vanguardia" in the Andes as it took on new meaning in Peru at the beginning of the twentieth century. She refers to a "vitality" within the same, explaining that a number of Peruvian avant-garde texts were able to strategically appropriate the term: "vaciarlo [the term "vanguard"] para asumir una posición vital de revisión, enjuiciamiento y apropiación original del patrimonio literario y cultural"[63] (emptying the term in order to assume a vital revisionist position, of judgment and original appropriation of the literary and cultural patrimony). Collections like *Ande* (Alejandro Peralta, 1926), which springs from Peralta's desire to "sembrar palabras" (to sow words) from the Puno region of Peru, underscore this vitality.[64] As a poet, he is described as offering "una nueva versión de la vida Cósmica"[65] (a new version of Cosmic life) by Luis Valcárcel, and his verses are described by Vallejo as "versos que andan y viven"[66] (verses that walk and live). Throughout the *Ande* collection, the vital landscape and ecosystem of the Puno region actively perform in his work, for instance as "sale el lago a mirar las sementeras"[67] (the lake heads out to look at the planted fields) and "Y el croar de las ranas se punza en las espigas"[68] (And the croaking of the frogs throbs in the sprigs). Because he animates the ecosystem around him, he merges an indigenous view of animate nature with a vanguardist material perspective that situates Puno as a place from which and toward which to be oriented. In his poetry, Peralta moves us beyond a view of only the human at center, as the lake too, and the impact of the croaks of the frogs, contribute to "life": the relationships themselves between things.

María del Mar, reading *Ande* from Mexico writes in a short piece titled "Estética andina": "Recogí *Ande*, nuevo en formato, en ideas y pujanza. Lo leí en compañía de varios poetas y todos estuvimos conformes en la briosa vitalidad que lo anima"[69] (I picked up *Ande*, new in its form, in its ideas and its vigor. I read it in the company of various poets and we were all in agreement with the spirited vitality that animates it). This "spirited vitality" is a result of the experience of the material book and its contents: what the poem actualizes in someone's body is as important as the content of what it says. The two are not in a hierarchical relationship but move together. It is this "spirited vitality" that animates the body of the human as one materiality among many. Alejandro Peralta and the Puno avant-gardes is an example of the way that early Andean avant-garde artists challenged the subject–object binary between the human and nature in a way that anticipates a cultural and natural continuum, rather than reinforcing a binary.

Vital Materiality

Vital materialist approaches to life, in my interpretation, capture the affective experience of "becoming alive" activated in material orientations and encounters, not contained in a single human, impervious to the substances around that human. They reflect the concept that materiality exists beyond the human ability to completely rationalize and represent it; a range of materials move on their own and do not need "us" to materially be, like Peralta's frogs or Churata's golden fish. In drawing in the concept of vital materiality to the discussion, the central question I raise is not just how do the Andean avant-gardes complicate humanism by accounting for material differences within the category of human, but also, how do they move beyond it by thinking outside the confines of its logic? Building on the Cartesian duality between mind and body, Western humanism has historically assumed as the exemplary norm, a disembodied, male, white, all-knowing and rational subject as both the starting point and the inevitable end point of a universal modernity to which an autonomous, and human, "we" will all arrive. In order to move, breathe, and be a human in the world is to be oriented in time and space. As Sara Ahmed argues, "bodies inhabit space by how they reach for objects, just as objects in turn extend what we can reach."[70] In order to not get lost, the other materials of the world guide us as much as we reach for them. So, how do the avant-gardes make sensible new objects and their relationship to the human?

In contradistinction to the word "human" and its various adjectival forms, the word "vital" appears just as many if not more times, within the Andean avant-gardes, and often in relationship to material culture and nature. I take "vitality," for instance, as what causes poet Vallejo to claim that "today" is the first time he feels the presence of life.[71] The affective experience conveyed in his observation that "Nunca, sino ahora, ha habido vida"[72] (Never, except right now, has there been life) is Vallejo's articulation of the materially contingent conditions of becoming, suddenly, more alive than a moment ago. Aliveness is experienced in the poetic voice in relationship to whatever unnamed materials are affecting him. It is a sense of "becoming-with" his surroundings. This aliveness is an affective result of material factors both inside and outside the visible boundaries of the human body and that comes to be in their relationship.

Portal describes the "esencias vitales" (vital essences) of her poetry as if the "word" or the poem itself were alive. As her career evolves, Portal becomes increasingly interested in her material existence as in relation to the cosmos, as her later collection *La esperanza y el mar* (1965) reveals, gradually articulating life at the juncture between the human body and other natural bodies, including the sea that she held so dear. And Bolivian poet-activist Paredes defines the relational movements between different bodies within a community as what makes up her vital community-based feminism. Paredes emphasizes the material body as part, not the whole, of "life" itself: "Comprendemos el espacio como un campo vital para que el cuerpo se desarrolle. Es espacio donde la vida se mueve y se promueve"[73] (We understand space as a vital field in which the body develops. It is space where life moves and perpetuates itself). Life does not "happen" in the human alone, but takes shape via the moving material relationships that form a given space, and that orient a community. In Peru, Arguedas portrays life as a relationship between multiple species and natural formations in the ecosystem. Based on this premise he declares, "no hay mucha diferencia entre una montaña, un insecto, una piedra inmensa y el ser humano"[74] (there is not much difference between a mountain, an insect, an immense rock, and a human being). The mountains orient insects, and the insects the mountains. The material basis of existence is what partially differentiates and partially equates beings and things.

Additional evidence of a vital materialism latent in the Andean avant-gardes also comes from Gamaliel Churata's eccentric *El pez de oro*, mentioned earlier. Churata and his brother, Alejandro Peralta, produced works from a relative periphery to Mariátegui and the intellectual lettered class of Lima, and have tended to be read as marginalized figures in the field of Latin American literature, although this is changing. In *El pez de oro*, Churata describes his work as "un nuevo punto de partida para la vida"[75] (a new point of departure for life) and refers to the need to "equilibrar los valores vitales"[76] (balance the vital values) of America. He then reminds readers that "Si vemos al arte vital del hombre, le sabremos transfundido de núcleos germinales. La belleza no es abstracción en él: es latido, orgasmo"[77] (If we see the vital art of man, we will see that it is based on germinal nuclei. Beauty is not an abstraction in it: it is a beat, it is an orgasm). Such descriptions of the "vital values" of America as originating from "germinal nuclei" deemphasize the human form and instead emphasize that the organic basis to life at the cell level is shared by other materials in the local context, like plants or animals. Churata's "text" is interrupted by other bodies, be they those of celestial forces, of animals, of raw materials like gold, of fragments from Nietzsche, Schopenhauer, Plato, and Bergson, and the myriad figures of the pre-Incan and Incan universe. Churata's vision of "life" extends beyond the "arte vital del hombre," as he weaves a book out of a web of diverse materials. In this mixing, he makes sensible new ways of conceiving of life as a negotiation between materials. He defines the human as "halpakamaska" (animated earth,) and the dead, he describes as seeds.[78] This terrestrial, material vocabulary is manifested throughout the text, but always in dialogue with other philosophic traditions. Churata's vision is a network, not a binary between the West and "pure" indigenous cultures, and anticipates life forms to come, like the "plurality" partially emphasized in Bolivian politics today, and mentioned earlier.[79]

In another text from Arequipa, Antero Peralta (neither a brother of Alejandro nor of Arturo), who also published in *Amauta*, and ran his own journal, *Chirapu* (1928), describes Andean art as being made from "el barro de nuestro suelo y el aliento de nuestra raza" (the clay of our soil and the breath of our race), and calls for a new art that extends from "lo profundo de las profundidades humanas y geoanímicas" (the deepest of human and geoanimic depths). The word "geoanimic" speaks to the vitality of the ground and the animacy of the natural world that surrounds Tahuantinsuyu, the four-parted Incan Empire. He also invokes "la materia prima del nuevo arte" (the primary material of new art) as the basis for life's "floración multiforme"[80] (multiformed flowering). The inclusion of raw primary materials "dirties" an image of a clean, neutral, disembodied, and rational human, placing the human into the clay of the soil, the water of Lake Titikaka, and the geological layers of Tahuantinsuyu. This imagery simultaneously causes readers to access the "geological energy" of another time that is nonetheless made present in the writing. The liveliness of the material world directly impacts the aesthetic result (life *is* in art) while the aesthetic object makes sensible new materials (art *makes life* newly sensible). The two are not in opposition or hierarchically divided, but enmeshed and entwined.

The Andean arts, as sites where the exploitation of both is made sensible as it is resisted, showcase plural ways of moving against dominant capitalist ways of organizing the world through making sensible vital material relationships at the center of life instead of the individual. Underpinning my interpretation of the avant-garde arts is the belief that the aesthetic realm anticipates political openings in ways that are sensible aesthetically prior to their (potential) realization in practice. In her book *Vibrant Matter: A Political Ecology of Things* (2010), Jane Bennett makes the political claim that inanimate objects act upon animate life in ways that have gone historically unperceived, or at least underperceived. She also traces the implications of the same, particularly as applicable within the rapidly growing subfield of environmental politics. She demonstrates the ways in which inanimate objects like trash, plants, stones, and metals, to name just a few, might serve alongside humans as what Bruno Latour names as an "actant." An actant is any person or object that can intervene even passively in the formation of a social network.[81] Bennett relies on literature as a reference, particularly the work of Henry Thoreau, to demonstrate "the recalcitrance of things" as they catalyze events in assemblage with other bodies—human and otherwise.[82] As environmental crises loom on the horizon line, if the matter of the human is not considered as embedded within a much bigger network from which we cannot be separated, then storms and droughts will continue to not be seen as material consequences of (human) behavior, but as Bennett argues, freakish acts of nature. In recognizing the relationships between materials, not the materials themselves, as central to life beyond the specific organized form of a human, the human might ironically perpetuate the species' existence much longer than if we consider nature as a separate sphere over which the human reigns. In other words, moving our locus of ethical concern beyond the human does not mean operating counter to human interest or romanticizing the power of trees to "fix" our problems, but in forming assemblages with those actors and actants with which and whom we share common alliances in the struggle for the continued vitality of life.[83]

Avant-Garde Assemblages

I structure the book in accordance with its arguments to emphasize the plurality, adaptability, and spiral nature of the avant-gardes, as present-day artists draw on the past in a way that does not repeat it, but grows outward from it. The materiality of the bodies of the artists are emphasized as what partially differs and is partially in common with the other beings of their ecosystems. In the Andes region, where nature daunts the human in a particularly acute way, the artists, while not "purely" indigenous, are susceptible to seeing the materials around them as animate and interactive, instead of wholly distinct from human beings. Because avant-garde art has historically juxtaposed unlikely materials, disorienting its recipients, it is particularly apt for the exploration of the ways in which humanism combined with the lively Andean landscape produces a vital aesthetic that transforms notions of what constitutes the basis of political life. Echoing the recent work of Matthew Bush and Luis Hernán Castañeda, the artists are linked by affinities and harmonies, which connects them at certain points of alliance and disconnects them at others.[84] I structure the book to look at what is common across both the historical and the contemporary avant-gardes in the Andes in the foreground of politics and art: the natural world from which both spring. In moving beyond the human, what becomes obvious is that the same cosmos and ecosystem is the common point of orientation. It is therefore around this common space that plural perspectives are oriented. Bodies are juxtaposed with other natural materials like rocks and stones, in the case of Vallejo, or water, in the case of Dorado, or the air as well as animals, in the case of Arguedas. I make manifest these material juxtapositions through close reading and visual analysis to demonstrate that life happens at the intersection between the human and other forms of animate and inanimate materials.

The historical (dis)ordering of the book reflects the interpretative frame of the assemblage model that I argue is at the crux of the avant-gardes. Time is an embodied sensation in my reading of the avant-gardes. The past crosses through our minds as much as the future; the present is right now, but never graspable. In regard to complexity of the avant-garde's question of time, Premat refers to "una vision paroxística de la temporalidad artística"[85] (a paroxistic vision of artistic temporality). Bush and Castañeda also refer to the "challenge to chronological time" proposed by the avant-gardes, because they look to the past to imagine the power of the present to transform a future yet to come.[86] The spiral nature of the avant-gardes is not only indigenous but rather a characteristic of the movements in general. An orientation toward time that occurs in the body, rather than objectively or scientifically, shapes the logic of my chapters. The power of art is its ability to invoke multiple coexistent and conflicting times at once, disorienting us to reorient us again.

Consistently the artists of my chapters defy classification. Not one of them is particularly concerned with fitting into a specific label or being globally recognized. In not wanting to be classified, they reflect "una postura y una energía sin capacidad de entrar en catálogo"[87] (a posture and an energy with no capacity to enter into a catalog). This is the essence of a relationship or an orientation: it does not "enter" into a catalog because by nature it is dynamic. I move forward and backward in history, juxtaposing both canonical and lesser-established avant-garde artists, including Vallejo, Dorado, Arguedas, Paredes, and Portal. This assemblage of artists produces from diverse bodies and artistic genres ranging from poetry to installation art to performance in the twentieth and early twenty-first centuries. The physical body is at the center of their projects in part to remind us that material differings matter in artistic renderings of life. But, ironically, their same diverse bodies serve not just to "humanize" a periphery—or what has been theorized in postcolonial studies as giving voice to subaltern subjects—but also to pivot our attention toward the common materiality of the physical body. They demonstrate the liveliness of the bare body behind the discursively constructed "human" by showcasing subjectivity as part cultural performance, part relationality to other materials. This transformation deemphasizes enlightened humanity and foregrounds materiality as the vital starting point for a relational ontology. By disorienting readers in language or space, the artists fold us back into material form as the starting point for life, challenging the hierarchical position of the human subject over the material body, as well as the autonomy of the human from other species, through an emphasis on material orientations in time and space.

All the artists of this project are partial subjects: they speak as a particular "I," and at the same time actively distance themselves from that "I" through an acknowledgment of the bare materiality that is common to any nameable individual. That bare materiality, which is what orients the human and is also that by which the human is oriented, is what enables these assemblages to form. In speaking of artistic production, we cannot access bare material life without acknowledging the subject that produced the object at hand. But also, each of these artists is an object in a material assemblage. The forms of resistance to considerations of life's end goal as the formation of rational political subjects therefore take different shape across the project, whether in Vallejo's active but only partially possible disavowal of his self in "Voy a hablar de la esperanza," (I am going to speak of hope) or in Paredes's insistence that she is *not* an artist, and that she does *not* write from a subject that is "I" in the book *Hilando fino: Perspectivas desde el feminismo comunitario* (2008). The disavowal of a biopolitical subject also comes up in Dorado's demonstration that her "self" is nothing more than a pastiche of so many who went before her and come "after" her: not only humans but tadpoles, dogs, and other animals. The subjects of this book, this is to say, recognize the prosthetic nature of their subjectivity and draw on this as a strength, not a weakness. They do not take subjectivity for granted, but demonstrate how easily it slips out of reach, as in when Portal, despite acting as and from a strong "I" in her era, is turned into a muse-like object when named "la primera poetisa" (the first poetess) of Peru by a well-intentioned José Carlos Mariátegui.[88]

In chapter 1, "César Vallejo's Lithic Poetry: Stones as Material Guides," I make three central arguments about the work of Vallejo in order to demonstrate the way he orients us toward a horizon line "beyond the human" via his poetry and prose. I turn to Vallejo's friend and compatriot Antenor Orrego, whose work underscores the animate materiality of Vallejo's poetry. Orrego's original "Introduction" to *Trilce*, first published in 1922, makes evident Vallejo's tendency to question the difference between the animate and the inanimate, the living and the dead.[89] Second, through an analysis of poems from *Trilce* (1922) and *Poemas humanos* (1937), I explore the ways that Vallejo animates rocks, stones, and statues—among other materials—to accentuate that the human body is one material form among many. Stones are evidence of the constancy of the material world of which the human is an inseparable part. While rocks might seem like the dullest of the natural matters, they are also not separate from culture, but interwoven into it, particularly in the Andes. Lastly, I argue that Vallejo's poetry acts as if it were a prosthetic addition to the human body.[90] His poems are prosthetic in the sense that they "hook up" the human to both concrete and virtual alternative worlds, orienting us to new ways of conceiving of life. In putting forward a nuanced relationship between biological life and cultural art, they challenge the liberal notion of a disembodied, knowing subject in favor of an open material body who affects and is affected by other beings and things. While his earlier work was produced in Peru, his later works speak at a more global scale to the common cause of resistance to fascism.

In chapter 2, "Alejandra Dorado's Installation Art: Material Transmutations in Contemporary Cochabamba," I juxtapose Vallejo's poetry with the installation art and digital media of Dorado (Cochabamba, Bolivia 1969–). Dorado, who began producing art in the mid-1990s, combines images, theoretical texts, and living bodies to make transparent the symbolic political and gendered violence that is metaphorically inscribed onto living bodies in twenty-first century Bolivia. In the first installation I discuss, titled *martirio* (martyrdom), Dorado uses the original "cut" that we all have on our bodies—the belly button—to symbolize a common site of disorientation that demonstrates our partial autonomy and our partial contingency on a material world that dwarfs the prosthetic self. The exhibit makes visible the paradoxical conditions of being: the ways in which we can work within our material conditions and the ways in which they confine us. This tension is where the potential for vital encounters and transformation among materials occurs. I then pay particular attention to a series of photos that Dorado and her friend produced called "Speculating on Myself or Speculating on the Same" as an example of the way that her incorporation of digital technology enables non-gender-conforming subjects to not just imagine but visualize and represent themselves beyond the physical confines of biology. By using new technologies, Dorado manipulates the body to demonstrate the vital component of possibility and play in making gender manifest beyond binary thinking. Digital manipulation and physical performance enable subjects to live out potential desires inorganically via technological manipulation, moving life beyond the confines of the organic world.

Chapter 3, "José María Arguedas's 1960s: The Air as Space of Material Encounters" spirals back to the 1960s to trace vitality as the relationship between people and other living things, as well as between knowledge systems (indigenous and Western) in the later works of Arguedas. Granted, Arguedas would have balked at being called an "avant-garde" artist, but at the end of the day, his concern is with the construction of community based on material relationships that challenge the status quo of his era. After I outline Arguedas's aesthetic philosophy and background, I focus on the concept of dislocation in his work, despite his intimate ties to place. I trace the air in his works as a space that puts different materials in contact with each other through their dynamic orientations, but not permanent locations. I discuss displacement first in *El Sexto* (1961), where I argue that Arguedas focuses on affective exchange, even though the novel takes place in one of the most disciplining of physical spaces, the prison. I move from *El Sexto* to an analysis of the ways in which Arguedas felt "colonized" as a writer during the now famous roundtable discussion held in Peru in 1965. I analyze the way that the air and wind operate in this hymn as well as in the collection *Katatay y otros poemas* (1972) as a relational field between different species and things. Air reminds us of the singularity of our breath but simultaneously the contact between our organism and those other living beings and objects that infiltrate us. I contend that air is vital to a life philosophy that takes as a starting point material contact between human beings, nature, and cultural objects. We cannot separate them. Formally, chapter 3 also serves as a center from which the other chapters unfold in either direction. It is a *chakana*, or crossing point, in Quechua.[91]

In chapter 4, "*Mujeres Creando Comunidad*: Communitarian Feminism from the Bolivian Soil," I return to Bolivia again to Mujeres Creando's (Women Creating's) early street "actions" as the group transforms the walls of La Paz. I describe the history of Mujeres Creando (officially founded in 1992) and gradually move to the 2000s to interrogate community activist, lesbian, and feminist Paredes's (1958–) writing and political actions as critiques of Western feminism from her embodied materiality as it moves through various communities: local and international; indigenous and feminist; rural and urban. My readings focus on performance and graffiti art as forms of vital "gifts" that create an affective connection between diverse material bodies while drawing attention to the common bare materiality to life regardless of sexual orientation. The early works that Paredes and Mujeres Creando produced challenged a capitalist market economy by treating cultural interventions as gifts. In the second half of the chapter, I analyze Paredes's early poetry from a few of her collections as well as selections of her text *Hilando fino: Desde el feminismo comunitario* (Spinning fine thread: Perspectives from communitarian feminism) Her work makes a contribution to the field of decolonial feminisms and methodologies through its challenge to Western models that espouse the liberal subject as center in favor of a relational approach to feminist thinking that provides a transcritique of both Western and indigenous knowledge systems in favor of an immanent community to come.

The last chapter, "Magda Portal's Bare Life in the Sea" spirals back to the historical avant-garde with new readings of Portal. I return to poetry and back to the 1920s, when Portal describes her poems as living substances that run through her body. She writes, "Amo la poesía, me recorre de arriba abajo como un licor de fuego o de sangre amasado . . . y vibro a su contacto"[92] (I love poetry, it races up and down my body like a fiery liquor or a thick blood . . . and I vibrate at its contact). Portal's description of the kinesthetic properties of poetry in her body reflects the liveness of "art-objects," or as Bennett has called them, "art-things," as poetry makes Portal "vibrate."[93] This is not to say that a poem simply creates itself without a subject. However, the aesthetic encounter between Portal and art is an event that makes the vitality of both of their disparate physical materials become sensible. The artistic encounter signals that symbolically "liveliness" happens partially beyond the human bodymind.[94] Portal's material differing as female mattered very much, but her poetry also moves beyond her biology to signal a commonality to the bare life force that runs through materiality, from the human to the sea.

In sum, this book revises the avant-gardes in the Andes by bringing materiality to the fore, not only to emphasize the plurality of embodied orientations that make up the Andes but also to move beyond the centricity of the human. Through an emphasis on the bare body and materiality, the authors at first might be said to reinforce an anthropocentric point of view through the comparison of art to the human body. However, through their projects, they diffuse the (false) unity of any human subject into a relational network. This project does not suggest that we discredit the offerings of Western humanism, but instead, reanimates the materialisms underlying that discourse in dialogue with Andean artists as part of a more open approach to life as an ecosystem of many different types of bodies. It looks beyond the human, toward a utopic horizon line as that which has informed the past and present, as well as that which is still becoming. It aims to think with and from the Andes, not just "about it," in an attempt to bring the vitality of plural Andean materials into collective thinking in an act of *pens-ande-ar*. The verb *pensar* is "to think" in Spanish; the verb *andar* is "to walk." The verb *pensandear* reflects an active thinking that is mobilized with the materiality of the Andes (*ande*); it holds vital life as the relationships among materials at the center as differing bodies move and are moved, oriented toward and orientated by, the local and the cosmos, and the common desire for their continued vitality.

1

César Vallejo's Lithic Poetry

Stones as Material Guides

The event that is bumping up against César Vallejo (Santiago de Chuco, Peru, 1892–Paris 1938) and his poetry has traveled countries and cities, couches, desks, pens, and air. It has settled into my elbows and ankles, my 20 (+ 1 virtual) fingernails and my hair, as the latter grow, and I read him.[1] Every Thursday that it rains, Vallejo. And every *¡Yo no sé!* (I don't know!), Vallejo in the bloodstream, a shrug, as his thoughts slip through me. In choosing to read Vallejo, my fingerprints touch his verse, and I meet him in the transient space of his words for a shared interpersonal moment, *entrambos* (among both of us). Although he is no longer physically present, *su cadáver* (*está*) *lleno de mundo* (his cadaver is full of world).[2] There is nothing conventionally alive about a cadaver, and yet, I sense what Vallejo wants to imply in this line as the logical ruptures in his language disorient me, leaving me reaching for something more: precisely, this "worldliness" that inhabits his language and the physical effect of the literary encounter. And "Vallejo" as a concept also gives off "world" through the energy that he invokes in readers as his poetry and prose continue to be read and transformed into new artistic forms, taken up even in the present.[3] The pull toward his grave, first in Montrouge then in Montparnasse, is one way in which the stone that stands in for him now magnetizes fellow human passers-through of the world to the call of Vallejo, no longer a living human, but still materially vital.[4]

In this first chapter, I approach Vallejo through the lens of a monistic material philosophy of life that sees the subject and the object, and the animate and the inert as coming-to-be together. I make manifest this vital life philosophy in Vallejo by looking at the way he troubles the differences between doll and human being, rock and body, stone and corpse as part of his disorientation strategy. He demonstrates the capacity of things like rocks, suits, and bones, to "act as quasi agents or forces with trajectories, propensities, or tendencies of their own," while not negating that the human subject partially differs from them. Instead, pebbles, stones, bones, boxes, chairs, drawers, lizards, and dogs also are granted partial agency and are called forth by the poetic voice, as if the corecipients of his poetry all along.[5] Sara Ahmed writes, "moments of disorientation are vital. They are bodily experiences that throw the world up, or throw the body from its ground."[6] Vallejo's disorientation of his readers is the starting point for his critique of human hubris. Each poem brings new materials into an ethical fold—that is, into something readers sense and approximate—as witnesses to, and agents alongside, the human. Vallejo's poetry is an example of a "poetic ecology of things" that makes sensible "the material agency or effectivity of not-quite-human things."[7] The not-quite-human things that Vallejo makes sensible demonstrate the inextricability of natureculture. The ways in which his poetry manifests these material relationships constitute the matter and the ongoing potential of his avant-garde orientation as it continues to move us closer to a new way of life in the present.[8]

I argue that Vallejo's poetry is purposefully disorienting because it pulls the ground from under the subject, destabilizing the material world. As has been said countless times, Vallejo's hermetic language is at times enigmatic and at others plain indecipherable.[9] His writing or *un*writing—what Julio Ortega names his "poética de tachadura" (poetics of erasure), and Julio Prieto names "escritura errante" (wandering writing)—returns readers relentlessly to the materiality of their body. Because language has been naturalized as what differentiates the human from other species, Vallejo undermines this difference by partially negating that which makes humans unique from other animals: the ability to reason and conceptualize the world through language. But as Manuel DeLanda recently reminds, "to assume that human experience is structured conceptually is to de-historicize the human species; we spent hundreds of thousands of years as a social species, with a division of labor (hunters, gatherers) and sophisticated stone tool technology. Language is a relatively recent acquisition."[10] Vallejo's stumbling poetic points to this very fact: humans' acquisition of language, considering geological time, *just* occurred. He uses language as a pretext to ironically orient readers toward life as it existed prior to its human form. As a result, the poems humble us before the absurdity of insufficient attempts at logic and the failure of language to fully express the concrete reality around us. By extension, subjectivity is undermined and shown to be partially a cultural performance in relationship to the naturalcultural web of worldly things. It is acquired through our interaction with the other living and dead materials of the ecosystem and the technology of language.[11]

In what follows, I embark on three interpretive inroads into, and out of, Vallejo. First, I turn to the writing of Vallejo's friend and compatriot Antenor Orrego, whose work serves as an initial entry point into our appreciation of the animate materiality of Vallejo's poetry. Orrego's "Introduction" to *Trilce*, published in the original 1922 version, makes evident Vallejo's tendency to trouble the difference between the animate and the inanimate, the living and the dead.[12] These two writers became friends as part of el Grupo Trujillo (The Trujillo Group) during the years when Vallejo was studying at the University of Trujillo and Orrego was the intellectual leader of the city's growing bohemia. Orrego walks us through his firsthand perceptions and description of that which differentiated Vallejo from his peers from the start. Orrego helps illuminate the intellectual trends of early twentieth-century Peru with which, and against which, Vallejo wrote.

Second, I interrogate the ways that Vallejo animates rocks, stones, pebbles, and statues—among other materials—to make clear that the human body is only one material form among many, via analysis of poems from *Trilce* (1922), *Poemas humanos* (1937), and the play *Piedra cansada* (c. 1936). Rocks are evidence of the duration of the material world, of which the human, in its current form, is at once an inseparable and a dispensable part. Rocks might seem like the dullest of natural matters, yet they are the concrete base of culture and interwoven into it, in the Andes and beyond. The materials of Vallejo's poems form an ecosystem that the poet might have described as "los enredos de enredos de los enredos"[13] (the knots of the knots of the knots). These knots symbolize the articulations of materials within natureculture as they are inextricably bound. Humans are simultaneously active travelers and passive passengers through those material planes, neither completely autonomous pilots nor fully inert bodies. When Ortega describes *Trilce* as presenting a "a conceptualization of the human in terms of what he or she lacks," he signals the ways in which Vallejo's language fails as an adequate representation of the experience of the world.[14] But the other side to that coin is that the poems also dwarf the human as a tiny speck in the chaotic cosmos. "To be" within Vallejo's corpus is to be within a poetic ecosystem that forces us to reorient before the materials in which we are embedded and to the evolutionary bare materials of which we, and the stars themselves, are assembled. This avant-garde philosophic contribution of Vallejo is increasingly timely in an era of contemporary environmental decay.

Third, I conclude by making the case that Vallejo's poetry acts as if it were a prosthetic addition to the human body. Because his vital materiality troubles the status of the human being as a closed system and demonstrates to readers their intimate connections to stones, to animals, and to other animate and inanimate beings, they, too, become a temporary addition, and a demonstration of the incompleteness of a single human experience.[15] The poems are prosthetic in the sense that they "hook up" the human to both concrete and virtual alternative worlds: to the "ciliado arrecife donde nací" (the ciliated reef where I was born) and to the offerings of journeys "a lo largo de otros mundos"[16] (across other worlds). Like Vallejo's "Sombrero, abrigo, guantes" (Hat, overcoat, gloves) in the *Poemas humanos* collection and the multiple "suits" that inhabit his world, his poetry is like a prosthetic material that revitalizes a mutilated, decrepit, and always partial subject. "Prosthesis" means "an addition, an attachment, or an add-on" to the human form. But in its original Latin, "prosthesis" also means to add a syllable or a letter onto a word—something Vallejo practices with his notorious neologisms like "hombligo," "heriza," "todaviiza," and "cuadrumano," among myriad others. Through prosthesis, I argue that Vallejo's poetry orients us to a beyond-the-human horizon line that approaches a human life as always necessarily lacking and thereby dependent on the naturalcultural worlds in which the human is embedded.[17]

In sum, I argue for the continued relevance of Vallejo's poetry to future transformations of our understanding not just of the human as he or she "is" today, but of the bare potential of life, as a materially based continuum and part of an ongoing avant-garde impulse.[18] Because Vallejo's poetry expressed so early in the twentieth century the relationality between nature, culture, and technology while acknowledging the blind spots of any human in understanding the ecosystem of which he or she is already partially made, I argue that it contributes to twenty-first-century discussion in the Andes on new approaches to transforming and organizing life that move away from the inert approach to matter of Marxist ideology while recognizing that the critical subject is a necessary agent in catalyzing social change alongside and in the interest of other materials essential to the sustainability of life in that subject's environment.[19] Vallejo's poetry makes us radically aware of objects that, even if they come from language in the poem, affect us in such a way as to throw us back to the bare material of the universe. Just because his poems start from a human body (his own), the rational human is not their only philosophic "end."[20] Instead, his ability to perceive and articulate the relationships between the single human, the terrestrial world, the globally connected world, and the cosmos keeps his work contemporary.

Vallejo's Early Search for Life's Secret

Antenor Orrego (1892–1960) and César Vallejo are related through their shared birth dates, their material conditions, and the complementary content of their early writing. Vallejo spent his university years at the Trujillo area and overlapped at the same events on numerous occasions as part of the bohemian cultural collective "el Grupo Norte" (The North Group) or "el Grupo Trujillo"

(The Trujillo Group) until 1918, when Vallejo relocated to Lima. Older than Vallejo, Orrego was one of his earliest teachers, readers, and promoters and, by all accounts, a lifelong friend. Orrego wrote the original and alluring prologue to Vallejo's *Trilce* (1922), one that Vallejo requested always accompany the work. However, because Orrego became a member of the polarizing Alianza Popular Revolucionaria Americana party in Peru, his Introduction was subsequently left out of some versions of the collection due to political animosity that shaped the publishing world.[21]

In addition to the Introduction that he wrote to *Trilce*, Orrego also wrote a biography on Vallejo that detailed the early years of their friendship, but that was left unpublished until 1989.[22] This book, *Mi encuentro con César Vallejo* (*My encounter with César Vallejo*), traces Vallejo's earliest years of production as part of el Grupo Norte.[23] Critic Luis Alva Castro summarizes: "En su valoración de la poesía de César Vallejo, por ejemplo, se constatará cómo Orrego fue el primer crítico literario en reconocer el valor artístico del gran bardo a quien le vaticinó un futuro fructífero y enriquecedor de las letras castellanas"[24] (In his valoration of César Vallejo's poetry, for instance, one concludes that Orrego was the first literary critic to recognize the artistic value of the great bard, for whom he foresaw a fructiferous and enriching future in Spanish letters). In retrospect, given the critical acclaim that Vallejo would later garner, Orrego's prescience in naming *Trilce* from the start as a transformative collection in the history of Latin American poetry attests to his keen critical eye, even amidst the personally threatening political climate that characterized Lima in the 1920s.

Orrego's prologue to *Trilce* presents a metaphor that contributes to our understanding of Vallejo's vital materialism; in this case, that inanimate materials influence and affect life. In his description of Vallejo, Orrego sketches a fictional scene for readers, positioning the young poet before a doll: "el niño [Vallejo] se llena de estupor ante el sutil juego dinámico, ante los gritos inarticulados de su muñeco. Su asombrada puerilidad toca por primera vez las puertas del misterio"[25] (the child is stupefied before the subtle dynamic toy, before the inarticulate screams of the doll. His surprised puerility comes face to face for the first time with the doors of mystery). The awe that a young Vallejo experiences before the material object, as related by Orrego, captures both writers' simultaneous wonder and fear before that which resembles life, but is not alive. The doll represents Vallejo's initial confrontation with the doubt that plagues human life, captured ironically in "the inarticulate screams" of the doll. This paradox of agency—the doll would seem to want to cry, but cannot—represents a melancholic hope that will also come to characterize most of Vallejo's poetry. This hope for life is expressed by Orrego as "el milagro que se produce en sí mismo, el milagro de la vida, le pueda ser revelado por esta criatura mecánica"[26] (the miracle that is produced inside himself, the miracle of life, it may be revealed to him by this mechanical creature).

Orrego describes the scene further as Vallejo pulls out "las entrañas de trapo y de aserrín tras de haber examinado atentamente la arquitectura de su juguete, tras de haber apartado pieza por pieza todo el montaje interior, tras de haber eliminado todo lo puramente formal en busca de las esencias, el investigador se encuentra ante el primer cadáver de ilusión, ante el primer conocimiento"[27] (the insides, made of rags and sawdust, after having examined the architecture of his doll, having taken it apart piece by piece . . . the investigator encounters his first cadaver of illusion, his first encounter with knowledge). Vallejo's encounter with this same cadaver of illusion comes full circle at the end of his writing life via, again, his own line "su cadáver, estaba lleno de vida" (his cadaver, it was full of life) of poem III of *España, aparta de mí este cáliz* (*Spain, Take this Chalice from Me*).[28] Both the doll and the cadaver are metaphoric prostheses for disillusioned subjects who look for that which enhances aliveness outside of themselves. This lack is filled, temporarily, by other materials of the world that orient the subject toward his or her own perplexing condition.

Orrego equates the relationship between Vallejo and the doll to the poet's artistic process. He elaborates in the Introduction to *Trilce* that the lifeless doll before the eyes of the inquisitive poet symbolizes "la posición fundamental de César Vallejo con respecto a la poesía. Niño de prodigiosa virginidad, busca el secreto de la vida en sí misma"[29] (Vallejo's fundamental position with respect to poetry. Child of prodigious virginity, he looks for the secret of life itself). The search for this "secret" via poetry and prose does not come to a close; it perpetuates itself throughout Vallejo's career. The poetic creation operates, as it does in all the artists in the following chapters, as an addition to him, her, or them. The prosthetic prose, poem, or object stands for the necessary noncoincidence between life and art discussed in the Introduction. Unable to "understand" life, the poetic expression enables Vallejo to point to the inadequacy of language to ever capture the embeddedness of subjectivity within the material world. "Life" happens outside the material form it takes (the body) as much as inside it because it is embedded in so many layers of material influence (the air, the soil, the trees, etc.).

Orrego differentiates Vallejo's aesthetic from that of others, including his own: "Los demás hombres vemos anatómicamente las cosas. Asistimos a la vida como estudiantes de medicina ante el anfiteatro. Nuestra labor es una labor de disección. Tenemos conocimiento de la pieza anatómica, pero no del todo vivo"[30] (The rest of us see things anatomically. We attend to life like students of medicine in the amphitheater. Our work is that of dissection. We have knowledge of each anatomical piece, but not the entire being). Orrego believes that Vallejo is exceptional in comparison to others because the poet does not recognize life as something to be dissected piece by piece, but instead he "percibe el panorama humano . . . retrae hasta su origen la esencia de su ser, bastante oscurecida, chafada, desvitalizada por su carga intelectualizada de tradición"[31] (he perceives the human panorama . . . he traces the essence of being, significantly obscured, flattened, devitalized due to the intellectual weight of tradition, back to its origins). In Orrego's description, the weight of the intellectual tradition devitalizes the human. He likens an implied set of artists, himself included, to scientists in an operating room in the pursuit of the objective identification of organs. Instead, Vallejo captures something additional and impalpable about life that is more than the sum of its physical parts alone but based on its adjacency and continuity with the other vital materials of natureculture.

In Orrego's writings unrelated to Vallejo, he demonstrates that he, too, was influenced by the materialist thinking as well as vitalist philosophy coming out of Europe in the early twentieth century, while engaged in forging his own take on the same.[32] In an essay published in Mariátegui's *Amauta* 27 (1929), Orrego defines an authentic American art as that which arises from a new material orientation. He notes: "Después de repetir malamente a Europa, en segunda edición desvitalizada,—no podía ser de otra manera—los americanos nos estamos convenciendo que América sólo saldrá de sí misma en la proporción del esfuerzo y del valor que tengamos para descubrirnos . . . cada nueva agrupación humana únicamente puede salir de sí misma, nutrirse de sus propias entrañas"[33] (After poorly repeating Europe, in a second and devitalized edition,—it couldn't be any other way—we Americans are now convinced that America will only come out of its shell in proportion to the effort and the bravery we put into discovering ourselves . . . each new human group can only come from itself, nourish itself from its own insides). Orrego diagnoses the necessity of an aesthetic in Peru that relies on its own material reality rather than imitating, and moreover poorly, Europe. The quote criticizes mimesis, which results in a devitalized aesthetic, detached from the local material conditions that are an integral part of the life of the artist and the artistic creation. In contrast to this mimetic aesthetic, Orrego argues for one that originates from the materials at hand. In Orrego's view, art must spring from the materials that sustain the bodies that make up "América," much like José Martí's version of "Nuestra América," as a product of its local resources.[34] This turning in, and even "on" oneself, while it smacks of an isolationist nationalism, is a means to a longer-term end.

In his 1928 *Siete ensayos de interpretación de la realidad de Perú*, José Carlos Mariátegui also speaks to the need for the organic material connection between artists and their creations, emphasizing the relationship between human and the environment. In this work, Mariátegui describes the ways that raw materials shape "life" in Peru. For instance, he explains how the *guano* (fertilizer) and *salitre* (saltpeter) "booms" did not sufficiently produce "una clase de savia y *élan* nuevos"[35] (a new class, made of vital sap and spirit), but instead only led to a mediocre transformation in the old dominating class. This material boom was stimulated by external domination as a result of The War of the Pacific

(1879–1883). In its wake, this war left a nation that was "desangrada, mutilada"[36] (bloodied, mutilated) and that, for this reason, suffered a metaphoric anemia. Implicit in these statements is that the "life" of Peru is affected by forces besides the human being: the impending "market force" of capitalism, the circulation of the *guano* and *salitre*, the flows of people, goods, and capital. These materials, the market, the human laborers, the event that is war, all contribute to the vitality of the precarious nation. And the nation, here, while it is an imagined space, is equated by Mariátegui to its own being—without blood, mutilated, anemic—but alive just the same. The human is not in complete control of the health nor the material resources of the nation because of the plural factors impacting life.

In "El proceso de la literatura" (The process of literature), much like Orrego as cited above, Mariátegui calls for an organic literature that needs to "alimentarse de la savia de una tradición, de una historia, de un pueblo" (feed itself on the sap of a tradition, of a history, of a people), spiraling temporally back to the past but in the name of fomenting change for the future. He goes on to conjure up blood and fat, noting that the "flaqueza, la anemia, la flacidez de nuestra literatura colonial y colonialista provienen de su falta de raíces"[37] (the thinness, the anemia, the flaccidness of our colonial and colonialist literatures comes from their lack of roots). Here, he echoes Orrego and relies on biological metaphors for the creation of a vital aesthetic.[38] Mariátegui's invocation of organic materials emphasizes the necessity of considering the raw material components of life as part of "authentic creation." The appeal to roots and cells adds up to a Peru that must come from its own materiality; a blood transfusion from Europe will not suffice. This articulation of a new orientation toward materiality works on a few different levels. On the one hand, it points to differings within the category of human based on the material context, implicitly reminding readers of their bodies as oriented in space. On the other hand, it points to the commonality of the bare material of blood, a substance that is shared by humans but that is also found in other species. In dismantling the idea of universal human creation, Mariátegui moves the attention to blood or fat instead of a rational subject. Mariátegui's writing metaphorically acts as a resuscitation device for the colonized nation, reorienting the "life" of Peru toward its own material potential and making sensible the potential for a new approximation to humans that accounts for their material surroundings.

Vallejo, like Orrego and Mariátegui, had his own take on the purpose of art. In his oft-cited chronicle "Salón de otoño" (1926), he asserts that art's role is to "elevar la vida, *acentuando* su naturaleza de eterno borrador. El arte descubre camino, nunca metas"[39] (to elevate life, accentuating its nature as eternal draft. Art discovers pathways, never goals). Returning to the beginning of the quote, the notion of poetry as "elevating life," is evidenced in Vallejo's prose poem "Hallazgo de la vida" (1926), first published in Trujillo's newspaper *La semana* the same year. In the first full sentence of the prose, the poetic voice refers to a "presencia de la vida" (presence of life), of which he has recently become aware. The poetic voice exclaims, with uncharacteristic excitement for Vallejo: "¡Señores! Hoy es la primera vez que me doy cuenta de la presencia de la vida. ¡Señores! Ruego a ustedes dejarme libre un momento, para saborear esta emoción formidable, espontánea y reciente de la vida, que hoy, por la primera vez, me extasía y me hace dichoso hasta las lágrimas!"[40] (Fine sirs! Today is the first time that I am aware of the presence of life. Fine sirs! I beg you to leave me alone for a moment, to savor this formidable, spontaneous, and recent emotion of life, that today, for the first time, brings me to ecstasy and makes me feel blissful to the point of tears!). The use of exclamation points three times in the few lines of prose communicate the excessive emotion invoked internally in Vallejo as a result of his experience.

Despite the fact that Vallejo was, quite obviously, alive for many years prior to the publication of this piece, the poetic voice notes the feeling of "firstness" that the present time and space stir within him. Employing the phrase, "por primera vez" (for the first time), he qualifies the present moment as qualitatively "more alive" than moments passed. As he describes it, he wants to taste the hyperpresent aliveness or ecstasy that he experiences, drawing attention to the impossibility to concretize in language the affect of the nuanced contours of a material experience. The assumption upon which Vallejo's momentary aliveness rests is that temporary material conditions have contributed to this affect. In other words, the conditions of this vitality are beyond human agency and form, and instead emanate from the material encounters occurring in the poetic voice's world; yesterday was different than today for reasons unnamed but nonetheless impactful. The vitality that Vallejo's poetic voice expresses in these lines is passed on to his readers, not through the syntax of the words but instead through the poem's resistance to name the very reason for his positive feelings of vitality. This, in turn, leaves readers back in their bodies with an affective experience of wonder as a result of the encounter with the poem.[41]

Material Witnesses: Stones and Statues

> Stone speaks differently from its sibling elements of air, water, and lightning-swift fire. Its injunction is always to step out of the breathless rapidity of anthropocentric frames and touch a world possessed of long futurity and deep past, a spatial expanse that stretches from the subterranean to the cosmic verge.
>
> —Jeffrey Jerome Cohen, *Stone: An Ecology of the Inhuman*[42]

In this section, I will primarily look at the way that stone and rock operate in his corpus as natural and technological agents in his poetry, alongside his own voice. In the past decade, Vallejo's emphasis on materiality has been experiencing renewed attention, in no small part due to the work of Michelle Clayton. Attesting to the predominance of the material in Vallejo, Clayton writes, "Curiously, critics have for the most part sidestepped various actual physical presences and tropes in Vallejo's poetry, preferring to focus instead on expression and abstraction, and almost entirely ignoring the enmeshment of matter—bodies, landscapes, and other natural and manmade objects—with the languages which saturate it and vice versa."[43] While Clayton has covered remarkable ground on this topic in *Poetry in Pieces: César Vallejo and Lyric Modernity*,[44] in this section I build on some of this work by homing in on just a few of the materials that repeat among his corpus. I organize what follows by materials rather than by poetry collection to emphasize the way they serve as a leitmotif in his poetry, particularly from *Trilce* on. The materials I look at come from various sources, and draw together the local and the cosmological as well as the concrete and the existential.

When we think about the vitality of the materials of the natural world, stones and rocks might seem like the absolutely dullest of the lot. They don't fly like birds or flow like rivers; they don't dance like flames or move like the wind. In their obduracy, they seem sucked dry of life, stubbornly lying there as a stagnant surface impossible to move and impenetrable to our touch. Vallejo, as Arguedas will, too, invokes them frequently in their various forms—as "piedra" (stone), as "guijarro" (pebble), in their Incan form as parts of fortresses, and in their Western-aestheticized form as statues. Vallejo's rocks are "found" in Peru, Spain, and France; in poetry, plays, and prose; alone, and with men and dogs and bones upon them. They are steadfast companions to Vallejo's poetic evolution and seem to call to him and draw near to him from myriad angles. If rocks were ever dull, in Vallejo, and later in Arguedas, they are brought to the fore of life as the material backdrop to its unfolding. They precede and outlast the expanse of the life of an individual. While I have been emphasizing the material aspects to Vallejo's poetry, I should clarify that Vallejo does not create an inverted hierarchy of object- over-subject, but instead centers the coexistence and mutually constitutive elements of both as to trouble the starting points for thinking.

Even though it is not the earliest poem to deal with the topic, the poem "Piedra negra sobre una piedra blanca" ("Black Stone on a White Stone"), published posthumously in the *Poemas humanos* collection, is arguably the poem of the Vallejo corpus that most quickly jumps to mind as referencing stones. This is likely due to the fact that not only is the material in the title, but the poem goes on to predict the poet's own death in a way that grabs ahold of readers' morbid fascination. Some critics have taken the black stone to be a gravestone or death itself and the white stone as the poetic voice/Vallejo's body. As the poem unfolds, the white stone seems to be his almost-human body, whose white color is emphasized via the references to bone in the poem; "húmeros" (humeri) and "huesos húmeros" (humeri bones) both appear. "Húmeros" appears in the colloquial phrase, "los húmeros me he puesto / a la mala," used as a way of emphasizing that even one's bones feel bad. The strange syntax of the phrase, "los húmeros me he puesto," deemphasizes the human-as-subject-in-language and instead draws to the fore of the imagination the bones that impact the human, and of which he is both made and that make him. Continuing in this vein, in the last stanza the bones take on a role of witnesses, alongside the rain, alongside "Thursdays," alongside walks or roadways: "son testigos / los días jueves y los huesos húmeros, la soledad, la lluvia, los caminos"[45] (they are witnesses / Thursdays and humeri bones, loneliness, the rain, the paths). Turning inanimate materials such as paths or rain or humerus bones into witnesses, the poet ascribes agency to material objects and draw humans into their reality rather than the reverse, within the context of the poem. The bones are made witnesses to the death of the subject. Like the cadaver with which we began, they too are transformed into perceiving objects of that which the dying, or even the dead, human, is unable to fathom.[46]

The weighty materiality conjured up by the poem offsets the ephemeral and fleeting human experience of life. In reducing human life to a white stone or a pile of bones, Vallejo parodies humanity's hubris while presenting an ironically humble poetic voice who delivers the news of his own death with a hopeful tranquility. The calm acceptance and clarity of vision conveyed via the future tense (I *will* die; not I *might* die), eradicates all doubt, and the attention to mundane details, like the weather and the (arbitrary) day of the week, turn human death into the most ordinary of events. The net impact of the poem is the almost comic realization that human life reduces to bones, made up of the same substance as stone, in fact. This minimalist reduction is both humbling and a relief because it enables readers to grasp that stones and bones remain as geological substrates to the fleeting lives, human and otherwise, passing through the cosmos. In orienting our attention toward this material inevitability, Vallejo pushes the rational, critical readers aside to let other materials come to the fore.

Moving backward in Vallejo's history for a moment while we advance the analysis of rock, Vallejo had already oriented his readers to his affinity for stones similar to those of "Piedra negra sobre una piedra blanca" multiple times in the *Trilce* collection. For instance, in *Trilce* "X," a "piedra" (stone) comes to life, ironically, through its poetic death. Vallejo writes, "la prístina y última piedra de infundada ventura, acaba de morir con alma y todo"[47] (the pristine and last stone of ungrounded fortune has just died with a soul and everything). The idea that a rock would die with a soul "and everything" both animates the rock through its act of dying and again parodies the exceptionalism of the human through the insinuation that this rock is inhabited with soul. In assigning a rock a soul, Vallejo materializes the immaterial, but partially negates the metaphysical concept of the same, through this lithic grounding. The symbolism of this "última piedra," also conjures up the bones of the body, linking human materiality and life to the surrounding world. This similarity is further reinforced at the end of *Trilce* "X," when Vallejo infers that a "patient" died, as if the last stone were a stand-in for this human body. The stone is made the permanent and only witness in the poem, though, because it is named as the "last stone." Through the word "last," Vallejo ascribes the material rock with a geological memory that outlasts and precedes whatever other life hypothetically existed inside the parameters of the poem. The last rock standing is the seemingly permanent material in and of the world, that, once gone, leaves a vacuum approximating nothing. Vallejo's bleak landscape brings us close to the edge of geological time, where the last rock dwells.

Spiraling backward in the Vallejo corpus, rock is conjured up again in one of his earliest poems "Las piedras" (1918), which is again used as a bridge between the human and the unknowable and outlasting cosmos. The rocks are brought to life as he writes, "Las piedras no ofenden; nada codician. Tan solo piden amor a todos y piden amor aun a la Nada."[48] (The rocks don't offend; they don't covet anything; they only ask everyone for love, they even ask Nothingness for love). As the poem continues, he describes that "the moon is a white rock," and addresses himself to "Our Mother," as if talking to a feminized Cosmos or Nature. The poetic voice explains "this morning, I have run with the ivies upon seeing the blue caravan of the rocks, of the rocks, of the rocks." Vallejo paints a nature-inspired canvas of green, white, and blue. Through the juxtaposition of the earlier mentioned white moon, now aside a blue caravan, and the (green) ivy, earthly nature stretches outward through a cosmic blue to the moon. All the while, the poetic voice is embedded within this web, as it runs alongside the ivies, compelled upon seeing this blue caravan of rocks. The repetition of the phrase "of the rocks" at the end of the poem suggests that they trail on into infinity, as if the blue caravan is visualization of their multiplication out into a limitless cosmos. In other words, the poem takes readers from the most local of rocks to the cosmos through Vallejo's formation of a constellation via this geological commonality. A pebble becomes the moon, and a caravan of potential worlds beyond human perception; the infinite rocks. The human is enveloped poetically within the lithic, drawing attention to cosmic movement that goes on regardless of the subject. And yet, like the Incan wall in Arguedas, this rock asks for love, even from Nothingness. The idea of the "rock last standing" from above again brings us to the edge of geological time: at the beginning or, conversely, at the end, rock remains among a vast Nothingness.

Continuing with the same motif, Vallejo invokes a similar moon and the blue, green, and white color palate in another early poem, "Deshojación sagrada" or "Sacred Defoliacity." In this poem, Vallejo transforms a white moon into "dispersed opals," then additionally described as the gypsy heart of the poetic voice. In the iridescent topography of the poem, the cosmological moon is scaled down to the smaller stone of an opal, that then becomes connected to the "heart" of the poetic voice. Via this constellation, again, of the material (from moon to opal to heart), the three materials are strung together as partially similar and partially differing. The cosmic, the terrestrial, and the corporeal planes intersect each other; their differing is less important than their relatability.[49]

In both "Deshojación sagrada" and "Las piedras," the human subject does not look for transcendence beyond nature. Rather, Vallejo sets up a plane of immanence wherein the "gypsy heart" or the "soul" is already contained within the material world of the body, the earth, and, moreover, the cosmos. Vallejo invokes concrete reality as a pretext to draw the cosmos to the fore, thereby subordinating the human experience to something much more encompassing and "beyond" language, but immanent to the affect of sensing these intersecting planes. Opals and moons will exist regardless of the human; again—they are (the last) rocks standing.

Vallejo's play, *La piedra cansada* (c. 1936), is inspired in part by the indigenous play *Ollantay*, and also calls upon rock as a metaphor for the material of the masses, and specifically, the indigenous base to Peru. In this Marxist-oriented play, Vallejo invokes the past and material base of the indigenous population to inspire revolution in the present. When the play opens, the dramatic, anonymous narrator begins by addressing the Rock Mother: "¡Mama Roca! ¡Hermosa piedra! ¡Un día más alumbra tu cansancio! Un día más que vamos a tratar de levantarte"[50] (Rock Mother! Beautiful stone! Another day illuminates your tiredness! Another day that we will attempt to wake you up!). Later, he refers to the "fatigued rock" and the "weary pebble," highlighting the exhaustion of the stones throughout. In act 4 the chorus again yells, "Mother Rock! Tired stone, How many years lodged there in the patient embankment!" and Vallejo refers to "your mysterious tiredness, your tenacious material indolence!"[51] The tired and beleaguered stone is transformed into a malleable and vibrant substance that, in relationship to the community within the play, becomes the source of Life itself. Vallejo, with a directness only characteristic of his most committed Marxist phase, writes, "Rock is the substance of universal life. The God of stone is Inti, the men of stone are the quechua peoples, plants and animals are made of stone, and even the stones themselves are made of stone!" Stone literally is the beginning and the end in this play—the basis for all other materials.

Masters of stonework and technology, the Incans often built their structures into the landscape, so that some rocks that were chiseled to take on a certain form were built around others that were a natural part of the environment, like the site of Sacsayhuaman, where the play takes place. The enmeshment of architecture into the landscape demonstrates the way that natureculture were thought of together, as often the stones in the natural environment served as part of anything built around it.[52] At another point, Vallejo elaborates: "In one rock, sometimes, an entire city is hidden. Another stone contains a bolt of lighting, another an echo, another the color of urine of life, the smell of the sulfur of death."[53] Vallejo emphasizes that these stones are not a separate part of Life but the material base to it, and a link to the past. Vallejo makes the stones sensible as witnesses to potential social change in Peru, and as that which also absorbs the affective realm: the light, the echoes, the smells of life and death.[54] These same stones exist in Peru and throughout indigenous sites in the Andes, steady material guides that orient the fleeting inhabitants of the land.

While his poetry incorporates plenty of bare stones or rocks, Vallejo is also interested in rock in its aesthetically produced form of the statue. In its statuesque form, rock in Vallejo represents, in the Venus de Milo poem, human's search for an unreachable perfect alignment between (human) life and its representation. Vallejo complements the references that he makes to natural stones (other stones appear both in *Trilce* "XVII" and *Trilce* "XXXI"), with references to the contrastingly refined materials of statues. *Trilce* "XXXVI" or "the Venus de Milo poem," tells the tale of the imperfectly incomplete beauty of the statue:

¿Por ahí estás, Venus de Milo?
Tú manqueas apenas, pululando
entrañada en los brazos plenarios
de la existencia que todaviiza
perenne imperfección.
Venus de Milo, cuyo cercenado, increado
brazo revuélvese y trata de encodarse
a través de verdeantes guijarros gagos
ortivos nautilos, aunes que gatean
recién, vísperas inmortales.
Laceadora de inminencias, laceadora
del paréntesis[55]

(Are you that way, Venus de Milo?
You hardly act crippled, pullulating
Enwombed in the plenary arms
of existence,
of this existence that neverthelessez
perpetual imperfection.
Venus de Milo, whose cut-off, increate
arm swings round and tries to elbow
across greening stuttering pebbles,
ortive nautili, recently crawling
evens, immortal on the eves of.
Lassoer of imminences, lassoer
of the parenthesis.)[56]

Vallejo animates the statue through the question directed "to her," this mythological figure suspended in the present, always, and places her gracefully within the "plenary arms of existence." These metaphoric arms seem to reach out from beyond the language of poem to envelop the statue, the poem itself, and all of the matter of imperfectly perpetuating Life. The plenary arms of existence are made concrete via the image of the statue, that stands in as a "cultural" intermediary, again, between the cosmic, the natural terrestrial world, and the human body—here in its culturally mimicked form. The statue, like the stones analyzed earlier, is part of the material natureculture that remains beyond the mortal life of one generation or community and that simultaneously precedes it. It is a witness to more of the cosmos, metaphorically, than any one life could ever see. This statue is brought to life in the present, however, via Vallejo's poetically alliterative "verdeantes guijarros gagos"[57] (greening, rolling pebbles) that emphasize the way that it seems materially alive, like the doll with which we began, before each viewer or reader.

The statue is a perpetually imperfect representation of human life that in its *not quite completion* reminds of a utopic impulse, those green pebbles rolling along that both the statue and the human long to lasso. Like the blue caravan of rocks from the earlier 1918 poem, "Piedras," these greening pebbles seem to roll in a perpetual "forever" of the poem. There is no teleological end to the quest nor a linear movement, just a constant reaching in plural directions at once on the part of the human, embedded in cultural and natural worlds. The imperfection of the uncreated or missing arm of the statue, Jean Franco reads as "related to the cosmos which is all process and unrealized potential."[58] And Christiane von Buelow reads the statue as an emblem for the imperfection of art itself, "*Venus* is thus an emblem for the experiential and aesthetic existence that continues perpetual imperfection."[59]

Like the crippled Venus de Milo, the natural world of Vallejo's poetry is also "mutilated," a description that serves to further downplay the exceptionality of the human and draw attention to substances taken for granted in the atmosphere. In *Trilce* "XVI" even the natural substance of the air is described as mutilated, making poetically physical the essential but invisible air in which terrestrial life is immersed. The poetic voice commands, "Dame, aire manco, dame ir"[60] (Give me, crippled air, give me a go). The "crippled air" is an enigmatic visualization that combines, the cosmos, the terrestrial, and the body again. In the poem, an agent that has power over the poetic voice metaphorically asks permission to take leave from this mundane container of life. The air, invisible, becomes tactile and visible through the description of it as crippled, giving it material form and weight and likening it to an injured human. While the projection of human characteristics onto the air is anthropocentric, it at the same time makes sensible the air as a partial agent with the human, and vice versa. The crippled air is a metaphor, it would seem, for a world gone so wrong that even the air itself is injured.[61]

The Bones of Bare Life

The rocks, stones, and statues in Vallejo link the terrestrial and the cosmic to the human body primarily via the materiality of all three planes. Whereas the rock of the moon brings us from the cosmos to the rocks of the earth, to the statues made of rock that imitate human form, Vallejo also works in the opposite direction. He concerns himself equally with bones, as they move from the human body outward to the earth and the cosmos. As we will see in the second chapter as well, the critique Vallejo performs of human exceptionalism sets the groundwork for a relational ontology among human beings and other things that takes as a starting point their "becoming together," not their different trajectories. To get down to the bareness of the bones of the body, Vallejo must peel back some layers that hide the "subject," to arrive at its base simplicity.

One of the materials that Vallejo takes up on numerous occasions in his poetry to literally undress the fancy superficial subject is a suit. In *Trilce* VI, Vallejo writes, "El traje que vestí mañana no lo ha lavado mi lavandera: lo lavaba en sus venas otilinas, en el chorro de su corazón"[62] (The suit that I put on tomorrow/my laundress has not washed it: she used to wash it in her Otilian veins, in the spouting of her heart).[63] The innovative and nonsensical mixing that occurs between the past (vestí) and the future (mañana) challenges sequential temporality through an illogical and disorienting sequence. This disorientation is further exacerbated as Vallejo uses a verb tense (the preterit) to signal the past, but adverbial noun (mañana) to orient us toward the future. The two come to have meaning only in relationship to each other, as in a before/after pair, not on their own. He also combines a materially connotative verb, like "vestir" (to dress) with the immateriality of "mañana," (tomorrow or "the morning"), a sensed space and time that unfolds, but not a concrete, locatable object. The sequence of the event in calendrical time is rendered irrelevant, because *mañana* becomes incongruous when juxtaposed with the preterit *vestí*. The "traje," a material container for a human, has now passed through the heart of another body, the laundress and her streaming blood. This line of poetry reorients a reader in the material world, startling us before an irreconcilable but alive world in which affect is shared between humans and other things; between a shirt and the bloodstream, and the outside and the inside of a permeable and permeating body. When we approach Vallejo's most well-known and enigmatic avant-garde collection, *Trilce* (1922), on the one hand, the poems it comprises "insistently foreground the process by which things come out of the body and take on their own form."[64] And, on the other hand, *Trilce* also demonstrates how materials from the outside infiltrate the porous human body, acting upon it as it, in turn, spills outward to the environment.

Vallejo emphasizes an open, porous body by juxtaposing the "traje," the material and inanimate object, with the first-person active subject embedded in the verb "vestí." When he observes of his *traje* that "no lo ha lavado mi lavandera" (my washerwoman has not washed it) he then adds an enigmatic statement that is *not quite* a counterstatement, but a juxtaposition that confounds what he just said, "lo lavaba en sus venas otilianas, en el chorro de su corazón." Here, the poet implies, if we were to even attempt a hermeneutic reading, that the *lavandera* absorbed the suit-turned-liquid into her own body, passed it through her veins and heart, and returned it to the body of the poetic voice. This poetic thought sequence overcomes what would be an unbridgeable divide between the poetic subject and his jacket, as the poetic voice enters the suit. He inhabits it, and re-creates it, from the inside out: his body is a jacket, as it were, for the organs of the suit. As the material object passes through the veins of a body, the relationship between nature and culture is transformed such that neither is privileged over the other. Instead, both coexist as open systems oriented toward each other.

Vallejo continues to strip down the human and reach closer to the core of the material existence of him or her. In *Trilce* "XLIX," another suit is animated as the poet writes, "Murmurando en inquietud, cruzo, / el traje largo de sentir, los lunes de la verdad. Nadie me busca ni me reconoce, y hasta yo he olvidado de quien seré"[65] (Murmuring in anxiety, I cross, / the long suit of feeling, the Mondays of truth. No one looks for me or recognizes me, and even I have forgotten about who I will be). The ambiguous gerundial phrase that begins the poem could modify "cruzo" or "el traje largo de sentir." Is the subject embedded in the "cruzo" (I cross) murmuring or is it the suit itself? The ambiguous syntax melds the suit and the potential "I" of the verb, again, undermining the agential capacity of the "human," as the suit is an agent alongside the "self" of the "I cross." As the poem continues, the poetic voice addresses itself directly to a wardrobe, now ascribed agency. "Buena guardarropía, ábreme tus blancas hojas"[66] (Good closet, open your white sheets for me), the poetic voice entreats. Then, the poetic voice goes on to reference the "bastidores donde nos vestimos"[67] (the wings of the stage where we get dressed). But these spaces wind up being empty: there is no one but the body-less suits falling off hooks, the shells of the humans who are not there: "no hay, no Hay nadie; hojas tan solo de par en par"[68] (there isn't anything, there is nobody; sheets so alone, pair by pair). This verb emphasizes a subject-less existence as the center of the poetic line; moreover, the combination of "Hay" with "nadie," is doubly effective at deemphasizing the human subject as central to the poem. "There is nobody" or "Nobody is there" is a paradoxical statement that begs the question of what "there is" if there *is* no one.

From the externally visible materiality of the suit, usually on the outside of the human body, the poem ends with the bone, usually hidden from outside view, at the bottom of the bowl. Both the suit and the bones emphasize the materials at the base of Vallejo's poetic ecosystem, as well as the performed, prosthetic "humanness" of the suit and the natural, species-ambiguous bones. The difference between human and nonhuman is therefore negligible by the time one arrives to the bare material at the end of this poem. Like a rock that becomes metamorphic under heat and pressure, the bones are boiled down to their bare mineral base. Vallejo deconstructs the subject of his poem, leaving us with a reduced stock from which to potentially reorient a deconstructed self. By the end of the poem, the "hojas tan solo" of the poem are transformed into a "gran caldo de alas," and ultimately boiled down, "Y hasta el hueso!" (And down to the bone!). The material bone at the end of the poem as a symbol of life as reduced to the barest of materials, an "Hay" at the bottom of a soup. This very material bone contrasts with the "feeling suit" at the beginning. From suit to bone, Vallejo undermines individual identity, equating it to an empty performance by the "nobody" that it is.

If in the previous poem the bones are abstract and unassigned to a particular person, Vallejo also references more specific bones—those of his mother—in *Trilce* "XXIII."[69] In this poem, the poetic voice directs himself to a mother: "Hoy que hasta tus puros huesos estarán harina que no habrá en que masar"[70] (Today even your pure bones might be flour without a place to be kneaded). In this verse, the bones are turned poetically into a pile of flour without a container, emphasizing material transformation and the conflation of the body of a mother figure with an act she might have (or, just as easily, might *not* have) performed: making dough out of flour. This mixing of materials again emphasizes the reduction of human beings to a mundane substance: flour/bone powder. A mother is not made sacred via the "holy" description of "ashes to ashes, dust to dust," but rather becomes "bones to flour," a much more terrestrial and pragmatic transmutation of life expressed through Vallejo's material alchemy. Reinforcing the point, "Tal la tierra oirá en tu silenciar / cómo nos van cobrando todos / el alquiler del mundo donde nos dejas"[71] (Just as the earth will hear in your silencing / how they go on charging everyone / the rent on this world you leave us). The earth is a sensible agent that, like the rocks above, continues in its "earthiness" regardless of human life. The land is called as witness to the violence of capitalism, as it will "hear" how an anonymous "they" "keep charging us all rent on the world that you leave us." The earth in the poem is implied to be prior to and beyond "tu silenciar," as if it exists beyond the relative present of the poem. The despair of the poet before what seems a broken world is allayed only by the ironic reception of the earth of the silence of his mother, and the plea to a nonhuman source (the earth) that it might "hear" even the silence left in Nothingness, recalling again, the last (terrestrial) rock standing from above.

To further link terrestrial materials to the materials of the body, Vallejo undermines an integrated, "whole" subject. His dilution of a unified subject does not go so far as to eradicate or sublimate it totally to the material world. A human subject exists but is contingent upon many other factors; the subject has agency, but always only partial agency. This is a cornerstone to what I see as Vallejo's monistic philosophy of life, but a nuanced one, and that continues in "Voy a hablar de la esperanza" (1926). Vallejo wrote his piece after founding a Peruvian cell of the Communist Party in 1923, and witnessing social revolution firsthand in Russia and to varying degrees in Europe. Therefore, this piece represents a desire to link a community to the common cause of hopeful revolution based on the negative experience of suffering.

In this piece, Vallejo practices a poetic of *not quite* negation. By "not quite negation," I mean that the poetic voice makes a series of statements followed by only partial negations of the same, thereby expressing a philosophy that is more about differing in degrees than difference as delineating a clean binary between two discrete and wholly separate categories.[72] If we try to interpret the title of this piece then César Vallejo, assuming the poetic *yo* of the phrase "Voy a hablar de la esperanza" coincides with César Vallejo, claims that he is going to speak about hope. The title projects itself toward an unknown future through the present tense form of *ir* as coupled with the infinitive, *hablar*, as well as marks its intention: to speak of hope. But the word *esperanza* never appears in the prose that follows, even though an affect of what "hope" might be rises to the surface of the prose. Therefore, the affect of the piece lies in the interpretive gap between the title and the content; that is, the "meaning" of the words in the title move toward something other than what is projected, undermining our reliance on language as decipherable and presenting vitality as what is to come: the "hope" literally unnamed. The same linguistic lacks or holes that we witnessed earlier when the Venus de Milo tries to lasso "parentheses" is duplicated, but not quite, as Vallejo tries to lasso hope, not aesthetic perfection, in this piece. In both, the object of the poem's orientation is kept out of reach.

Beginning with the title and ending with the last word, the text is a circular paradox. It writes and unwrites itself as it unfolds. Each affirmation is not a negation of itself, but it is neither able, nor unable, to be proved. This beyond dialectical logic moves us into an ontology of becoming: we do not know from what the text comes forth, nor to where it heads.[73] It is not the result of anything, nor is it not the result of anything. It represents the potentiality of neither here nor there, neither this nor that; rather, it resides outside of binary logic. The first line of the text, "Yo no sufro este dolor como César Vallejo" (I don't suffer this pain as César Vallejo) exemplifies a pattern of affirmation and *not quite* coincidence. Vallejo begins the sentence with an emphatic assertion of self: "Yo," a grammatically unnecessary first person pronoun in Spanish because the verb ending has already determined the number and voice of the person speaking. Although Vallejo asserts the first person through the "yo," he then explains that he is not suffering as César Vallejo. This not quite negation confounds personal identity and moves toward an identity based on potentiality and immanence. The line poses many questions: perhaps most obviously, if the poetic voice is not suffering *as* César Vallejo, the proper name, then from where does this suffering originate? As critic J. Patrick Duffey describes it, "Vallejo escribe un poema de su dolor personal, pero al mismo tiempo cuestiona el aspecto personal del poema, y juega con la imposibilidad de definir precisamente el <<yo>> poético"[74] (Vallejo writes a poem about personal suffering, but at the same time he questions the personal aspect of the poem, and plays with the impossibility of defining precisely the poetic "I").

Again, as mentioned earlier, the "I" is both material and immaterial, immanent from the already enmeshed naturalcultural and materialdiscursive world. Vallejo does not completely negate the personal aspect to the poem, but through his partial disidentification leaves the poem open to other narrators of life besides himself. He questions, in my reading, the individual aspect to the poem, through a radical questioning of the name that makes him particular. He opens up the "yo" to multiple voices, all of whom could step into the body of his poem, or, as Julio Ortega has recently described, "no es que el yo poético se deba al yo biográfico, sino que el yo es, más que enunciado, enunciación"[75] (It's not that the poetic "I" is owed to the biographic "I" but instead that the "I" is, more than enunciated, an enunciation). The idea of a "yo" that is an "enunciation" is a future-oriented potential that attests to Vallejo's almost negation of self in the poem, but that creates an open locus in the poem for personhood as anticipated in a future yet to come.

The poetic voice explains that he does not suffer as an artist, as a man, or even as a simple living being. If César Vallejo were dead, the poetic voice would still suffer. In this performance of almost negation, Vallejo's individuality as proper name is eradicated. And here, in the contemporary moment of our rereading of the poem, "he" still does suffer. Suffering, itself, is still suffering. Vallejo relies on the body of his poem to convey a suffering that extends beyond the rational scope of exceptional, single human life. When he writes, "Hoy sufro desde más abajo. Hoy sufro solamente"[76] (Today I suffer from farther below. Today I only suffer). He is not able to eradicate the self entirely from language, as the verb form indicates first person voice but gestures toward the destruction of that exceptional being. This "más abajo" is like the bone at the bottom of the soup bowl, "the zeros to the left" that are in *Trilce* "XVI," the bare life that precedes the individual. The potential for suffering in life is the topic of the poem, beyond the identifiable single subject. Suffering is life: it is the hope of a potential vitality to come. Despite the references to "dolor," or pain, "hope" is the potential to think from an ontological space resistant to the logic of rational selfhood and characterized by radical alterity outside of fixed placement or naming. "Voy a hablar de la esperanza" is exemplary of a much larger project for Vallejo: one that brackets the centrality of the rational subject in order to cut across subject–object duality through the recognition of vital immanence among things and beings, or what William Rowe has described as "un dolor cósmico"[77] (a cosmic suffering).

Vallejo negates causality and the logic of origins when he says that he suffers *sin explicaciones*. Such an undoing of causality sheds light on a condition of life: to be unable to name what it is that is catalyzing an event or response. The poet poses questions: What could be the cause of said suffering? Or even more enigmatically, where is that space (*aquello tan importante; that so very important*) that would have stopped being the cause of such suffering? When he answers his own question, *Nada es su causa* (Nothing is its cause), he declares that nothing is the cause of this suffering, but he reinforces his critique of causality. If causality is thrown into question, then like Gilles Deleuze and Félix Guattari challenge causality in *Anti-oedipus*, a genealogical concept of origins and offspring is also biologically and historically challenged. As Vallejo famously writes, "Yo creía hasta ahora que todas las cosas del universo eran, inevitablemente, padres o hijos. Hoy sufro solamente" (I believed until now that the things of the universe were, inevitably, fathers or sons. Today I only suffer). A world without biological causality is an untethered and frightening world, but also an open world of potential material encounters rather than a linear world of direct cause and effect. Such a world would enable new configurations for culturalnatural social groupings like "family" or "humanity" itself, outside the parameters of representation as it stands today. This disruption of logical ordering or a sequential chain of being is the "hope" of which Vallejo does (not) speak: it is that utopic horizon line toward which the avant-garde is oriented, but to which it will not arrive. The poem's secret, as it were, is contained in that which, like Edgar Allan Poe's purloined letter, is not ever said but simply is. It lures us back in an always postponed hope of discovery for that missing arm of the Venus de Milo, that seems to float in the material past and future at once.

The same idea that the affective experience of life and its suffering stems from an encounter is seen in the poem "Los nueve monstruos," of *Poemas humanos*. In this poem, Vallejo refers to "el dolor que crece en el mundo a cada rato," adding that such dolor happens "dos veces." The repetitious "dos veces," as well as the "do-" sound of "dolor" and "dos," emphasizes the duplication of pain between a potential poetic "yo" who may suffer and the deterritorialization of such suffering into, or onto, its social context. A doubling that encompasses the singular and the collective occurs in the poem. The single human being's suffering is such that it would also seem to be felt and shared by inanimate objects: "Y el mueble tuvo en su cajón, dolor; y el corazón, en su cajón, dolor; y la lagartija, en su corazón, dolor"[78] (And the furniture had in its drawer, suffering; and the heart, in its draw, suffering; and the lizard, in its heart, suffering). Vallejo's poetry ingeniously mixes the natural and the cultural. Humanmade objects, like the piece of furniture, mix with biological forms, such as the heart. Furniture with a drawer becomes a heart with a chamber, which then morphs into an animal, a reptilian lizard. In fact, in his study on stone and literature in the medieval period, Jeffrey Jerome Cohen speaks about the "vertebral bone" that links the human with other species, "vertebral bone is the architect of motion, the stone around which the flesh arranges itself to slither, run, swim, fly."[79] The bones and the rocks of Vallejo's corpus help us see the common substances reflected between human and other natural substances, and in addition, between species as different as the reptile and the human.

Ignacio López Calvo provides an analysis of "Los nueve monstrous" in his article, "El fluir de conciencia en César Vallejo." He writes of this poem that "es muy común encontrar en su [Vallejo's] poesía elementos cotidianos evocados con gran ternura, como el cajón que aparece en este verso relacionado al corazón, seguido de palabras más prosaicas o conversacionales como 'lagartija'"[80] (it's very common to find in his poetry mundane elements invoked with great tenderness, like the drawer that appears in this verse related to the heart, followed by more prosaic or conversational words like "largartija" [gecko]). However, whereas López Calvo describes the mixing in terms of the way Vallejo finds an equilibrium between the "eloquent" and the "mundane," we might also consider the broader philosophic underpinnings to such asynchronous mixings. In order to explain "distinctions" and overlaps between species, Judith Butler has written, "For the human to be human, it must relate to what is nonhuman, to what is outside itself but continuous with itself by virtue of an interimplication of life. This relation to what is not itself constitutes the human being in its livingness, so that the human exceeds its boundary in the very effort to establish them."[81] Vallejo draws attention to this "interimplication" of life among animate and inanimate objects: to the way that our personal suffering emanates outward toward material objects, and vice versa. The recognition of what it is to be "human" is contingent on a sense of shared vitality that, while it happens between humans, also occurs in the encounters between the human and the nonhuman.

In order to think through the relationship between Vallejo's subversion of subject–animal–object hierarchies, as well as his aforementioned overturning of causality and single origins, Deleuze and Guattari's work, especially in *A Thousand Plateaus*, runs partially in the background. For the latter, "Becomings-animal" are neither dreams nor fantasies. They are perfectly real. By "perfectly real," they mean that *becoming* produces nothing other than itself: the abstracted movement from one state of desire to another. As they write, "We fall into a false alternative if we say that you either imitate or you are. What is real is the becoming itself, the block of becoming, not the supposedly fixed terms through which that which becomes passes."[82] As a reader brackets his or her own body to enter that of the poem, the reading process enables the reader to *become* something or someone else. In this way, the poem itself enables a series of *becomings* for the poet, the reader, and the text itself. The relationship between these three challenges the confines of a territorialized space (the form of the poem), a singular body (yours/mine/the author's), and the fundamental subject–object hierarchy that determines otherness relative to the human. The vital aesthetic Vallejo creates ultimately demonstrates how the artistic object serves to draw our attention to the knowledge structures that foreground our beliefs about the difference between animate and inanimate things, instead of the relationships between them.

Poetry as Prosthetic

The crippled air and the armless Venus of *Trilce* "XXXVI" evolve into the description of literal physically crippled bodies as a result of the violence in post–World War I Europe and the lead-up to the concrete events of Spanish Civil War. While Vallejo's early poetry is marked by the influence of his experiences in Peru, in his later poetry he takes the common cause of the Civil War in Spain, which brought so many artists together, as the impetus for his poetry. In his *Poemas humanos* collection, we find countless descriptions of mutilated or maimed bodies. In writing poems that expose readers to this collective loss, the poems stand in as prosthesis, to staunch the pain of the the poet and that of his readers.

In one of his most literal poems about physical injury, Vallejo writes, "Existe un mutilado, no de un combate sino de un abrazo, no de la Guerra sino de la paz. Perdió el rostro en el amor y no en el odio. Lo perdió en el curso normal de la vida y no en un accidente. Lo perdió en el orden de la naturaleza y no en el desorden de los hombres"[83] (There exists a mutilated man, not from combat but from a hug, not from the War but from peace. He lost his face in love and not in hate. He lost it in the normal course of the day and not in an accident). Vallejo paints a picture of a man literally without organs, "Yo conozco al mutilado del órgano, que ve sin ojos y oye sin orejas"[84] (I know the one with mutilated organs, that sees without eyes and hears without ears), and he tells us that this being "nació en la sombra de un árbol de espaldas y su existencia transcurre a lo largo de un camino de espaldas"[85] (was born in the shadow of a backless tree and its existence unfolds across a pathway of backs). Vallejo paints a dystopic, lifeless world for his readers without light or meaning, but that serves as a reflective space of hope for abstract loss. This living yet mutilated life continues in the "aire inmortal e inmemorial"[86] (immortal and immemorial air) that sustains its body-turned-into-trunk. In spite of the physical destruction the being has suffered, there is a vitality to the life of which Vallejo writes that exceeds its categorical human form and seeps outward to us, "por los brazos y las piernas y los pies"[87] (through the arms and the legs and the feet). The poem stands in for the "eyes" and the "ears" that the human life of which it tells does not have: a partially restorative prosthesis for the violence incurred in the world, even in times of peace, and absorbed by the immortal air in the foreground.

Vallejo makes an even bleaker statement about the dilapidated state of the world around him in another poem of the same collection. This time, it is not a man who is mutilated, but what seems to be "life" itself: "Cesa el anhelo, rabo al aire. De súbito, la vida se amputa, en seco. Mi propia sangre me salpica en líneas femeninas, y hasta la misma urbe sale a ver eso que se pára de improviso"[88] (Longing ceases, tail in the air. Suddenly, life amputates itself, sharply. My own blood splashes me in feminine lines, and even the city itself comes out to see what stops unexpectedly). Vallejo creates a poetic sensation of "longing," as if it were an animal, tail in the air. Desire, in the form of a tail in the air, is juxtaposed with a trademark Vallejo reflexive verb, "se amputa," and the active subject of the sentence, "la vida." The poetic voice captures something bigger than his own life in these verses, but rather a stopping or ceasing of a collective longing on the part of a shouting but nebulous "urbe" that appears as witness. The urbe is an agent, consisting of materials and bodies unnamed, that witnesses the autoamputation of life, calling this partial collectivity to the scene as ethical witness to a violent undoing.[89] By the end of the end of the prose poem, "cesa el anhelo, a la altura de la mano enarbolada"[90] (longing stops, at the height of the raised hand). The poem circles back to its initial longing, a longing that ceases at the height of the raised hand. The poem enables this mixing between culture, nature, and human, resuscitated here for each reader. In the poem, life itself as more complex than the sum of its components appears on the horizon, in its knotted sculptural, physical, and natural lines of articulation. The poem is a prosthesis to "life,": both metaphorically staunching the blood flow of the amputee, and reinstating a longing for life that is only seen via the vital form of the statue as it sprouts new life.[91]

During the years he spent in Paris from 1923 until his death in 1939, with travel to both Russia and Spain, among many other places, Vallejo's preoccupation with his own death as well as with the momentum that would lead up to the Civil War in Spain resulted in a growing focus on mortality in his poetry.[92] Even more so than rock or bone, death—in all its elusiveness—would seem to be the opposite to human life. However, as we have already seen in this work, Vallejo presents death not as the opposite to life but an active agent that is not heading toward a definitive end. In his last collection *España, aparta de mí este cáliz*, while death is happening around him, poetry seems to serve as a temporary prosthetic affective solution to the very real physical loss that Vallejo witnesses around him. In the first poem of the collection, "Himno a los voluntarios de la República," Vallejo names twelve different body parts—huesos (bones, again), corazón (heart), and espalda (back)—to name a few. A stray limb or seemingly "unattachable" body part like a *pecho* (chest) or a *frente* (forehead) is transformed from a once-integrated part of an organism into material detritus left to the world. The poem is directed to any number of "voluntarios de España," the Republicans who are fighting against Franco's fascism, but they carry the burden of an "agonía mundial." Vallejo moves from the particularity of "tu corazón" (your heart) personalized through the possessive adjective "tu" or "mi pecho" (my chest) again personalized through the possessive adjective "mi," to speak of this diffuse agony that emanates from the poem. The poem materializes "loss" through the reference to the body, and also serves as a replacement, metaphorically, for stray limbs. In this sense, the poem is a prosthesis for a collective body that "lacks." It is a cultural production that hooks into a reader as a temporary fix for the lost vitality caused by political violence.

In the third poem of *España, aparta de mí este cáliz* Vallejo writes about Pedro Rojas, a synecdoche for the Republican forces engaged in an active resistance of the fascism espoused by Franco's Nationalists:

> Solía escribir con su dedo grande en el aire:
> ¡Viban los compañeros! Pedro Rojas,"
> de Miranda de Ebro, padre y hombre,
> marido y hombre, ferroviario y hombre
> padre y más hombre, Pedro y sus dos muertes.[93]
>
> (He used to write with his big finger in the air:
> "Long libb the comrades! Pedro Rojas,"
> from Miranda de Ebro, father and man,
> husband and man, railroad worker and man,
> father and more man, Pedro and his two deaths.)

I am interested first in the assemblage that is formed with the string of descriptors: "padre y hombre" (father and man), "marido y hombre" (husband and man), "ferroviario y hombre" (railroad worker and man), and yet again, "padre y más hombre" (father and more man), "Pedro y sus dos muertes" (Pedro and his two deaths), Vallejo casts the proper name *Pedro* as a synecdoche for innumerable living people. He emphasizes that the Pedro Rojas, who lived as a father, or as a husband, or as a railroad worker, represents the multiplicity of potential *Pedros* that died. Each descriptor of Pedro indicates another one of his relationships to others, relationships that when named manifest the web of relationships in which Pedro comes to have meaning. Meanwhile, the second death that Vallejo mourns stands in for the consequences of the death of the one on humankind, represented by the "hombre y hombre y hombre y hombre." Because of the poetic repetition, the term "hombre" becomes one component of a much broader community. This community is, syntactically and metaphorically, made up of the relationships between the singular being as well as his or her relationship to other animate beings and inanimate objects. A community is forged on the strength of the "and," the bond between one *and* another. But it is not the simple sum of the parts. Rather, it is the exchange between the various persons of a community that serves to bind the one to the many: the *hombre*, plus *hombre*, plus *hombre*.

The chain of *hombres* that Vallejo names captures a Deleuzian notion of conjunctional becoming instead of a singular ontology based on the verb "to be." As Deleuze and Guattari write: "The tree imposes the verb 'to be,' but the fabric of the rhizome is the conjunction, 'and . . . and . . . and . . .' This conjunction carries enough force to shake and uproot the verb 'to be.' Where are you going? Where are you coming from? What are you heading for? These are totally useless questions."[94] "Pedro" is an arbitrary name that stands in for the myriad potential lives lost during the Civil War. He is not a person, per se, but rather a figure who is always *becoming* someone or something different, here in the poem; he is the next life that might be lost; the potential of more lives lost to come. Arguably, it is not of concern to Vallejo where Pedro Rojas has gone or who he ever "was," but the effect of his existence on a community. The poem serves as metaphoric prosthesis to ameliorate the loss of life: to give to the lives that receive it an affective experience to alleviate pain as it makes "pain" materialize through words.

A life-affirming approach to death is reaffirmed in Vallejo's later description of Rojas's *su cuerpo, un gran cuerpo* (his body, his great body) that is discovered after Pedro Rojas is dead. Rojas's single physical body is transformed into a sacred metaphoric body, as the adjective "gran" poetically permits that this single body is offered up to the world in a scene reminiscent of a New Testament death and resurrection scene. This time, however, a Marxist everyman working in alliance with others through repetition and conjunction stands in as the promise of change in the moving contemporary. As an extension of the life lost, the elegy stands in as the Pedro Rojas and the *y, y, y, y hombres* whose bodies have gone before, who are reading the poem, and who will potentially read it in the future. The elegy performs the role of (re)vitalizing the body: through the act of reading, or listening to the poem being read aloud, a community of readers is called as witnesses to this loss. Pedro Rojas is therefore *not quite* dead but continues to affect us through the materiality of the poem itself. The poem and Pedro Rojas rest in latent states of potential, able to come up and haunt us at any moment. The elegy holds the memory that, each time enacted, brings Pedro back to not-quite life.

Julio Ortega observes that the fact that Pedro writes, in the quotation above, with his "dedo" suggests "una escritura natural; y escribir en el aire, una escritura cósmica . . . esta escritura 'natural' y 'cósmica' está hecha con el propio cuerpo, tal vez con la propia sangre, y es una pre-escritura, una huella oral, que irá a ser también una post-escritura, una marca transnatural"[95] (a natural writing, writing in the air, a cosmic writing . . . this natural and cosmic writing is made with his own body, maybe his own blood, and is a pre-writing, an oral trace, that will also be a post-writing, a transnatural mark). Ortega's reading of Rojas's "transnatural" writing is in line with my interpretation of Vallejo's vital aesthetic: the exchange between the human finger and the natural air brings the terrestrial, the cosmos, and the human body together. The notion of a "pre-escritura" or "una huella oral" draws into the poem the distinction between *zoë* and bios. It is the hand of a human (nature) writing in nature (the air). In this sense, the poem is about Nature: that which facilitates any relationship to exist. If "life" is a central trope of the turn-of-the century aesthetic, and obviously a major concern during the charged period of both the Spanish Civil War and the extremism to come out of World War II, Vallejo's poem speaks to sacred life—not just biological quantifiable life but rather life as a bare potential, to be transformed. Bare life precedes and supersedes, in the sense of being "felt" after it is gone, the particularity of nameable species, individuals, and bodies. The use of the finger as a writing instrument, is crucial to a cuerpocentric reading of Vallejo's approach to writing. In naming the finger, Vallejo reduces humans to their bare material existences and the imperceptible traces of life that are given off in the air, moving through it after an agent's death. These traces of cells, of molecules, of the very iron-filled blood of which the stars are also made, permeate back into the cosmos.

In Cornejo Polar's reading of the same poem, the links he makes to Arguedas are particularly relevant in the context of this project. For Cornejo, he reads the "Pedro" of the poem as "piedra," or rock, and the "Rojas," in its redness as a reference both to blood and to communism. As he notes of Vallejo's concept of Piedra Rojas, "es algo que está misteriosamente comunicado con la imagen de la 'piedra de sangre hirviendo' que surge vigorosa e iluminadora, ante las milenarias piedras cusqueñas, en la visión de Ernesto, el entrañable personaje arguediano"[96] (this concept is mysteriously communicated with the image of "stone of boiling blood" that comes up so strong and illuminatingly in the vision that Arguedas's beloved Ernesto has before the rocks in Cuzco). In both the texts, the "alchemy" between the written word and the spoken sound is enacted through the authors' writing. The reference, however, to the the rock of boiling blood demonstrates the intimate link between the physical body of Pedro/Ernesto and the materiality of the rock, beyond the written or spoken word. Their bodies are intimately linked to the terrestrial and the cosmic via these "millennial rocks" that affectively bring readers back to a past, ground them in the present, and throw them into a transformed future. The starkness but solidity of the stone returns us to the bones of bare material life that run throughout Vallejo and Arguedas's texts.

In Poem IX of *España, aparta de mí este cáliz*, written with the title, "Pequeño responso a un héroe de la República" (Short Response to a Republican Hero) (1937), Vallejo reanimates innumerable "heroes," but via their transformation into cultural artifacts or nature. Vallejo refers to an untitled book that "retoñaba de su cadáver muerto" (a book that sprouted up from his cadaver). By selecting the verb *retoñaba*, which has botanical origins and translates as "to shoot," or "to sprout," Vallejo emphasizes the vital materiality of the book by way of its eerie juxtaposition with a once-living, now dead, body. The prefix of the verb, *re*, implies that this growth is happening for at least a second time, if not a third or fourth, speaking to a cycle of life, death, and material transformation. Vallejo's selection of the verb *retoñaba* in the context of both a dead body and the product of a "book" merges, once again, natureculture as well as deathlife. The poem centers becoming-something-else as the vitality of Life itself: the movement from one form into another. By means of the material book, the text and the body converge; this is the same process occurring at a metalevel, as I read Vallejo's poetry as prosthetically serving to remind humans of what any given individual lacks. The body of the reader comes into contact with the "poem" and realizes upon reading that there is more power in nature than a single body nor a single mind nor a single cultural artifact could possibly ever lasso together. The coexistence and collision of the body, the sprout(ing), and the book encapsulate Vallejo's vitalist aesthetic as it mixes the animate and the inanimate in the poem to make sensible the impact of cultural production on the human, even if produced by the human.

Later on in the same poem, Vallejo enacts a collective and metaphoric "carrying" and honoring of the Republican cause of the Civil War in Spain by resuscitating lives gone by through the poem.

> Se llevaron al héroe,
> y corpórea y aciaga entró su boca en nuestro aliento;
> sudamos todos, el hombligo a cuestas;
> caminantes las lunas nos seguían;
> también sudaba de tristeza el muerto.[97]
>
> (The hero was carried off,
> And corporeal and ominous his mouth entered our breath;
> We all sweat, under the load of our navehalls;
> Moons were following us on foot;
> The dead man was also sweating from sadness.)[98]

The lines present a concrete visual image in the form of a group of people carrying a body, either over their shoulders or in a casket. In the next line, however, Vallejo writes what veers into the surrealist, as a physical description and more tangible word, *corpórea*, or "corporeal, bodily" and a sensorial, intangible word, *aciaga*, or bitter, are juxtaposed to describe the physical "mouth" of the soldier. This mouth enters into *nuestro aliento*, or our breath. The material mouth serves as an ironic metonymy for the intangible life of the soldier, a vitality that Vallejo transforms and distributes among the invisible molecules of our "shared breath." In transforming this other body into "shared breath," Vallejo draws attention to a shared, neutral plane that belongs to no one but is simply the minimal condition for exchange between animate materials. No human life is not somehow immersed in the air, and yet the air is hardly only human. It is a plane that moves freely in and out of bodies, human and animal alike, and that moves germs to and fro and weather currents here and there. Even though the soldier's biological existence has passed, his materiality is transformed back to the air, but not into any one individual. This vital air is made sensible through Vallejo's art, and will be retaken up again in the third chapter on José María Arguedas.[99]

To conclude, Basque sculptor Jorge Oteiza (1908–2003) designed an abstract rendition of Vallejo during a visit to Lima in 1960. His work was considered the first abstract work of art in Lima and is a short few blocks off the Plaza de Armas, in front of a baroque church, in the Plaza de San Agustín. The heavy iron form is sturdy, made of negative space as much as positive: the cutouts from the iron suggest the absences in Vallejo's language, the words that leave us seeking potential or hope. It is not a literal representation of Vallejo as human, it is a representation of the philosophy of becoming that Vallejo's poetry enacts. It is a material form transformed from the memory of his life. The iron abstract form sits atop a large stone engraved with the name "César Vallejo," almost as if a tomb.[100] Touching this sculpture is not touching Vallejo but rather just one ways that "he" has been materially transformed, becoming alive again in the material world: "Oh piedra, almohada bienfaciente al fin" (Oh stone, well-doing pillow at the end). Vallejo's vitality is redeposited into his gravestone, into the rocks, the pebbles, the sculptures, and the poems, that affect and attach to us, prosthetically, with more world than the human alone can ever hold in his or her mutilated arms. The stone's tiny accretions are the demonstration of a cosmos that extends outward from the books and corpus of Vallejo: a pebble in the process of greening, rolling perpetually toward the future of Life.

2

Alejandra Dorado's Installation Art

Material Transmutations in Contemporary Cochabamba

Cochabamba, Bolivia (a compound of the Quechua words *cocha* [lake or body of water], and *bamba* [plain]) took front and center on the national and global stage during the water protests that erupted there between 1999 and 2000.[1] Even though Bolivia had returned to civilian rule in 1982 after a string of consecutive dictatorships, the political and social instability that ensued resulted in acute skepticism among the popular classes of the government's ability to provide them with essential resources.[2] Under the second constitutionally elected presidency of ex-dictator Hugo Banzer (1997–2001), the government signed a legal contract to privatize water under the auspices of a company named "Aguas del Tunari," (Tunari Waters) a subsidiary of the multinational giant, Bechtel. When the price of water began to skyrocket, peasants and retired union workers, led by activist Oscar Olivera, took to the streets of Cochabamba, demanding that the contract with Aguas del Tunari be dissolved.[3] When the government refused to heed their demands, civilian protests continued until Banzer was forced to sanction a government siege of Cochabamba due to mounting tension. The national army was dispatched, only exacerbating the conflict. Finally, after the conflict and its media coverage reached a tipping point when a Bolivian army member fired a rifle into a crowd of demonstrators and killed a high school student, the government met with Olivera. As an end result of the meeting, government officials signed a formal agreement guaranteeing the ousting of Bechtel and turning Cochabamba's resources over to the public sector again. Nevertheless, despite the legal victory, "by the time the state of siege was lifted, on April 20th, the confrontations had claimed five lives, four of them civilian."[4]

What has become known as the Cochabamba Water War brought to the fore of the Bolivian imagination underlying structural instabilities to the neoliberal nation. The water war was an important event in a long history of confrontations between those in power and those without. Because a significant portion of those affected by the water crisis were peasant-class farmers, and self-identified as indigenous, the privatization of this essential resource was another drop in the bucket of their historical marginalization. As Jonathan Assies observes, "At the root of the problems in Cochabamba was a rather classic 'urban contradiction': the precarious and class biased distribution of a scarce collective consumption good."[5] The population that needed the water most was precisely that which could not afford the bills that saw water prices spike as much as 150 percent. Water, or *yaku* in Quechua, is a vital natural substance essential to the maintenance of human and animal life, as well as to plants, the food supply, and the health of the environment. The water is an entry point into Cochabamba and the predicament of its twenty-first-century citizens as they advocate for the vital resources that create and sustain the life of an ecosystem, not just for humans. Water, like other natural resources, brings together and connects diverse actors, Andean and international, human and nonhuman alike. And Bolivia, landlocked and the poorest country in South America, is particularly attuned to the dependency on internal resources for livelihood because there is no port. These events in Cochabamba partially fueled the momentum that led to the election of Evo Morales in December 2005, and that ultimately would lead to the new 2009 Constitution.[6]

In this chapter, I build on the arguments made in chapter 1 by looking at "beyond human" from the perspective of the feminist, queer, and transhuman art of Alejandra Dorado. By "transhuman art," I refer to the ways that installation, digital, and performance artist Dorado makes sensible the ways that technology can both harm and free the human from the confines of biological identity. In this chapter, I make sensible the ways that humans are material, active beings made up of DNA as well as passive surfaces for cultural, natural, and technological inscription. However, beneath biopolitical differences metaphorically etched onto the surface of the body, the moving vitality of bare material life links beings together and reorients humans to consider life beyond the dualities of subject–object, human–animal, or nature–culture, as we will see most explicitly again in chapter 5 on Magda Portal. What is common in community is not only what is contained within the human but also that which connects the human to other forms of life, be it the lives of animals or nonhuman entities, that which makes up the *zoë*, or bare life, of a community, and the influence of technology on the same.[7]

Dorado's projects manifest a vital materialist approach to life in two ways. On the one hand, her art makes sensible the physical body as it superficially looks in contemporary Bolivia, drawing attention to the commonality of the body. She produces exhibits in which she puts her own body and those of other fellow citizens and visitors directly into the exhibit. Citizens are represented, for instance, in photographic forms that make visible the way that the state regulates bodies through the construction of national archives, registers, and normative language. On the surface, Dorado's installations make the relationships between real people and their images visually sensible, causing them to confront the ways that images, as well as the visual component to words and language, can devitalize and objectify life by representing it as if it were something to capture or contain, not something emergent. But this work ultimately reinstates the bare materiality of the human as a source of agency and pure, moving potential.

In this second way, a reinstatement of bare life makes sensible what Claire Colebrook has theorized as a "passive" vitalism. Dorado's art, this is to say, demonstrates that "life is a pre-individual plane of forces that does not act by a process of decision and self-maintenance but through chance encounters."[8] This second type of aesthetic is what Colebrook names "queer" because it is "distanced from the already constituted images of life as necessarily fruitful, generative, organized and human."[9] Dorado transforms materials in her exhibits to critique the notion that life is "as it is represented" and instead consistently demonstrates that it is in a process of becoming that is partially under a human subject's control and partially a result of the human's positioning among objects of the world. Like José Muñoz's work on queer futurity as cited in the introduction, Dorado's work too points to life as that which is to come via her exposure of the confined subject as trapped in language to the potential for its embodied movement among other materials. The human experience of "life" is partially passive in the sense of being orientated by the material world as much as orienting oneself in the same. Her work contributes to new materialist thinking because it looks at humans as partial agents in and partial surfaces *for* the enactment of life, not the sole proprietors and creators of the world.

In what follows, I look at three of Dorado's multimedia installations. First, in her exhibit *martirio* (martyrdom) (2006), she combines images, texts, and the participants' bodies-in-motion to demonstrate that archives are not closed structures but instead underwritten by infinite combinatory possibility between letters, images, symbols, and moving bodies in space. The material encounters that the installation enacts demonstrate that life is a series of positions and orientations before others and objects, not a linear or predetermined path. In a place like twenty-first-century Cochabamba, where linguistic and racial diversity are defining factors to the community, as well as the natural resources with which we began, a recognition of difference is essential to building community but so is an awareness of the bare material vitality to life, beyond divisions that parse people into hierarchical categories based on gender, race, class, sexuality, and their intersections.

In my analysis of *martirio,* I pay particular attention to the poetic trope of the unstable anagram to demonstrate that, beyond a linguistic term, this functionality in language serves to relate different letters while remaining outside the meaning system itself. In other words, the anagrammatic function of language facilitates the combination of various semiotic registers: visual images combine with letters, bodies, and texts to reflect back the way that, for Dorado, life is partially facilitated by *zoë,* which fuels a series of material encounters that are open to chance. Like the anagram itself, "life" is what is *not* ever able to be represented. It lies, as in my interpretive concept of the avant-gardes, at the margins of representability because it is unfixed by the institution of art, but yet is the outside that defines the institution. Likewise, the anagram is a function that makes mean that which is inside the language system and therefore representable. This "outside" might be likened to *zoë,* or bare life, that is already part of bios—politically qualified life—that links humans, animals, and other life forms.

In the second section of this chapter, I analyze Dorado's critique of domestic violence and her denaturalization of "disciplined bodies" in her installation *Castigadores domésticos moderados* (Moderate domestic punishers) (2008). In this exhibit, Dorado draws attention to the domestic violence women continue to experience, particularly in Bolivia, while simultaneously parodying the prolific visual representations of the historically masculinized, militarized, and heteronormative nation. She juxtaposes pictures and the recorded spoken words of Bolivian women to critique their (self)-objectification in society: an ambiguity that can sometimes underlie "gendered" behavior. When the installation is considered as a sum of its parts, it never forms a "whole" per se, but hinges on the fluctuating network of relationships it reveals. Like the anagrams Dorado uses in *martirio,* the exhibit only functions through the tensions it makes sensible between its relational components. Because there is no prescribed direction in which to walk or look at the exhibit, life is presented as a moving experience that is impossible to look at without already acknowledging one's embedded location in the network of relationships that make up the material experience. The exhibit is not a reproducible image. Its vitality, like that of life, is the event that it causes: a movement of bodies through the time and space of the exhibit in relationship to the other materials around us.

Lastly, I look at the ways that Dorado reflects on human life as it is increasingly mediated through, enhanced, or controlled by technology. For instance,

Dorado produced a series of digital images with a gender-nonconforming friend of hers. The digital art medium gives Dorado and her friend the potential to visualize alternative potential bodies to those that they possess. This projection enables them to imagine the singular self beyond its DNA coding and genealogy and in relation to desires that delink sex from the outwardly visible performance of gender. These images underscore the arbitrariness of physical "organs," in comparison to a contextual and fluctuating material orientation dependent on more than DNA. With these images, Dorado lays bare the potential for material transformation as an integral component to vitality in the world. In addition to her use of digital media in the context of gender and sexual identity, Dorado also uses the digital to contemplate interspecies relationships, one of the first Bolivian artists to recognize the theoretical implications the virtual might have on topics of identity formation. In sum, the material manipulations in language and images she catalyzes point to life beyond the confines of the biological human. In addition, Dorado's digital manipulation of humans in combination with animals and other forms demonstrates the way that nature, culture, and technology traverse each other in increasingly inextricable ways that resonate with and depart from that which we saw in the previous chapter.

In my discussion of all three exhibits, I analyze the common thread that runs through Dorado's projects: a consistent attention to the tension between bare material potential and the "represented" life of a partially differing subject. The tensions she creates reveal the power that metaphoric "bodies" like gender discourse or the "military" have on constricting the movement of real human lives. However, she also draws to the fore that life does not have to be approached from the perspective of the two-eyed, seeing subject, but could be conceived from the perspective of a series of porous bodies in contact with each other. Materials that are "added-on" to the bare human, like our reading of César Vallejo's poetry as partially prosthetic, demonstrate that life is immanent; that is, it is an emerging concept that springs from the assemblages between diversely oriented humans, other forms of life, and the objects in and around them.

Encounters in Cochabamba

I first "met" Dorado in Cochabamba, Bolivia, in July of 2006. As I found myself walking along a narrow sidewalk on Calle España, a few blocks north of the Plaza del 14 de Septiembre, a black and white poster affixed to an otherwise empty granite wall jumped out at me. The poster was no more than two feet by three feet, a replica of the exhibit cover to Dorado's interactive art installation *martirio* (martyrdom), to open later that week at the Centro de Cultura Simón I. Patiño.[10] The poster was a stark aberration from the images I typically saw on my walk across the colonial part of town. It displayed a provocative bare

FIGURE 2.1. *martirio* catalogue cover, by Alejandra Dorado. 2005.

abdomen that was slightly gender-ambiguous. The central image of the belly button was neither ugly nor beautiful, and in its paradoxical obviousness, seemed to mock the dressed performance and differentiation of the myriad people walking down the street. In its bareness, it appeared to challenge the exterior public construction of self we perform. Underneath our clothing each person's abdomen looks relatively similar. However, the belly button is the trace of a unique but also universal event: a particular subject's birth and cut from his or her mother. Below the surface of the body there is not an essential "self" to be found but a site of potential that emanates from our material form as it circulates in the material world. The encounter on Calle España—myself looking at a resemblance that was other than me—hinged upon the recognition of similarity and difference at once as it played out in the already dense web of discursive and material threads through which I roamed in Cochabamba.

This first encounter on Calle España recurred a few days later when I walked by El Centro Cultural Simón Patiño in Cochabamba, a contemporary art space, permanent museum, and education center, on the other side of town.[11] Here I saw the poster again, and coincidentally, the artist herself bringing in pieces of her soon-to-be installed *martirio*. The imagined perception I had of the artist became actualized, as her material form took shape before me. I later learned that the poster was based on a photograph of the artist's body. The top of the photograph began just below her chest and the bottom ended just below her belt. The image revealed a slender torso dressed in a black T-shirt that was raised by her own hands to hit just below the area where a bra might start, and she donned black pants adorned by a silver-studded belt. The exposed midriff of the artist highlighted her compositionally and physically centered belly button, offset by a two-inch tattoo of a slightly surreal-looking sun. She was visually alternative to the most ordinary of abdomens, due to her tattoo, and for those who could already name her as a result of that inscription, due to her singular proper name.

Born in Cochabamba, Bolivia, on September 24, 1969, Dorado grew up as an only child to parents Toni (Antonia) and Mario, lifelong residents of Cochabamba. Her father is an accomplished architect and carpenter and her mother a Spanish teacher to foreign exchange students. Dorado initially got involved in the arts through dance, participating in modern dance performances throughout Bolivia beginning in 1979, until she moved to Chile. Her continued participation in dance contributes to the motion of bodies through space, upon which the effectiveness of her art tends to depend. After studying art and architecture for two years at the Universidad Mayor de San Simón in Cochabamba, she moved to Santiago, Chile, where she continued her formal art studies, majoring in fine arts with a minor in painting at Universidad ARCIS (University of Art and Social Sciences). Since returning to Bolivia, she has worked primarily in Cochabamba as an art professor, an installation artist, and a performance artist. Since 2008, she has organized and participated in the only annual performance workshop in Bolivia, which brings national and international artists together for a series of professional and creative events. In this first exhibit that we will analyze, Dorado makes the material-discursive construction of bodily production sensible through the ways she critiques the ways in which we classify and delineate the human.

Anagrams: *martirio* as Material Critique of Biopolitical Discourses

In her poem "Frente a la vida" (Confronting Life), the Peruvian poet Magda Portal situates herself before the sea. She writes, "I estoy aquí—enorme Mar / Humano Mar / Mar mío"[12] (And here I am—enormous Sea / Human Sea / my Sea). In this poem, Portal repeats the word "mar" three times in three lines in order to draw attention to the relationship between the poetic voice and the vast sea, the "human sea" that the "I" wishes to possess, but that also serves as the place that ultimately contains the poet: Portal is of the sea more than the sea is hers. In Alejandra Dorado's exhibit *martirio* (martyrdom) she also relies on the word "*mar*" (sea) as well as the concept of the moving water, to emphasize the fluctuating relationships among the material and the discursive as the two co-constitute each other. To create her exhibit, Dorado relates many disparate components—digital photography, ink stamps, excerpted texts, and material human bodies—to make sensible the tension between bare life (taken here as the material) and political subjectivity (taken here as the discursive). Dorado makes sensible the ways they are bound together and thereby criticizes the notion of universal subjects who could detach themselves from the material sea in which they swim, and the material body in which they come to be.[13] In relating the various material components to her exhibit in a specific way, she is able to make visible and critique the ways in which cultural scripts are imprinted upon us and the ways in which the human is object and subject at once. We will turn directly to the installation—installed in Cochabamba, Santa Cruz, and La Paz at different times—in process.

As a potential participant in the installation, one is thrown into a ring of forty life-sized colored photographs.[14] Each of these photos captures the head-to-toe body of a unique Bolivian who exposes his or her torso, and specifically, the belly button. Dorado affixed the photos carefully to the four walls of the exhibit space so that a continual chain of bodies rings the room. There is no clear "start" or "end" for the viewer, defying a teleological history. The people captured in the photographs are of various ages, some female, others male; some in *polleras* (traditional skirts worn primarily by indigenous women), some in jeans; some very light skinned, others with darker complexions; some young, some old. All of them, however, expose their belly button.[15] While there are only forty of them, they represent the members of a plural community whose differences are superficially visible but become quickly secondary in the space of the exhibit. In fact, the register-like chain of bodies moves our attention to what they have in common: their exposed abdomens.

To gather these materials, Dorado invited her subjects—around town, friends, people she encountered in her daily life—to lift up their shirt to expose their belly button before her camera lens. Once she had gathered enough photos, she neither digitally nor otherwise enhanced their quality because they were supposed to serve as a raw, very partial register of the Cochabamba population. Dorado's act of photographing a bare stomach with a camera makes physically visible and sensible the violence of the camera's gaze. Because these images overtly expose physical vulnerability, they make the symbolic violence of a disembodied "eye of the state" sensible, drawing attention to the far from neutral status of something like a state register or census. The exhibit gives rise to a questioning of the violence of the archive, and the way that state control over clas-

FIGURE 2.2. *martirio* installation, photographs detail, by Alejandra Dorado. 2005.

sifiable life can lead to violations of the very lives it would espouse to protect. Dorado insinuates that the artistic space is like a political space through the employment of this type of register.

Photographic registers have been and continue to be used to record, monitor, archive, and even falsely represent the existence of bodies within the state and the institutional apparatus of the same. Deborah Poole's comprehensive work on the ways that images of the people of and the place called the Andes have circulated on both sides of the Atlantic. Her work is concerned with the ways in which images were produced, traveled, and accrued value while contributing to evolving notions of race and its hierarchical violence from the late eighteenth to the early twentieth centuries.[16] To be seen and captured on film is to be partially colonized because moving life is transformed into an object on display, and an "object," often taken out of its material context.

But Dorado's installation is not a static representation of an archive but rather a provocation to critique the ways in which visual and discursive registers can be disrupted. The photos take on their full significance in relationship to the rest of the materials in the installation space.

The photographs are put in conversation with the various textual elements that transverse them, creating a complex semiotic game. This further emphasizes the tensions and the imbrications between materiality and discourse. At the center of the exhibit is a small table with a square glass-box placed on top of it. Inside the box, at its base, rests a small photo of Dorado's belly button illuminated from below—the same photo from the exhibit catalog. Directly above this glass a transparent thread hangs from which dangles a small photo of the artist, in swim gear, including a bathing cap and goggles. She poses as if launching herself from an imaginary diving board directly toward the belly button in the illuminated box. The artist dives into the shadowed depth of her *ombligo*, "the door of birth and the place of deathly return," as described in her exhibit catalog.[17] This self-reflexive component to the exhibit mocks the unknown aspects to her singularity—that in part include her unknown birth and death—as part of the installation. By including an image of herself in the exhibit, Dorado "the artist," or "the photographer," purposely temporarily separates her proper named self from her bare material life via this representation. This gesture is important because it draws attention to the distance between one's lived, embodied experience and the subsequent aesthetic representation of it within a potential political realm. It is in the interval between physical reality and its interpretation by the state in which political power resides.[18] Dorado makes this space sensible by invoking the audience to participate actively in the exhibit.

To that end, on a table next to the aforementioned glass box and "diving" artist, there are wood stamps, each of which represents a letter of the word *martirio*. Anyone in the audience can pick up a stamp, dip it into the ink, and imprint the massive photos with it. No one is "asked to," but the installation prompts viewers to act, attesting to the pull of the artistic materials over the viewer. As participants stand before each photo, they can perform their own anagrammatic game by using the stamps Dorado provides. Grabbing hold of the chosen stamp, a participant can create new words, phrases, or figures out of the letters of *martirio*. Spectators can also mix the letters with the representative "bodies" of the photographs, creating tattoos of sorts on the surface of another. The letters gradually begin to obscure the body of the person in the photo, muddling its details behind a screen of ink. Again, the role that the technology of writing plays in defining, confining, and altering material bodies is made sensible through Dorado's visualization of the entanglement of the subject, the object, and the writing instrument.

The choice of stamps, as opposed to a pen or a marker, emphasizes the mechanical aspect to the textual screen that is layered upon the photographs. A stamp invokes the transgression of one human's physical movement onto the surface of the body of another's. The stamps lack the intimacy of handwriting and recall Franz Kafka's "In the Penal Colony," as the harrow inscribes the prisoner with his "sentence" in a mechanized, but now outdated, sign of corporeal punishment.[19] To "stamp" a photograph, an audience member has to press the letter with some vigor onto the image as well as think about the placement of the mark. The act of stamping serves multiple purposes. On the one hand, it places power into the hands of the person who does the stamping.

FIGURE 2.3. *martirio* installation, stamps detail, by Alejandra Dorado. 2006.

But on the other hand, it draws attention to the common body of actor and recipient because of the neutrality of the belly button, as if to say, "you, too, are being stamped all the time and have been since the day you were born." When I looked at the visual register of photos after they were stamped, the stamps revealed something about the energy of the body from which they originated. In some cases, someone had stamped the same letter many times in one spot leaving a very dark imprint on the photograph. Once the lettered layer is thick enough, the physical details of the person as well as what is written on the image mix and mingle in an anagrammatic visual/textual game. The title of the exhibit, *martirio*, becomes distorted as viewers rearrange the letters on the bodies, making sensible the literal but more importantly symbolic traces of one person on the "body" of another.

An additional component to the exhibit is a meticulously placed paragraph extracted from a relatively unknown essay by Michel Foucault titled "Siete sentencias sobre el séptimo angel" (Seven sentences on the seventh angel).[20] This essay was originally published as part of the introduction to the nineteenth-century book *La grammaire logique* (Logical grammar), written by the French linguist, Jean-Pierre Brisset. Brisset self-published this text in 1883, but it remained little known until it was republished with Foucault's piece in France in 1970. The selected text extends itself around the exhibit, running along the ground, in a font large enough to be easily legible from wherever one stands in the space. The paragraph that Dorado excerpts from the full text (which is about three thousand words) is anagrammatic and playful, and yet at the same time, unsettling in that it starts with the word *el demonio* (the demon):

> *El demonio* = el dedo mío no. El *demonio* presume de dos dedos-dedos de dos-, dado el dedo de Dios, su sexo. . . . Invertida, la palabra *demonio* da: la *monda* = una mondadura = un mundo de altura. A lo alto del mundo = yo empino el mundo. El demonio se convierte así en señor del mundo en virtud de su perfección sexual. . . . En su *homilía* él se guiaba por su *ombligo*: su *ombliguía*. La *homilía* es la mira del *maligno*. De un mar *igneo*, ven tú, el *más digno*: el maligno es una criatura del mar, de un *mar tibio*. Ahí salta y sortea el *martirio*. Con mi salto al *mar me tiro*.[21]

This ludic text, only one of myriad anagrammatic structures Foucault includes in "Siete sentencias" (Seven sentences) continuously transforms words and the phonemes that compose them, as each semantic unit is deconstructed and reconstituted into something that resembles what it just was but is also a transformation of its previous form. As Foucault exploits each phoneme and its potential permutations, an empty center to the paragraph holds, enabling readers to sense the movement of the text, but not its meaning, like the "holes" we find in Vallejo's poetry. The empty center that enables a reader to track motion is the common, nonsignifying nucleus of decipherable language that brings us, literally, full circle if we "read" along the ground of the exhibit space. The subtext at the ground is in constant dialogue and tension with the mingling bodies in the exhibit space and the mixing of images and visual words over the course of the paragraph and our circling around the room. Freud writes, "There is often a passage in even the most thoroughly interpreted dream which has to be left obscure; this is because we become aware during the work of interpretation that at that point there is a tangle of dream-thoughts which cannot be unraveled and which moreover adds nothing to our knowledge of the content of the dream. This is the dream's navel, the spot where it reaches down into the unknown."[22] The center of the paragraph is like this Freudian knot: the navel, meaningless on its own, but yet the cipher that enables the motion and tension within the system.

The Foucault text that Dorado includes in the exhibit continually mutates, deconstructs, and reconstitutes itself from beginning to end. Once it has gone through a number of permutations, the traces of a given word's starting point are still present despite the metaphorical distance their transfigurations. Like the experience of reading Foucault's text, as viewers read the text and circle the exhibit space, they never return to the same starting point, but experience the different relationalities between the bodies on the wall, the stamps, the letters of *martirio*, and the text. The aesthetic effect of the exhibit resides in the movement and friction caused between the materials. In fact, without the movement

FIGURE 2.4. *martirio* installation, stamped photographs details, by Alejandra Dorado. 2006.

of bodies through the exhibit, it would not make the vitality of life despite systematized linguistic or visual constraints sensible.[23]

Now, beyond the description of the exhibit, what does it all amount to? The artist's statement about the installation opens the exhibit catalog, and begins midstream. Here I have translated the Spanish to English:

> the language of the image that circulates through all strata: social, cultural, economic; the axis: the belly button, open to all transformations. The text decomposes in its most primitive form to regroup an idea many times . . . the root of the signified is in the nature of the significant; both fundamental in semantics, as much with respect to the image as the text: in sum, in the plastic arts. The hermetic symbolism of the signs; the asexual belly button, the androgynous belly button: door of birth.[24]

The *ombligo* (belly button) is the first written mark on the body of all humans, regardless of gender, and simultaneously is a physical symbol of our entrance into society as an autonomous being, cut from our biological mother's body, but dependent on a larger social body for our sustained existence. As the cord is cut, the body comes into contact with other bodies that have a complexly different DNA sequence but can still be deciphered as *alike* yet *different* from one another. In Dorado's reading, the belly button is metaphorically the door of birth, through which the body enters gradually into the domesticity of a societal archive, like the register of photos that ring the exhibit symbolize.

The idea of being born androgynous and then "gaining" gender or sexuality presents the cultural aspects to identity, as that which is embodied and that which is made or "done upon us," by the networks in which we are embedded. Part of the traumatic experience of being born is the violence of the proper name that is bestowed upon us through language—written or nonwritten, according to Derrida. Jacques Derrida's reading of such violence in the seminal "Writing Lesson" in *Of Grammatology* considers the obliteration of the proper as even prior to writing, "When within *consciousness*, the name is *called* proper, it is already classified and is obliterated in *being named*."[25] No matter who we might think we are, behind our countenance, our hair, our sexual or asexual body, we will be classified as a gendered subject, and assigned an identity by others at birth, an identity that is and is not our own making. In *martirio* the idea of the bare body open to other bodies and languages, stamps and registers, draws attention to the ways in which technology can be violent. However, just as easily, as we will see later, the ways in which technology and the natural mix can be positive in enhancing vitality.

When considered as a whole, the mechanism that enables the installation is an anagram: the playful shuffling not only of words but also of materials. As a biological example of the same linguistic concept, the human body and identity itself are made up of similarly functioning DNA. Our DNA holds the genes of those who went before us. If in the twentieth century humans tended to know their lineage, technological advancement increasingly changes and challenges that genealogy. DNA is and has always been the repository of mutational possibility, as well as a systematic code that undermines individuality not only as a human but also as humans given our only slight deviation with the DNA constitution of an ape. Whereas Vallejo expresses his confusion upon realizing that not everything in the world is either father or son, Dorado's corporeal-based art, perhaps more obviously than any of the artists of this project, reinstates the inextricable relationship between nature and culture, as the body, both her own and other people's, as the base of her artistic process. In this sense, her installation challenges Foucault's passive approach to the body as site of disciplinary inscription because active audience participation is the hinge upon which the exhibit operates. The visible language-centered aspects to the exhibit are challenged by the invisible code of the body that makes sensible the vitality of our DNA: that which moves us in ways beyond the human.

Andrea Bachner writes in her article "Anagrams in Psychoanalysis: Retroping Concepts by Sigmund Freud, Jacques Lacan, and Jean-Francois Lyotard" that although metaphor and metonymy have been the privileged tropes within the context of psychoanalysis, an anagrammatic approach to psychoanalysis opens up new avenues of exploration that reveal the "ana-grammar" of the unconscious. Bachner writes, "The anagram is the site which makes the combinatorial character of sign systems visible. This visibility can be achieved by different means (and their combinations): through a potential incompleteness of the anagram, through a palimpsestic thickening of a text (in its widest sense), through a mixing of units of different sign systems, or through a destruction of the conventional textual units. The anagram as a figuration shows itself to be only the petrified trace of the anagram as a process, a permutation beyond the laws of specific discourses."[26] According to Bachner's analysis, the anagram is less important as a linguistic figure and more relevant to study as a process. The movement between letters and registers that also transforms the word or image is what makes the anagram vital as a trope. But the vitality is not what the anagram was before (from where did it come?) or what it will be after (where is it going?) but rather the process and potential for mixing in its pure potential.

When we consider Dorado's work through this trope, the relationship between sign systems functions through a combinatorial process that is in excess of the regulatory laws of any one discourse, and is the vitality that keeps it perpetuating itself. This combinatorial process of DNA plus linguistic code plus bodies moving opens up new spaces of enunciation for marginalized subjects because it goes beyond one privileged way of expression into a realm of anagrammatic semiosis.[27] There is a common nucleus that connects the one to the many and facilitates transformative relationships: the vital materiality to bare life. Life happens in the space of the installation only with the participants present. Without them, language and image lose their controlling power. Dorado's installation illuminates the fact that, "in bringing people and things into a common frame of 'bodies,' the idea is not that things are enchanted with personality but that persons *qua* materialities themselves participate in impressive thing-like tendencies, capacities, and qualities."[28]

In total, the exhibit makes sensible, like Vallejo's work, the notion of a nomadic, partial subject; that is "a contested space of mutations that follow no technological directives and no moral imperatives."[29] The installation helps reveal the nonunitary subject—a nomadic, dispersed, fragmented vision, which is nonetheless functional, coherent, and accountable, mostly because it is embedded and embodied. The result of this installation is that Dorado returns us to our bodies and to the sea (The "mar" of *martirio* refers to the sea), to where it begins and ends, just as it does for Magda Portal as well. Rosi Braidotti explains, relying partially on Donna Haraway's work, that bodies as objects of knowledge are material-semiotic generative modes. Their *boundaries* materialize in social interaction. Boundaries are drawn by mapping practices; "objects" do not preexist as such. Objects are boundary projects. At the end of this exhibit, one is left as a witness to the absurdity of the anthropocentric fixation on a bound identity, as a *martirio* is transformed into *mar me tiro* (sea, I throw myself). The image of an artist "throwing herself" to the sea expresses an agency to move the material body and an acceptance of the discursive, material, natural, and cultural elements in which the human is already immersed. If we take Donna Haraway's "Cyborg Manifesto," Dorado's *martirio* demonstrates that we, like a machine, are an informational pattern that happens to be instantiated in a biological substrate.[30] Language capabilities and critical reasoning aside, at the end of the day, we are just DNA always under the potential of moving out of the "human" phase that we are in to something beyond our current configuration.[31]

Critique of Violence and Hypermasculinity

In this second section, we will look from another angle at the ways in which feminist materialist work has contributed to new materialist thinking via analysis of a second exhibit of Dorado's *Castigadores domésticos moderados*. This exhibit criticizes gendered violence, particularly against women. Silvia Rivera Cusicanqui has observed that, "A lo largo de la historia colonial y moderna la sociedad había visto y internalizado la imagen implícita de las relaciones entre los géneros incluye: varones ocupados exclusivamente de la representación pública de la 'familia,' en la que se subsume a la mujer ya los hijos . . . mujeres dedicadas exclusivamente a las labores reproductivas y decorativas"[32] (Throughout colonial and modern history, society has seen and internalized an implicit image of gender relationships, which includes: men occupied exclusively with the public representation of the "family," under which category his wife and children are subsumed . . . and women as dedicated exclusively to reproductive and decorative labors). To critique domestic violence, both physical and symbolic, and the colonial and modern circulation of images that can contribute to violence against women, Dorado re-creates domestic space in this multimedia installation to make sensible the network of factors that contribute to dehumanizing gender binaries.

Of note is that this installation, unlike the more conceptual *martirio*, was inspired by a real case of domestic violence that occurred in 2006, in which an indigenous woman killed her husband in self-defense.[33] Dorado was able to meet the woman, who was imprisoned in Cochabamba. Dorado visited her in prison and got to know her; eventually the woman related her story to her. With her permission, Dorado recorded the woman's story, which became a central axis to her exhibit. As the exhibit recounts, the woman's life was one of constant hardship with a series of family complications and mental and physical abuse.

In the installation, Dorado did not want to simply retell this specific story; she also wanted to present the way that doubt enters the equation so frequently in questions of violence; the shadow of doubt about what really happened, whether it is in regard to the specific case or to the more abstract question of violence.[34] Dorado therefore wanted to open up a space through which viewers could experience the underlying hypocrisies and ambiguities to gender dynamics in society as the complex problems they are, not as stereotypical truths.[35] To make sensible the material and discursive layers to violence, the installation creates a multimedia web of images that evoke forms of physical and psychological violence or suffering. Dorado uses four primary components to create the exhibit: a video, a series of portraits of women, a series of portraits of men, and photographs of physical scars. Temporally and spatially, as was the case with *martirio*, the installation does not ask to be experienced in any particular order, providing the participant with partial agency to connect the dots between the multiple contents Dorado provides.

In one area of the exhibit space, a single-channel video runs in a ten-minute loop and flashes images of different women sitting alone in kitchen chairs, backs turned to the camera, facing the corner of the room. These women appear to have been punished, banished to the corner of a space that has traditionally been "theirs." The fact that Dorado is videotaping them, however, now makes what was an invisible concrete reality suddenly repetitively visible on the screen, consequently exposing an aspect to women's lives not sensible in the public sphere of society. The women's physical position in the video cues a number of possible readings. On the one hand, their hidden faces symbolize shame and convey a fear of being seen. Backs to the screen, the women are also metaphorically "faceless." While they represent a singular person, they also stand in for a potential site of injury for any number of women. The video is also filmed with a rose-colored filter. This pink color, integral to the entirety of the exhibit, is a purposefully clichéd nod to the female gender, but also to pop culture, in the sense that Dorado implies through association that pop culture reproduces gendered stereotypes.

In addition to the video, which runs simultaneously in a loop with the audio testimony of the imprisoned woman, Dorado also includes a group of portraits of Victorian-era soldiers, set off in a corner. The photographed portraits of the men are small, no larger than eight by ten inches, each a black and white print displayed in a stand-up, antique frame. As critic Pedro Albornoz notes in the catalog, they are "men with a Victorian air, embodying social virtues thought to be positive for their virility—detachment, stoicism, lack of expression, dignity."[36] The original portraits are in sepia tones lending an ominous air to them, and the expressions of the military seem almost smug, as they cluster together on the floor of the exhibit room, surreptitiously surveying the space (as well as the visitors and the other components of the installation) from one corner of the room. A given viewer almost does not notice them because they are placed in a subordinate spatial position.

In thinking about Foucault's concept of the Panopticon as elaborated in *Discipline and Punish*, from which the gaze of the disciplinarians can see those that they discipline while those disciplined cannot see them, Dorado ironically

FIGURE 2.5. *Castigadores domésticos moderados*, video installation detail, by Alejandra Dorado. 2008.

reworks the dominant gaze of surveillance from above by inverting the hierarchical spatial order attached to predominantly male and military scopic regimes.[37] By transforming the spatial arrangement between those who traditionally represent authority and the bodies who pass through the exhibit, Dorado critiques the coloniality of vision: who has the power to see whom, and from what vantage point.

Just as she critiques the coloniality of space, Dorado keenly critiques the ways that gender and sexuality also operate within the coloniality of power. As María Lugones makes evident, heterosexism as practiced by the colonizers brought with it a new gender system "that created very different arrangements for colonized males and females than for white bourgeois colonizers. Thus it introduced many genders and gender itself as a colonial concept and mode of organization of relations of production, property relations, of cosmologies and ways of knowing."[38] Gender and heterosexuality as predominant modes of societal organization are part of what Dorado critiques. Therefore, to reveal and mock the hyperenacted masculinity of the military, Dorado mockingly adds effeminate details to each portrait. She adds bright pink rosy cheeks to the men's faces, and other chromatic details; a flower on a lapel or a ribbon on a hat, pink buttons on a military jacket, or a cute bunny peeking out of a corner don the portraits. Each stoic, steely-eyed, and seriously dressed man has been turned into a *cursi*, effeminate version of himself. Because Bolivia has a long history of military dictatorships that did not cease until the technical return to democracy in 1982, Dorado's critique compounds years of history.

Dorado parodies a *machista* attitude but also underscores the fact that such attitudes are embedded in the historical national imaginary, exemplified in her choice of antique portraits instead of contemporary images. The use of antique photographs also performs a metacritique of the antiquity of a *machista* attitude, while it simultaneously grants modern-day viewers the benefit of the doubt that they may have outgrown such a perspective. Through these photos, Dorado mocks the military institution by urging viewers to see its stoic heroes as no more than aestheticized images that represent prosthetic selves. Because the additional details are so obviously "artificial" they draw attention to the act of representation itself, not actuality, undermining more obvious tangible representations of masculinity and virility by turning them into transvestites. The obvious performativity of identity is emphasized, as a denaturalization of masculinity and its associated disembodied gaze.

The third component of the exhibit is a series of enlarged portrait photographs of diverse women, captured in black and white. These portraits are enlarged to expose close-up details of their complexion in comparison to the small eight- by ten-inch frames of the military men. The women are shown in intimate detail: the lines around the women's eyes are visible, their dimples, their dry lips, or their high cheekbones The visual proximity we experience relative to the women creates an intimacy between them and the viewer that is lacking in relationship to the materially diminished men. While the men's faces are serious and neutral, these women convey vulnerability but are still steadfast in their gaze. Unlike the men, these women appear "current," with haircuts and clothing that evoke the present. And spatially, they hover at the viewer's horizon, in a much more prominent place than the vintage photos on the ground. The materiality to the set of the images of the women contributes to their impact on viewers: each photo is printed on a plastic latex material that resembles the standard white shades one might find on the windows of an ordinary house. By choosing this material, Dorado makes a connection between the women and their connection to the domestic space. Dorado uses her own hair as thread that she embroiders onto each of the portraits, using variegated "styles" of stitching. The end result is that it appears as if each woman either has an exaggerated scar or stiches beneath her eye, or more poetically, that she is crying. By incorporating her own hair into the exhibit, Dorado emphasizes her own material trace upon the exhibit, implying that she just as easily might be one of the women on the shades. The hair also, again, emphasizes the materiality of the body and its potential transformation into a fragmented object.

FIGURE 2.6. *Castigadores domésticos moderados*, portrait installation detail, by Alejandra Dorado. 2008.

The scars along the faces speak to the simultaneous ubiquity and singularity of domestic violence. Each woman's face is marked distinctly from any other woman's face, but the differences are indiscernible from a distance. This tension between uniqueness and similarity provides a powerful critique on societal attitudes toward domestic violence. Dorado insinuates that there is a collective capacity to gloss over domestic violence or to simply pull down the shade and ignore it. But in tension with the passivity of societal reactions, Dorado makes hypersensible women as those who have historically suffered. Additionally, the women's images are each adorned by a cartoon animal that has been digitally added to each portrait, emphasizing the relationships between the various materials and media. The apathetic women seem somewhat oblivious to "male" cartoon characters (wolves, dogs, tigers, jaguars) who stare outward at the viewer. The bright pink cartoon animals are the imagined perpetrators of the literal or symbolic violence inflicted on the women, as well as perverted symbols of childhood innocence. The bright pink color of the animal matches the same pink detailing on the portraits of the military men that oppose them, creating a dialogue between both sets of portraits. And, because animal decals exactly like those that Dorado chose frequently adorn urban minibuses and micros throughout Bolivia—which are almost exclusively driven my men—they make further reference to the pop cultural materials that reproduce gender stereotypes. Additionally, the game between the innocent animals that adorn the portraits of the military heroes and the aggressive cartoon figures on the women complicates simple binaries between men and women. Because cartoons are abstractions of the real, they serve as a counterpoint to the physical realness of the women. Natasha Lennard and Cary Wolfe, in a recent article on posthumanism, write, "The sketches of the 'human' or 'the animal' or 'nature' that we get from the humanistic tradition are pretty obviously cartoons if we consider the multi-faceted, multidisciplinary ways in which we could address these questions."[39] The juxtaposition Dorado makes of black and white photos with hypercolor cartoons is a strategy that begs for more complex inquiry into the difference between representation and real life.

Still another component to the exhibit is the series of photographs that Dorado took years earlier during a visit to Cuba. Each photo captures a visceral, raw scar of a recently performed cesarean section. The graphic photos invoke physical discomfort and pain, an integral part of their ability to affect viewers' sense of their own bodies. In order to convey the rawness of the wounds, Dorado enhanced the photos digitally, saturating the skin around them in a bubblegum pink tone. The wounds themselves are five to six inches in length and are stitched with a visible dark-colored thread (these wounds were stitched in the hospital, not like the case of the shade images where the women's tears/scars were added synthetically). The skin that is pulled together by the stitches looks very tender and slightly curled on either side of the stitching, opening the wounds to a few different interpretations. If I did not know their origin before seeing them, it is not implausible that the sewn-up slit in the photos could be representative of a vagina. The fleshiness of the skin on either side of the stitching as well as the magenta color of tender skin folds contributes to this reading.[40] Dorado's wounds more abstractly resemble the sewn together lips of a mouth, representing in a corporeal image the silence that women have kept historically and fearfully continue to keep, regarding domestic violence of any form. But the wounds also criticize the reduction of women to the labors of childbearing and the domestic space.

In sum, as an assemblage of objects and bodies, images of the living and the dead, sounds, sights, and even smells, this exhibit operates through the relational tension between its parts to initiate a range of critiques of gender, sexuality, and power. While the deep rose color unites the disparate components of the installation, the meaning of any one component is contingent on its articulation with the image or an audio component next to it, as was the case with *martirio*, emphasizing the experience of vital life as contingent upon material context and relationality. The discrete pieces are experienced as a field of potentiality, as they can be rearranged, mixed, and added to or subtracted from in an ongoing story of emergent interpretation, all dependent on the way that the person participating in the exhibit experiences it and walks through it. Through the complexity of the components of her exhibit, Dorado makes sensible the ways in which women, and specifically women's bodies, are the form and surface that carry the symbolic burden of failed partnerships, the scars of physical labor or abuse, or the confines of the domestic space. Maria Lugones has asked, "How do we understand heterosexuality not merely as normative but as consistently perverse when exercised across the colonial modern gender system so as to construct a worldwide system of power?" Dorado's work attends to part of this question by making sensible the violence incurred within heteronormative relationships.[41]

Domestic violence continues to be a problem in Bolivia but has received more attention in recent years than in the past. In March 2013, Morales proposed Law 348, which protects women against violence and proposed three areas of action: prevention, protection, and sanctions against aggressors. In 2013 the Special Forces in the Fight Against Violence in Bolivia registered 15,000 cases of violence against women reported, whereas in 2012, prior to Law 348, there had been over 50,000 cases.[42] Dorado's art works toward materializing the isolation of gender and domestic abuse. In moving about the exhibit, the entanglement between viewers and the materials among which they move is brought to the fore. While *Castigadores domésticos moderados* emphasizes the way that power dynamics of stereotypical heteronormative relationships can repress and punish women, in other digital works, Dorado prompts an approach to gender difference that privileges invention and play beyond the confines of biological DNA, as enhanced by becoming with prosthetics, drag, and digital manipulation.

Queer Vitality

In a photographic series in which she actively participated, Dorado problematizes the notion of her own fixed gender, puncturing categorical definition and the confinement of her "self" in favor of playing with the potential openings in art for the expression and representation of a different orientation in the world. In the provocative series of photos *Speculating on the Same* or *Speculating on Myself* (Dorado offers both as titles) she subordinates the organizing principles of difference and individuality as secondary to those of similarity and doubt around one's own sexuality and desires. In the images, she combines parts of her own body and parts of other bodies digitally to demonstrate the inventiveness that is part of gendered identity and the power of technology to enable us to play with virtual aspects of self that otherwise would be less easily accessed or explored in a pretechnological age. To produce the images of this series, Dorado and a friend of hers who identifies as male but regularly performs in drag created a series of images together that were digitally manipulated to point out the ambiguity of gender and the spectrum of ways in which "female," "male," "one," or "many," are constructed both biologically and socially.

Dorado and her friend "Bianca" produced these images together. Bianca and Dorado cross dress in the images and Dorado plays with color so that Bianca is captured putting on mascara with a pink background behind "her," while Dorado in "typically" male briefs is shown with blue behind her. If one does not know either of them nor the specifics of the context, both Dorado's and Bianca's biological sex is opaque. Dorado adds in digital details, too, for instance, black and white graphic overlays that reference anatomy as well as hermaphroditic figures that hark back to classical mythology.[43] These photos demonstrate a dialogue as much between Dorado and Bianca as between each with a spectrum of selves. When Dorado chooses the phrase, "speculating on the self, or speculating on the same," she communicates first that the self contains more than one "gender," so to speak, and is able to hide or reveal different parts of his or her identity within. And then, in another sense the idea of "speculating on the same" equates Bianca to Dorado in a way that emphasizes the performative nature of *any* gender, not just that practiced in drag. The images in the collection—sixteen in total—are powerful individually, but even more so as a group.

In the images, Dorado mobilizes a process of disorientation in that the origins of gender and sexuality are shown not just to be given but rather that they can also be acquired. As Braidotti writes, "de-familiarization is a sobering process by which the knowing subject evolves from the normative vision of the self he or she had become accustomed to. The frame of reference becomes the open-ended, interrelational, multi-sexed, and trans-species flows of becoming by interaction with multiple others. A subject thus constituted explodes the boundaries of humanism at skin level."[44] The poetic "explosion of the skin" of which Braidotti speaks is visualized by the digital manipulation Dorado does to alter the idea that identity is a stationary concept. *Zoë*, a life force that is not classifiable but that which potentiates life and moves across species, is the catalyst behind this transformation: the spark to play,

FIGURE 2.7. *Especulando sobre lo mismo* photo 1, by Alejandra Dorado. 2004.

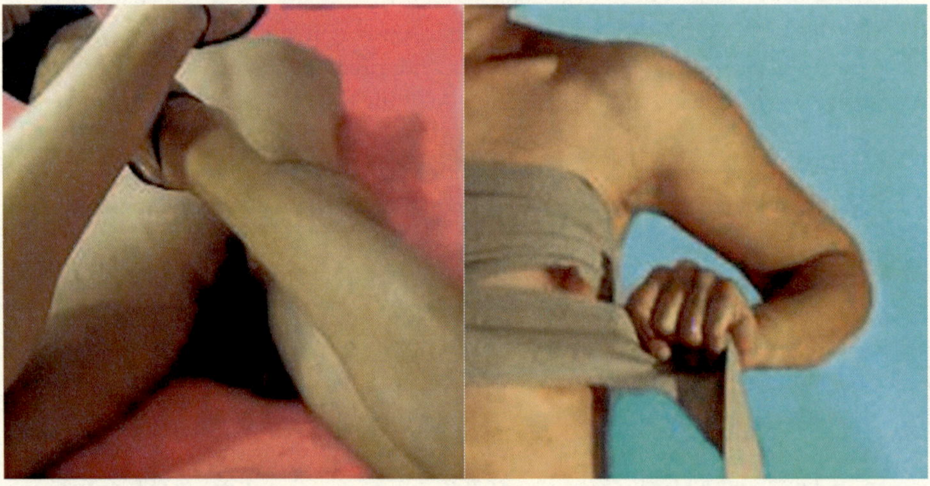

FIGURE 2.8. *Especulando sobre lo mismo* photo 2 (left) and photo 3 (right), by Alejandra Dorado. 2004.

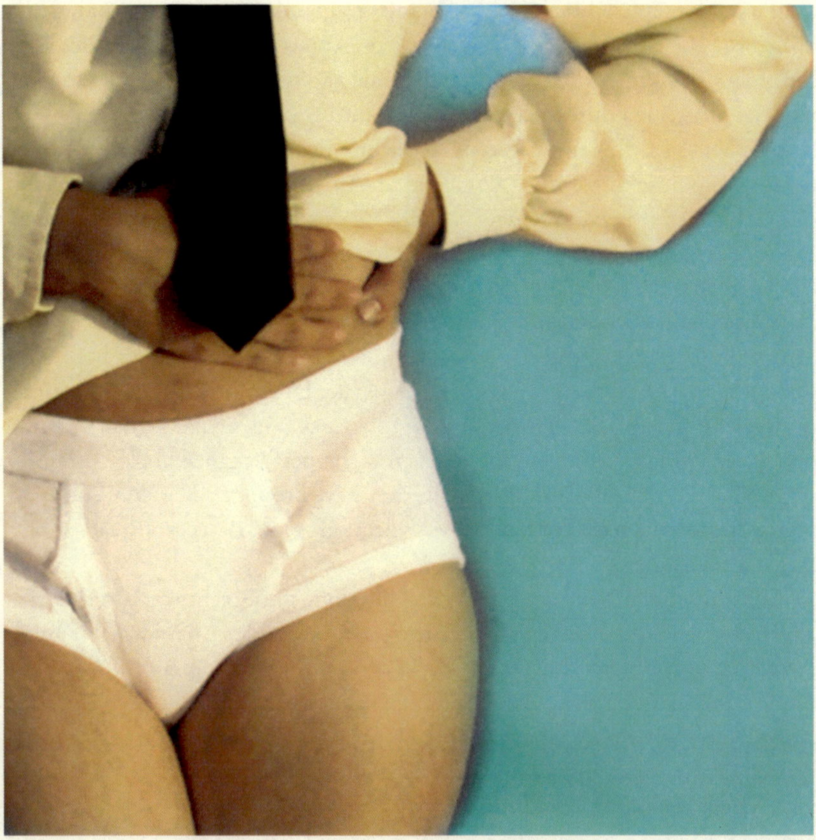

FIGURE 2.9. *Especulando sobre lo mismo* photo 4, by Alejandra Dorado. 2004.

to open one's self to the potential lives that lie beyond the skin level of humanism.

Because she manipulates the stereotypical blue and pink associations of girl and boy and the physical appearance of the body, Dorado complicates gendered identity that stems from the underlying urge that she has to "play" to challenge cultural norms that put forth material gender as if it were a simple binary. The title of this series of images subordinates difference and individuality espoused by neoliberal capitalist discourse as secondary to a tendency toward similarity and doubt, enabling nondualistic possibilities to enter the realm of sensible possibilities via her art. Dorado uses her imagination to combine parts of her own body and other digitalized details to demonstrate the inventiveness and prosthetic possibilities of sexuality that are available, to various degrees, as well as the power of technology to enable us to play with virtual aspects of self that are not yet actualized. The image in purple represents an androgynous figure, as Dorado overlays a hermaphroditic character on top of a double representation of her and of Bianca. The blurriness of the image is representative of Dorado's challenge to the binary thinking of self and other or male and female in favor of a monistic model of degrees of difference never locked into any position.

In 2011, the Bolivian press reported: "Se calcula que en Bolivia existen al menos 1.500 miembros de la comunidad transexual, lésbica, gay y bisexual (TLGB)"[45] (In Bolivia, calculations indicate that there at least 1,500 members of the transsexual, lesbian, gay, and bisexual community). The article leads by clarifying that the number of gay and lesbian identified people in Bolivia is actually incalculable because the majority of them are not yet out. While speculation can go on forever, the topic is receiving more attention than it has before, in some respect thanks to more visible groups like La Familia Galán, an activist transvestite group that has brought trans-issues and sexual rights into the popular imaginary through their activism, street performance, and community outreach.[46] Perhaps most importantly, they have brought a new conception of family to Bolivia, based on collective "selection" and alliances instead of biological genealogies.[47]

Andean scholar Michael J. Horswell has done important work to theorize alternative gender and sexuality in the colonial Andean world in his book *Decolonizing the Sodomite: Queer Tropes of Sexuality in Colonial Andean Culture* (2005). In his book he cites Santacruz Pachacuti, a well known indigenous chronicler—who knew Spanish and Quechua—and one of the earliest historians of the region now known as Peru and Bolivia. Santacruz Pachacuti's text, *Relación de antiguedades deste reyno del Perú* (*List of Antiquities from the Kingdom of Perú*), is a compilation of narrative descriptions of Incan traditions, accompanied by drawings accompanied by basic Spanish mixed with phrases in Quechua and Aymara. Dating to approximately 1620, it was discovered and published in 1879 by Marcos Jiménez de la Espada.[48] Santacruz Pachacuti chronicles various events but talks specifically about a ritual that occurred in Cuzco during a time of "pachacuti" or "cataclysmic change": "Los curacas y los mitimais (de Carabaya) trae a *chuqui chinchay*, animal muy pintado de todos colores. Dizen que es apo de los otorongos, en cuya guarda da a los ermofraditas yndios de dos naturas"[49] (The curacas and the mitimaes (Incan nobles) bring a chuqui chinchay, an animal painted in many colors. They say that he is the protector god of the jaguars, and who guards the hermaphrodite Indians of two natures). Due to a cataclysmic change, the Inca summoned a queer figure, the *chuqui chinchay*, to Cuzco. This was a revered figure in Andean culture, and its human *huacas*, or ritual attendants—what Horswell calls "third gendered subjects"—were vital actors in Andean ceremonies. These quariwarmi (menwomen) shamans mediated between the symmetrical spheres of Andean cosmology and daily life by performing rituals that at the same time required same-sex erotic practices. Their transvestite attire served as a visible sign of a nondualistic space that negotiated among the masculine and the feminine, the present and the past, the living and the dead. Their shamanic presence invoked the androgynous creative force often represented in Andean mythology—a force that brought together reciprocal energies, described by Julieta Paredes, as the reciprocal pair. This pair is not based on gender, but rather on complementariness in degree, and not in kind.

In his manuscript, Santacruz Pachacuti also includes a famous drawing that depicts the reciprocal relationality between masculine and feminine forces within the Quechua cosmovision. The sacred *chakana* (bridge) is in the center, the central axis to balance and mixing. And there is a blank oval toward the top that scholars have recognized as androgynous energy that sparks creation and creativity in the world.[50] Andean androgyny functions as a synecdoche in which the androgynous whole is greater than the sum of its feminine and masculine parts. Grammatically, unlike Spanish, all Quechua nouns are nongender specific, and again, in the drawing the *chuqui chinchay* animal is brought in to facilitate "bridging" during times of crisis—bringing, again, differences into a relational model that draws out the similarities and coexistence of humans within the Andean cosmovision to the fore. Dorado's photographic experimentation and challenge to gender binaries in digital form relates to the open oval of Santacruz Pachacuti's drawing. This open oval symbolizes the potential for bare life: that which is exceptional and that which is common among species. "Human" as a category has been a limited one based on a spectrum of exclusions. In recognizing the need to move beyond the limited Western position of human as naturalized, disembodied, white male, the category can become more nuanced and less symbolically violent, to incorporate agents that have been marginalized. It is then that the "proper framework to study the posthuman condition . . . based on the complex human interaction with nonhuman agents" can emerge.[51] Looking beyond human requires that we make entirely more nuanced the human itself, as a material being oriented in the world in myriad ways, dependent on factors outside and beyond human DNA.

Interspecies Points of Contact

Classical humanism needs to be reviewed and opened up to the challenges and complexities of our times, writes Braidotti, as she calls for "a sustainable ethics for a non-unitary subject [that] proposes an enlarged sense of interconnection between self and others, including the non-human and or 'earth' others, by removing the obstacle of self-centered individualism."[52] Reflecting a turn toward something broader than the individual, in an image Dorado titled, *Todo lo que empieza con A* (Everything that begins with A), Dorado transforms an old family portrait so that each of the bodies has an image of the artist's head on top of it, from when she was a slightly different age. One of the bodies is

FIGURE 2.10. *Todo lo que empieza con A*, by Alejandra Dorado. 2004.

that of Alice in Wonderland, and there are also dogs. Off to the side, in the corners, is a hand representing "the hand of fate," and along the bottom a series of ancient scientific images that begin with a tadpole and evolve into a frog.

The image reflects playfully on the similarity of forms. The parallel track of which the tadpole evolves alongside the images of the artist draws attention to the shared material conditions of both species, drawing attention to parallel evolutionary cycles within an imagined ecosystem. Dorado's work with family portraits visualizes Vallejo's antioedipal genealogy by juxtaposing humans with animals, in many cases to emphasize the *zoë* that runs through not only generations but through the process of evolution as a whole, with multiple species coexisting and overlapping at the same time.

The potential advantages to society in looking beyond the human fall within the ethical realm of recognizing animals as on the same ontological plane as humans. New materialist scholars Lennard and Wolfe argue that our "position has always been that all of these racist and sexist hierarchies have always been tacitly grounded in the deepest—and often most invisible—hierarchy of all: the ontological divide between human and animal life, which in turn grounds a pernicious ethical hierarchy."[53] Dorado's art shows, most recently, the way that animals and humans interact as in a flux between nature and culture in her light but amusing series of portraits of family members as dogs. As she did in her piece *Todo lo que empieza con A*, she transforms old portraits of seemingly "distinguished" men and replaces their heads with those of dogs, deer, or other animals. The manipulation of the portraits humorously downplays the seriousness the subjects seem to convey, while also undermining human exceptionality and self-importance. The portraits that she uses were found, she tells me, among her aunt and great aunt's possessions. In most cases, she does not know who all the figures are, but the custom of taking family portraits among the upper classes was a prevalent practice in Cochabamba and throughout South America during the first half of the twentieth century. In an amusing and ironic way, the images cause viewers to question the difference between man and beast as the animals look out at us with the same blank gaze as the human beings. The images cause us surprise because the animals seem so out of place, but the humans also seem out of place in the stylized settings and formal backgrounds that were the custom of the time. Through Dorado's work, we are made aware of the relationality between humans and other species, even on this quite literal level.

Because family portraits hinge so predominantly on genealogical relationships, the medium is an ideal one for the critique of evolution as a teleological project that ends with the perfection of the human. Instead, they suggest there is a way of looking at things from a different orientation that sees the evolution of Life as a project that preceded and will continue beyond the human in its current form. Reflecting on this concept, Diana H. Coole and Samantha Frost write, "If human perfection or redemption is no longer understood as the destiny of history, neither is it the goal of evolution. While it does not follow that cognitive capacities for symbolism or reflexivity are no longer valued, the new materialism does prompt a way of reconsidering them as diffuse, chance products of a self-generative nature from which they may never entirely emerge."[54] Dorado's images precisely mock the idea that the end of history is human. Perhaps we have reached a tipping point from which we are becoming something else, emergent and new, not just a "better version" of ourselves.[55]

Commenting on the posthumanist turn and the notion that perhaps the human will one day be "minoritarian" (again), Braidotti writes, "considering the extent of this posthumanist turn, to become animal or minoritarian you are better off cultivating your inner housefly or cockroach, instead of your 'inner child'—that is, forming anomalous and inorganic alliances, not oedipal and hierarchical relations."[56] If at the end of the day we are materials bound up with the other inorganic and organic ones around us, it is not such a stretch to imagine interspecies and intermaterial relationships. Prostheses and technology create a transhuman that is dependent on other materials or that changes due to their additions. These alliances can lead to thinking about Life as a network to be cared for and to be cared with from various moving and evolving alliances. From a new orientation toward Life, humans might protect

FIGURE 2.11. *Forest*, by Alejandra Dorado. 2013.

not only each other but the materials upon which the human, at least in its current form, is dependent.

In conclusion, across her corpus, from *martirio*, to *Castigadores domésticos moderados*, to *Especulando sobre lo mismo*, Dorado's multimedia installations bring critical insight into the multiplicity of representational registers that order and place subjects in language, in images, and in space. Through the use of an untamed anagram as a strategy for the undoing and undisciplining of fixed sub-

FIGURE 2.12. Untitled, by Alejandra Dorado. 2013.

jectivity in language, she underscores the agency that each person potentially has to challenge the labels and linguistic markers imposed on the self. This can make sensible the potential to transgress the imposition of externally imposed cultural codes as well as the gendered expectations seen in the popular media. Through the material tensions she sets up in her exhibits, Dorado reaffirms the socially constructed nature of being human but also moves beyond the human to demonstrate interspecies points of contact. While her artistic spaces are materially constrained in some form, the participatory power she hands over to her audience has the potential to make average viewers more aware of the ways that they are complicit with a given system of representation and the role they might play in transforming other humans and materials, not as resources for their consumption or benefit but as coagents in the construction of a sustainable community.

In the past decade, Bolivia has undergone substantial political changes as part of Latin America's pink tide. Luis Tapia, a contemporary political theorist from Bolivia, has pointed toward what he sees as the need for the location of a *nucleo común* (common nucleus) to forge a new governmental model that draws on the multiple political models that exist in the country. He explains, "tenemos que revisar críticamente el origen y la estructura de la concepción de derechos en las sociedades modernas, para luego establecer algunos puntos de comparación con otros modos en que históricamente se han organizado la dimensión de las leyes y por lo tanto, la forma de inclusión de las personas y las colectividades"[57] (We have to critically revise the origin and the structure of the conception of rights in modern societies, in order to then establish points of comparison with other modes in which the legal dimension has been organized, and by extension, forms of inclusion of people and communities). The critiques that Dorado's work brings to the surface point to the potentials of thinking about life outside the notion of the white male subject of the nation at center. Her exhibits demonstrate the material contingency of multiple bodies, images, and languages in motion, reconfiguring the human subject as a partial subject, open to transformation, and part of a network of life that precedes and unfolds well beyond humans or their belly button. Dorado's work serves as an example of an avant-garde orientation in the Andes that thinks not about what Life is but rather what is yet to emerge from dynamic material assemblages.

3

José María Arguedas's 1960s

The Air as Space of Material Encounters

> Viento, viento que rugía. De pronto, dentro la tiniebla se perfilaron sombras silenciosas; y de los cuatro que vocifera-ban tres temblaron, de asco, o de miedo. Fue entonces que un ronco maullido rompió los bramidos del viento.
>
> (Wind, wind that roared. Suddenly, in the darkness, silent shadows came into profile-view; of the four that were shouting three trembled, of dread, or of fear. It was then that a hoarse meowing broke the bellowing wind.)
>
> —Gamaliel Churata, *El pez de oro*

A few years before he accepted the Inca Garcilaso Prize in 1968, José María Arguedas published the poem "Llamado a algunos doctores" (A call to certain academics), dedicated to Carlos Cueto Fernandini and John V. Murra.[1] The work was originally written in Quechua but published in Spanish in the Sunday supplement, "Dominical," of the Lima newspaper *El Comercio* on July 3, 1966. In this poem Arguedas invokes something essential to the existence of all life forms but that tends to pass by unnoticed: the wind, or air. In his words, "el viento que va de mi tierra a la tuya es el mismo; el mismo viento respiramos"[2] or (the wind that goes from my lands to yours is the same; we breathe the same wind). Despite the fact that this quotation references a substance shared by humans and nonhumans alike, most of the critical questions that Arguedas poses throughout his work address differences, not similarities. In story after story, Arguedas demonstrates a preoccupation with the viability of lives of people marginalized by the intersections of race, class, gender, and language. Arguedas concerns himself, whether in short stories like "Agua" or his longer novels, like *Los ríos profundos* (1958), with the fundamental distinction between what it is to be biologically alive—a body that breathes—and what it is to live vitally in a society plagued by difference and its resultant political injustices.[3]

In this chapter I focus on Arguedas's works of the 1960s to analyze the life philosophy he creates based on diverse material encounters. In his creative production, disparate beings, forces, and knowledge systems come together in the air, a space that is always moving, and that I read as a potential plane from which to think about relational ontologies. While scholars like Martin Lienhard in his book *La voz y su huella* (1989), and Antonio Cornejo Polar in *Escribir en el aire* (1994) have explored in depth the role of orality as it relates to the "air" in Arguedas, I argue that the air is an invisible orienting axis to Arguedas's philosophy of life—not only a metaphor for the tension between writing and orality, or Spanish and Quechua. The air is the plane where Spanish and Quechua and species and things come to orient each other and be oriented around each other. Unlike land and other natural resources, it cannot be bought.[4] In contrast to light, it never goes out. If territory emphasizes location, based on borders and fixed geographic coordinates, air emphasizes movement toward or away, and the passage from inside to outside, as in breathing. The air is everywhere and nowhere, predominantly insensible but that which enables all senses. It makes relationships between species and materials possible and is often a catalyst for their contact.

Here, instead of engaging in a discussion of the social inequalities that Arguedas diagnoses, I argue that beyond a telluric poetic of difference, the air serves to uproot differences and "set them aflight" in order that their relationality rather than their difference serve as the starting point for *being with*, rather than *differing from*, other materials.[5] In the Andes, where different epistemologies have operated side-by-side for centuries to the point that one cannot distinguish neatly the enmeshment between them, this approach to ontology is particularly relevant. Physical differences originate in territoriality and corporeality: the perceived distinctions between human beings are the result of geographical variation, biological diversity, and the discursive fields in which such characteristics come to signify. The experience of living the world through Quechua versus Spanish is paramount to the way that persons perceive their world, as Arguedas's works have attempted to communicate.[6] However, and I make this case throughout the chapter, Arguedas is also worldly because, like César Vallejo, he presents the cosmological, the terrestrial, and the embodied as intimately linked. In this way, Arguedas's work is a valuable resource for thinking about nature as inextricably part of humanity and vice versa.

Air has two primary significations in the Arguedian corpus. On the one hand, as manifested in some of his works from the sixties, the air operates as an unstable metaphor of flux and permutation. In this first modality, the air symbolizes a threatening loss of stable identity for Arguedas. This loss is directly related to his personal crisis as an author who historically navigated between two or more cultures. His unstable identity results in a corresponding literary crisis (and the inverse) reflected in the erratic form and a disintegrating language, manifested at the end of his career. The end of Arguedas's life may, on the one hand, represent the difficulty in practice of living in and with difference. However, in contradistinction to this first troubling signification, the air is also a hopeful metaphor that facilitates exchange between human and nonhuman subjects and objects. The presence of the air, in this second sense, is charged with hope because it is a common substance shared between all beings and things. My objective is to think from the productive tension between air as destabilizing and air as possibility for sustained relationality, instead of trying to resolve it, in order to theorize the critical possibilities of Arguedas's vital air and the contributions his work makes to environmental concerns that plague society today.

In what follows, I explore the air through a range of close readings of Arguedas. I interpret the role of the wind and the air in *El Sexto* (1961), *Katatay y otros poemas* (1966), and *El zorro de arriba y el zorro de abajo* (1971) in order to "remember" the air in Arguedas as it facilitates interspecies contact and links the terrestrial earth, suspended in air itself, to the rest of the cosmos.[7] Through the readings I undertake, this chapter will go beyond terms like "heterogeneous" and "hybrid," which carry the rooted legacies of heteronormative biological reproduction, toward a new paradigm of relationality that contributes to long-standing and well known discussions about Peruvian identity within critical Arguedas studies.[8]

Claustrophobia and "the Most Formidable Hope" in *El Sexto*

As is well known, most of Arguedas's novels take place at least partially outdoors, whether in the small town settings of Puquio or the bustling city space of Chimbote. Detailing Arguedas's concern for geography, Antonio Cornejo

Polar has observed that the Arguedian narrative has tended to systematically expand its spatial parameters from the 1933 short story "Agua," situated in the small town of Puquio, to *Yawar fiesta*, which takes place in the capital of a province, to the "territorio humano y geográfico más vasto y complejo"[9] (more vast and complex human and geographic territory) of *Los ríos profundos*, and the migratory and urban space of *Los zorros.* At the same time as his geographic referent evolves, various critics, including Sara Castro-Klarén, Roland Forgues, and Rubén Bareiro Saguier, note significant changes in the form and the content of Arguedas's early versus mature works. His literature, in fact, seems to advance "toward a crisis" captured in the first diary of *Los zorros*: "En abril de 1966, hace ya algo más de dos años, intenté suicidarme"[10] (In April 1966, now more than two years ago, I tried to kill myself). The author's personal crisis influences his literary life, as his form becomes more chaotic, his language, delirious, and his characters, less developed.[11] An outlier to many of his other novels, however, *El Sexto* does not take place outside, but rather is based on the author's own experience in the notorious prison of the same name.

Here, I consider the way that the air and the wind interact in *El Sexto*, a novel that Arguedas wrote over the course of a few years, beginning in 1957, but based on an earlier period of his life. Because of the confines of its prison setting and the corporeal containment the space implies, it may seem like the last place from which to think about air and breathing. However, it is precisely for this reason that the air comes more sharply into focus as the symbol of an emancipatory outside relative to the psychological and physical confines of the prison's interior. It is also one of the very few elements of nature, besides their own bodyminds, to which the prisoners have access. While Anne Lambright observes that "*El Sexto* as novel serves as a means of mapping Peru and its subjects and of providing a (narrative) space for resistance against dominant culture and the dominant imaginings of Peru at the time of its writing," I frame the air in the novel as metaphoric of the potential unmapping of the territorial divisions of Peru and as a substance that represents movement and flux, even in the most stagnant of environments.[12]

Arguedas wrote *El Sexto* based on his personal experiences during a period distinguished by its social instability and extreme politics—as much in Latin America as in Europe—between 1937 and 1938. During this era, European fascism was gaining momentum under the directives of Mussolini, Hitler, and Franco, and the ripple effects of these extremisms reverberated across the Atlantic. In addition to the conflicts abroad, Peru was undergoing an intensely divisive political period. Oscar R. Benavides was a military leader who was twice president in Peru, first between 1914 and 1915, second from 1933 to 1939. At the beginning of his second term, he granted political amnesty to many of the Alianza Popular Revolucionaria Americana/Popular Revolutionary American Alliance (APRA) leaders and supporters who had been imprisoned and to those who had been exiled. Most significantly, Víctor Haya del Torre, leader of the APRA party, was liberated from prison. However, shortly thereafter, these same radical APRA militants incited an internal revolution, with a willingness to resort to violence for political ends.[13] Benavides subsequently outlawed the APRA party on the basis that it was not a national political party, but international, and by extension, directly affiliated with communism. And so, predictably, this resulted once again in a renewed persecution of APRA affiliates and an increased militarization of the central government. During this tumultuous period, both in Peru and abroad, university strikes and protests ensued. Because of his participation in a political uprising related to an antifascist international political movement at the Universidad de San Marcos, Arguedas was sentenced to eight months in the prison El sexto in Lima. As José Alberto Portugal summarizes it, "cayó preso por participar en una protesta antifascista. . . . Eran los años del segundo gobierno dictatorial del general Benavides"[14] (he fell prisoner because he participated in an antifascist protest. . . . This was during the years of the second dictatorial government of General Benavides).

Based on the concentrated and intense prison experience, Arguedas published *El Sexto* years later in order to recount the story.[15] It would seem fitting that it was published during the 1960s, a tumultuous era of large-scale countercultural movements, and the beginning of what would become an increasingly psychologically dark period for Arguedas. As a demonstration of the book's autobiographical nature and the slow process of finishing it, Arguedas wrote to John V. Murra, an anthropologist and his close confidant, in 1960:

> Lo malo es que tengo abandonados dos relatos que había comenzado cuando Matos me fue a sacar del Museo para hacerme cargo del Instituto. . . . Uno de los relatos, una novela corta, trataría de mostrar el Perú del 37 al 40 a través de la vida en una de las prisiones más inmundas que pueda imaginarse. . . . Mi propósito era mostrar esa prisión y las luchas de comunistas y apristas. Estuve un año en esa prisión y fue tan terrible e intensa la vida, tan lóbrega, tan triste y al mismo tiempo tan cargada de la más formidable esperanza.[16]
>
> (The bad thing is that I abandoned two stories that I had already started when Matos came to get me from the Museum to put me in charge of the Institute. . . . One of the stories, a short novel, would aim to show the Peru of [19]37–40 through the life in one of the filthiest prisons imaginable. . . . My purpose was to show that prison and the struggles of the communists and the *apristas*. I was in that prison for a year, and life was so terrible and intense, so sad, so gloomy, and at the same time so charged with the most formidable hope.)

On September 28, 1960, Arguedas writes to Murra again, happily relating that he has finished the short novel. As we see in this quote, the novel was based on his own painful personal experience, but despite the gloom and doom, the common cause of the Apristas and Communists inspires hope, even from the most abject conditions.

The prison is symbolic of the violent displacement that the prisoners have recently undergone during the dictatorship of Benavides. They have been uprooted from their respective homes—the Sierra, the center of Lima, the coast, Máncora, Morococha, and Cerro, to name a few places mentioned. They have also been dislodged from their discursive communities; for instance, university students have been taken out of their political parties or their families and placed into this microcommunity that aims to discipline and deprogram their political agenda. The spatial organization of the prison follows a compartmentalized ordering: each of the three prison floors is inhabited by those who have committed a certain type of crime and, politically, the majority of the prisoners are placed in the "discursive field" to which they would belong on the outside: the international Communists associate with each other as much as the Apristas, with a few exceptions.[17] The protagonist Gabriel, a prototype of Arguedas, however, does not align himself formally with any of the different groups in the prison. He is a fluid character who defies the "order" that the Communist and APRA party leaders want to promote within the prison, and by extension, outside. This reflects Arguedas's own "outsider" status, as he explained once: "Intervine en las luchas sociales no como militante de un partido sino como individuo siempre próximo a los movimientos que intentaron liberar al Perú de las férreas trabas que desde la época colonial no le permiten desarrollarse"[18] (I intervened in social struggles not as a militant from a party but instead as an individual always close to the movements that intended to liberate Peru from the rigid obstacles that impeded Peru's development from the colonial era). The refusal to be grouped within a community was also part of Arguedas's resistance to the label of the avant-garde. He preferred to remain unaffiliated and unincorporated, a move that frustrated some of his contemporaries but that is also part of his allure and the continued contemporary relevance of his projects: he resists categorization or institutionalization.

Arguedas presents various violent and unforgettable scenes, with eschatological passages and gay relationships, both construed as indicative of the demise of society. However, in contradistinction to the filth of the prison, the air and the wind represent subtle apertures in what would otherwise seem to be a totalizing hell. For example, when Gabriel meets his cellmate (Alejandro) Camác, an older Communist and unionized miner, the latter tells him, "Yo tiendo tu cama, compañero. Hay que saber tomar la dirección del aire que entra por la reja, y del andar de estos chinchecitos"[19] (I'll take care of your bed, friend. You've got to know how to work with the direction of wind that comes through the bars and the path of the bedbugs). Cámac gauges the wind, so to speak, so that Gabriel doesn't have to experience any undesirable contact with the bedbugs.

The presence of the air here facilitates and makes possible a mixing of what is outside the prison and what is inside. It puts the human species in direct contact with another that affects them, regardless of biological classification.[20]

As he is becoming accustomed to his new environment and community, Gabriel observes: "Con la humedad de la noche y el viento, la fetidez del primer piso subía, invadía las celdas, iba a la calle; llegaba a todas partes, junto con el ruido de las cucharas que los asesinos del primer piso hacían tocar para marcar el compás de valses, polkas y pasodobles. La fetidez ahogaba las celdas aquella noche; llovía"[21] (Combined with the humidity at night and the wind, the fetid stink of the first floor rose, it invaded the cells, went out to the street, it spread everywhere, together with the noise of the spoons that the first-floor assassins would play to mark the steps of the waltzes, polkas, and two-steps. The fetid air drowned the cells that night; it was raining). The porousness of the prison's configuration means that collective sounds, smells, and airflow affect all floors and spaces. One cannot materially locate "la fetidez" because it is a sensation that charges the environment or air of the prison, and that spreads through the contact with various bodies, surfaces, and molecules. Even though Arguedas uses the metaphor of "drowning," which carries a corporeal connotation because it implies, conventionally, the inundation of the body in water, in this case such a drowning happens to the entirety of the prison. The fetidness infects the water molecules that float in the air, falling from the exterior sky into the interior of the prison and the lungs of the prisoners. The rain infiltrates the prison and the prisoners even though they are in a theoretically contained space. At the same time, the music from the spoons that the prisoners play infuses the air, creating an antagonistic mix of sounds, smells, and sensations in the fetid air as it travels between floors. The prisoners are immersed in an ecosystem that changes constantly according to the "air" and the energy that it holds.

Later in the novel, we learn of the imminent death of Cámac, a character who Gabriel has come to admire for the lessons this more seasoned radical has taught him about social justice, even within the prison. Therefore, when the failing Cámac finds himself at death's door, Gabriel plants himself faithfully at his side. Gabriel narrates to us: "Su ojo sano se mantenía cristalino, como ciertos manantiales solitarios que hierven en las grandes alturas. Hierven levantando arenas de colores, rojos, azules"[22] (His healthy eye remained crystalline, like certain solitary springs that bubble up in the highest of mountains. They bubble up, raising colored sands, reds, blues). The crystalline water, infused with the oxygen of the air, "hierve,"—or boils—like the boilings of *Los zorros*—agitating the sands.[23] Arguedas links the visual image of Cámac's eye to a process he has witnessed in nature, uniting the corporeal and the terrestrial via the moving sand and aqueous water/eye. Before he dies, Cámac says to Gabriel: "El Perú es de fierro. Sobre el fierro hay arena, ¿no es cierto? Llega el viento, se lleva la arena y las pajitas; el fierro después brilla fuerte. La arena sucia con los gringos, los gamonales, los capataces y los soplones; los traidores. El viento de la revolución los barrerá"[24] (Peru is of iron, but over iron there is sand, right? The wind comes, it carries away the sand and the straw, the iron shines fiercely. The sand gets dirtied by the gringos, the landowners, the foremen, and the snitches; the traitors. The wind of the revolution will sweep them away). Here, the wind is ascribed a role in catalyzing revolutionary change, that while made somewhat cliché through its overuse in songs and literature from the 1960s, also signals that there is an aspect to change that is immanent: that is, it is vitally present but not necessarily predictable; it is as easily a chance encounter that brings about material societal transformation instead of an exclusively human plan. The wind or air of the implied outside is the antidote to a growing U.S. imperialism that receives the majority of the blame in the novel for Peru's situation: "Odio a los gringos malditos y moriré luchando contra ellos!"[25] (I hate those damn gringos and I will die fighting against them!) is Cámac's anthem, and will continue after his death. However, Arguedas clarifies the following, in a letter to Murra about *El Sexto*, "No hay odio contra los Estados Unidos como país en el libro"[26] (There's not hatred toward the United States as a country in the book), just against some of the gringos in Peru and their unscrupulous practices. This critique of growing capitalist imperialism will continue and develop much further beyond *El Sexto*, reaching its culmination in *Los zorros*.

After Cámac's death, Gabriel declares, "Cámac no está muerto" (Cámac is not dead), performing Cámac's material continuation. While some of the prisoners sing a hymn in memory of Cámac's life, Gabriel notes, as the singing begins to wane, that "El cielo gris que el himno iluminó, alzándolo, empezó a caer de nuevo al penal"[27] (The gray sky that the hymn illuminated, raising it up, began to fall again on the prison). As the prisoners look toward the sky, their voices metaphorically alter the physical aspect of the sky. In the act of emitting sound, the prisoners impact the air that surrounds them through the multiplicity of different voices that intermix and interact, producing a collective effect on the "lifting" sky. Through the hymn, a vital piece of Cámac's life is replicated, not biologically, but socially, through the contact he had with other prisoners. This (re)production of Cámac is facilitated through the creative act of singing and its dispersal into the air. While the prisoners cannot give Cámac his biological life "back," their own bodies absorb the passing of his. The air that leaves Cámac's body is the connection between the corporeal, the terrestrial, and the cosmos, as it disperses itself through those planes. Cámac, in dying, is part of the formidable hope that remains as potential for new forms of orienting life in Peru.

As an additional act in memory of Cámac's death, at another place in the prison, Pedro—one of the international Communist leaders—observes after the song: "Estos períodos de malestar, de mala tranquilidad, y de paz verdadera, se alternan en la prisión . . . de repente se carga el ambiente, el mal humor se contagia de uno a otro; la amargura se extiende por toda la cárcel"[28] (These periods of ill-being, of disquiet, and of true peace, alternated in prison . . . suddenly the environment would become charged, a bad mood would become contagious; the bitterness spread itself throughout the prison). The description of a "charged environment" also implies that there is an invisible but shared substance in the air that is affected by the negative energy or interpersonal tensions that exist not inside one individual body, but that come to be relationally in the air, among material beings.

In sum, despite Cornejo Polar's interpretation of the prison as "un monstruo devorador, de 'tétrico cuerpo,' que tritura y traga a los hombres"[29] (a devouring monster, a "dark body," that grinds and swallows up men), and Arguedas's own equation of it to a cemetery, a formidable hope of the community within it remains intact. In destabilizing the promise of total isolation that defines a prison, the air symbolizes the cracks in the disciplinary institution and the disciplined subjects that they aim to form.[30] My reading supports a strategy that Sara Castro-Klarén would suggest behooves students that want to critique colonialism: "to look and act in the cracks and crevices of the system in order to break open the homogenous surface that power/knowledge is always smoothing over."[31] The air is what inhabits, as well as contributes to the formation of, the cracks and the crevices of the cultural environment. It literally sweeps things toward and away from each other, spreading the positive along with the negative. Arguedas said, "Y bien sabemos que los muros aislantes de las naciones no son nunca completamente aislantes. A mí me echaron por encima de ese muro, un tiempo, cuando era niño; me lanzaron en esa morada donde la ternura es más intensa que el odio y donde, por eso mismo, el odio no es perturbador sino fuego que impulsa"[32] (And we know well that the isolating walls of nations are never completely isolating. They threw me over that wall, one time, when I was a kid, they threw me over that wall where tenderness is more intense than hate and where, for that reason, hate is not a disruption but a fire that inspires). The walls of the prison that snuff out and stifle life also, as Arguedas said of his own work, are infiltrated by and emanate outward a "formidable hope" in the relationships between humans, their material environments, and the natural resources beyond and within their reach.

The Winds of *Katatay*

About four years after the publication of *El Sexto*, Arguedas composed a series of poems that were published posthumously as one work under the title *Katatay y otros poemas* (Trembling and other poems) in 1972. While not stated explicitly by Arguedas, most of the poems in the collection present his reaction to ongoing debates around international development that emerged in Peru in the 1950s. Priscilla Archibald, in her book *Imagining Modernity in the*

Andes (2011), makes evident the politics that shaped the decade through a discussion of the development paradigm that grew out of the social science fields. This paradigm was premised on the belief that indigenous peoples who had lived for years as inferior servants to the hacienda-owning elites could be educated to "advance" socially.[33] As a reaction to developmentalist anthropology, a movement that through its belief in Western modernization directly impacted the indigenous cultures of Peru, Arguedas published "Huk Doctorkunaman Qayay," or "Llamado a algunos doctores," in 1966. Even more than a reaction to the 1950s debates, however, this poem was also written in response to the now famous roundtable discussion that had been held about Arguedas's novel *Todas las sangres* in Lima on June 23, 1965.[34]

By way of a brief summary, during "La mesa redonda," Arguedas felt criticized for what he seemed to internalize as a failure of his novel to effectively represent the "reality of Peru." The fallout from the episode is evinced by the sudden interruption in Arguedas's otherwise fairly consistent letters to, alternatively, either the aforementioned John Murra or his psychoanalyst, Doctor Lola Hoffman, throughout the early 1960s.[35] Instead, during the year that followed—from June 1965 until July 1966—Arguedas struggled, as was most acutely revealed by his first suicide attempt on April 11, 1966. After this attempt, he spent almost three months in the hospital.[36] It is fair to say that he was still experiencing a degree of personal crisis when he published "Llamado a algunos doctores" on July 3, 1966. This particular hymn, "Huk Doctorkunaman Qayay," was dedicated to the ex-rector of the University of San Marcos, Carlos Cueto Fernandini, and to John Murra, both of whom were close to Arguedas. It initially appeared in Spanish in the Sunday supplement of *El Comercio* de Lima, in July 1966, and then two weeks later in the same place, in Quechua.[37]

In the poem, Arguedas reacts not only to the doctors of the "north" but also somewhat sarcastically to those that "se reproducen en nuestra misma tierra"[38] (are reproduced right here on our own soil). The poem is a partial reaction to how difficult it was during that era to forge common ground with professors and experts from distinct academic territories and geographic regions. For example, at some moment during the roundtable, Arguedas had also responded to some of the commentaries of Henri Favre, a French ethnomusicologist, who was questioning the social framework within which the conflicts of class and caste were realized within the novel with the following contribution, "Esta es la terminología de un profesor"[39] (This is the terminology of a professor), marking the distinction he perceived between the discursive positions of some of the participants of the roundtable. Arguedas had to defend his work of fiction *as if* it were a social science report, a genre that he neither set out nor purported to write.

Therefore, the critique at the heart of Arguedas's poem is that some of the educated doctors from urban areas and disconnected from the rural sectors of Peru arrive to these same regions with the intention of practicing occidental methodologies and imposing occidental solutions to problems that require alternative remedies. Arguedas challenges a purely scientific or disciplinary approach to the social problems of his country, and instead proposes a more holistic solution to knowledge production and community formation that reflects the diversity of the Peruvian reality. For these reasons, Arguedas dedicates the majority of the poem to a detailing some of the natural solutions to health problems in Peru.

> Curaré tu fatiga que a veces te nubla como bala de plomo, te recrearé con la luz de las cien flores de quinua, con la imagen de su danza al soplo de los vientos; con el pequeño corazón de la calandria en que se retrata el mundo, te refrescaré con el agua limpia que canta y que yo arranco de la pared de los abismos que templan con su sombra a nuestras criaturas.[40]
>
> (I will cure the fatigue that sometimes clouds you like a lead bullet, I will re-create you with the light of a hundred quinoa flowers, the image of their dance when the winds blow; with the tiny heart of the lark that contains a portrait of the world, I will refresh you with the clean water that sings and that I pull out from the walls of the abysses that cool our creatures with their shade.)

Arguedas, like Vallejo, connects the cosmic to the terrestrial to the tiniest of structures via the image of the lark's heart, as it represents "the world." This vitality in Arguedas's writing may stem from the Andes, but it travels outward and beyond it as well, as the "call" outward to doctors in the name of organic medicinal practices and resources reverberates into the twenty-first century. In these beautiful lines, Arguedas's poetic voice observes that he will even "re-create" the doctors, meaning, open their minds to another way of thinking about holistic health, through an image of quinoa moving in the breeze. The wind that causes the quinoa to dance is a vital force shared between the viewers and the plant, as well as between the doctors and Arguedas. The wind destabilizes the tangible and material image of the quinoa and animates it, transforming a static object into a moving image.

These verses hinge upon the transfiguration and conversion of one thing into another, a process mediated by the invisible but essential air. For example, when he affirms that "Estoy junto a las montañas sagradas: la gran nieve con lampos amarillos, con manchas rojizas, lanzan su luz a los cielos"[41] (I am with the sacred mountains: their grandiose snow with its yellow flashes, with red spots; they launch their light to the skies). As the light emanating off the snow on the mountains flashes upward toward the sky, it is mediated by the air, that fills the space between the two images—the mountain and the sky—and that facilitates as well as communicates their relationality to readers. The material effects of light and space, of air and the snow, are made sensible via Arguedas's language.

When he assigns possession to the light flashes, the sacred mountain is shown to be an agent in a sense, drawing attention to the active role of nature in Arguedas's vision. In the same way, Arguedas later transforms condors into an "arco iris," that appears in the atmosphere. At the end of the poem, Arguedas refers to "la eterna vida mía, el mundo que no descansa, que crea sin fatiga, que pare y forma como el tiempo, sin fin y sin principio"[42] (my eternal life, the world that doesn't rest, that creates without weariness, that stops and forms like time, without and end nor a beginning). The sense of temporality that Arguedas creates, with neither a beginning nor an end, deemphasizes the centrality of the human being while assigning the "world" an ongoing vitality beyond its human form in a way that grants access to an alternative perception of nature.

It is not only in this first *haylli* (hymn), "Huk doctorkunaman qayay," that Arguedas speaks of the wind and the animate ecosystem around him. The collection includes this plus five other hymns in Quechua. Arguedas translates El jaylli, o jaylli-taki, as "himno," "himno-canción," or "oda," in the margin notes. Jesús Lara, in *La literatura de los quechuas* (The literature of the Quechua) (1961) explains that *haylli* were sung among farmers (to celebrate their harvests), or as "heroic" songs of triumph, or as sacred hymns offered to Pachakamaq, tiksi Wiraqucha, Inti, or Killa or to the gods or spirits of the mountains.[43] He also published the long and inspiring poem "A Túpac Amaru," in the same collection. Like Magda Portal, he breathes new life into this past hero through the *haylli* genre. For instance, in a hymn in honor of Túpac Amaru, the poetic voice directs himself to the fallen Incan hero and animates all the forces of nature to revive him. Arguedas employs the present progressive in Spanish, which is equivalent to the ongoing present in Quechua, to speak to the ongoing presence of not just Túpac Amaru but the Quechua knowledge system in the present.

Está cantando el río,
está llorando la calandria,
está dando vueltas el viento;
día y noche la paja de la estepa vibra;
nuestro río sagrado está bramando.[44]

(The river is singing,
The calandria is crying,
The wind is spinning around;
Day and night, the straw of the steppe vibrates;
our sacred river is roaring.)

As Arguedas's river sings, Magda Portal's river will later talk. The wind churns, symbolizing the movement of the interconnected web of nature. The river and the bird move with the wind, causing the straw to vibrate. As the air is "dando vueltas," things are changing, in that a positive time of change and renewal—Pachakuti—associated with Túpac Amaru, is imminent. As Arguedas sings to him, "Padre nuestro," he exhorts him to "escucha atentamente la voz de nuestros ríos; escucha a los temíbles árboles de la gran selva"[45] (listen attentively to the voice of our rivers; listen to the frightening trees of the huge jungle). Arguedas describes the earth as vitally connected to the spiritual world above. Through the limitless and uncontainable space of the air, the trees affect the top of the mountain, or the molecules in the sky above affect the terrestrial earth. Arguedas often names the "wind" in his poetry, not the still air, because the wind is a force in motion: it is what animates the objects that it passes through, linking them relationally to other forms of life. In the same poem, Arguedas refers to Túpac Amaru's "wound," one that is still raw and open before the present generation: "De tu inmensa herida, de tu dolor que nadie habría podido cerrar, se levanta para nosotros la rabia que hervía en tus venas"[46] (From your immense wound, from your pain that no one would have been able to close, the rage that boiled in your veins rises up for us). In his poem, Arguedas expresses indirectly, that the wounds of one generation are passed on to the next, as Túpac Amaru's suffering continues in the present.

Arguedas revitalizes Túpac Amaru by poetically perpetuating his presence in the nature around him and draws together through his poetic access the cosmic, the terrestrial, and the human body all at once, much like Vallejo.

> Al helado lago que duerme, al negro precipicio,
> a la mosca azul que ve y anuncia la muerte
> a la luna, las estrellas y la tierra,
> el suave y poderoso corazón del hombre;
> a todo ser viviente y no viviente,
> que está en el mundo,
> en el que alienta o no alienta la sangre, hombre o paloma, piedra o arena,
> haremos que se regocijen, que tengan luz infinita, Amaru, padre mío.[47]
>
> (To the frozen lake that sleeps, to the dark precipice,
> To the bluebottle fly that sees and announces death,
> To the moon, the stars and the earth,
> The gentle and powerful heart of man;
> To every living and nonliving being,
> That is in the world,
> in which blood breathes or doesn't breathe, man or dove, stone or sand,
> we will make it that they may rejoice, that they have your infinite light,
> Amaru, my father.)

In these lines, Arguedas's reference to "to all living and nonliving beings / that are in the world / in which blood breathes or does not breathe" is followed by a bringing together of disparate objects again, "man" or "dove," "rock" or "sand," all of which metaphorically breathe in his vision. The combination of animate and inanimate things, brought together through Arguedas's poetic breath, then resuscitates Túpac Amaru. The Arguedian world is not human-centric here but spirals around an axis that brings the animate and the inanimate at the cosmological (the moon), the terrestrial (the sand), and the corporeal (the heart of man) together as part of life.

The Vibrations of the World: Arguedas's Ecosystem in *El zorro de arriba y el zorro de abajo*

On December 16, 1966, Arguedas wrote to his psychoanalyst Dr. Lola Hoffman, "Ayer pasé un día promisor. En la ruta a La Molina volví a sentir los árboles y el canto de los pájaros en todo el pecho, como algo vivificante"[48] (Yesterday I had a promising day. I felt the trees and the birds' song in my chest again, it was something exhilarating). Arguedas explains to Dr. Hoffman, his psychoanalyst from approximately 1960 on, that he began to "feel the trees again," connecting the natural world outside his physical form to the inside of his body, specifically his chest. This letter, written about a year and a half after his first suicide attempt, expresses the intimate relationship Arguedas shared with the natural world around him. As a child, Arguedas suffered anxiety that he attempted to ameliorate by walking around outside, immersed in nature. In a letter that he wrote to Lilly Caballero, the widow of his friend Carlos Cueto, on November 24, 1968, he references this disquiet again: "Me llegó tu carta cuando más denodadamente lucho contra la antiquísima depresión. . . . Cuando muy niño me atacaba esa angustia en las noches. Entonces llamaba a mi padre: él me sacaba al corredor y al contacto del cielo y el aire también se me pasaba"[49] (Your letter arrived to me when I most relentlessly fight against my depression of old. . . . When I was really young, this type of anxiety would attack at night. Then I'd call my father: he would take me out into the hallway and the contact with the sky and the air would also help it pass). The way that Arguedas describes the "contact" with the sky and the air emphasizes that the air is not a neutral substance to him, but soothes him in an active way, as it passes through his system. Both of these letters implicitly name the break with his broader natural ecosystem as a root cause of his anxiety.

Arriving at the culmination of his personal crisis, in *El zorro de arriba y el zorro de abajo*, Arguedas's posthumous novel published in 1971 but written in 1969, Arguedas symbolically gasps for air as he writes. He began writing this novel in 1966 or 1967, and he relates his trips to Chimbote to John V.

Murra as well as to Dr. Hoffman in his letters. This profound struggle becomes very obvious in the four diaries of the novel, which represent Arguedas's last literary breaths and that demonstrate what Cornejo Polar has named "la quiebra absoluta del lenguaje"[50] (the absolute break of his language). Cornejo Polar explains that the word and language become incapable of signifying in this last novel, submerged in an emptiness. The air remains at the end of this text, however, as do the dancing foxes who are left to metaphorically "complete" his text. In this sense, I share the open-ended reading that Martín Lienhard makes of the novel: "La desaparición del narrador (el suicidio de Arguedas), convertida en articulación estructural del texto, instaura una apertura utópica: el escritor, testigo del pasado, abandona el escenario a favor del <<hombre de Vietnam>> peruano, capaz de provocar el vuelco cósmico-social del mundo"[51] (The disappearance of the narrator (the suicide of Arguedas), converted into a structural articulation in the text, initiates a utopic moment: the writer, witness to the past, abandons the scene in favor of the Peruvian "man of Vietnam" capable of provoking the cosmic-social overturning of the world). When Arguedas "abandons the scene," he leaves the novel open to future revolutions.

Because so much research has already been done on the diaries and Arguedas's life, I focus only on the sections that illuminate further the role of air and nature in Arguedas's struggle. From the outset of the novel, Arguedas is undergoing a grave psychological crisis, and his intention to write is the only energy that sustains him, a point he himself emphasizes when he confesses in a letter to don Gonzalo Losada that "Claro que escribir este libro es parte sustancial de lo que necesito para seguir viviendo"[52] (Of course writing this book is a substantial part of what I need to keep on living). Cornejo Polar echoes, the novel is a "desesperado gesto vital, como una apuesta a favor de la superviviencia"[53] (a desperate vital gesture, like a bet in favor of survival).

In the second diary, Arguedas talks about his novel *Todas las sangres* in which ancient Peru and demon-possessed Spain—met each other and mixed in "el aire de los abismos andinos en cuyo fondo corre agua cargada de sangre, así está, cierto, en esa novela, el constreñido mundo indohispánico"[54] (the air of the Andean abysses at whose base runs water full of blood, that being how it is, of course, in that world, the constrained indohispanic world). Even though in *Todas las sangres* the "*yawar mayu* andino vence bien" (the Andean blood river wins), here in his last novel, the air is charged with the multiple conflicts occurring in Chimbote and expressed in the chaotic diaries. Arguedas's identity and that of the Peruvians is no longer a negotiation between the sierra and the coast because the majority of the characters of the book have been uprooted from these spaces in order to find themselves in a more fluctuating city where the referents have lost their symbolic stability. However, due to this flux and the multiplication of difference, there is more urgency to find commonality in the shared natural resources.

Later, in the third diary, Arguedas continues his fight via his writing in order to sustain his own tenuous life, referring to the sensation of being asphyxiated: invoking the air as that which he cannot grasp. As an elixir, Arguedas juxtaposes this physical asphyxiation with another more hopeful image, that of a large pine tree:

> ese pino llegó a ser mi mejor amigo. No es un simple decir . . . los cortos troncos de sus ramas, así escalonados en la altura, lo hacen aparecer como un ser que palpa el aire del mundo con sus millares de cortes . . . un árbol de estos . . . sabe de cuanto hay debajo de la tierra y los cielos. Conoce la materia de los astros, de todos los tipos de raíces y aguas, insectos, aves y gusanos; y ese conocimiento se transmite directamente en el sonido que emite su tronco, pero muy cerca de él; lo transmite a manera de música, de sabiduría, de consuelo de inmortalidad.[55]
>
> (that pine tree became my best friend. It's not a simple matter of saying it . . . the short trunks of its branches, arranged like that up so high, make it appear like a being that touches the air of the world with its thousands of cuts . . . a tree like that . . . knows how much there is under the earth and the skies. It is familiar with the materials of the stars, of all the types of roots and waters, insects and birds and worms; and that knowledge is transmitted directly from the sound that its trunk emits, but only very close to it; it transmits it as a form of music, of knowledge, the comfort of immortality.)

Arguedas knows his world with and alongside the tree, a friend as well as a source of consolation. The tree, too, serves as a link between Arguedas's sensorial body, the terrestrial plane of earth, and the cosmos. The way that the tree stretches up to the sky and down below the surface of the soil enables it to serve as an intermediate plane between the world below and the world above. The human body is part of nature, not separate from it. This interconnectedness between layers of the earth and the cosmos as mediated via the tree and Arguedas's friendship with it represents the way that the human and other aspects of the ecosystem are in and of each other, not isolated entities. The air, in this second example, is a tangible backdrop—the tree "lo palpa"—and an invisible force that connects Arguedas with the tree through their mutual dependency on this substance. It is through his intimate relationship with the tree—"Yo le hablé . . . y que puedo asegurar que escuchó"[56] (I spoke to it . . . and I can assure you that it listened)—that Arguedas becomes reanimated. Likewise in describing the tree as "knowing" what is below the earth and what is up in the sky reminds humans of the life forms that have been here much longer than their individual body and that will long outlast them. Enthused and infused with vitality, Arguedas describes with exceptional optimism: "I returned from Arequipa in such a state of animation and with such lucidity that I thought I would be able to conclude writing the book." As a result of this shared relationship with the tree, Arguedas is rejuvenated before the work at hand; the air that they breathe together is vital to his life but also to the tree.[57]

This newly acquired energy carries him along to Valparaíso, Chile, where he visits a friend, Nelson Osorio. Arguedas relates the following:

> En esa casa del Nelson, como en la de Pedro (Lastra), intrínsecamente normada, mi cuerpo se movía con una libertad nunca antes conocida en las ciudades; todo estaba a mi disposición, especialmente el aire que respiramos. Porque es mentira que ese aire sea tan libre y tan propiedad pura de todo el mundo. El aire dentro de un cerco ajeno, de una casa ajena, aun en la de muchos amigos, está enajenado; el pecho no lo puede tomar con la misma alegría o inconsciencia con que lo respira en los campos, también todos con dueño, pero donde si estás solo, el aire, allí, sí es tuyo, como los altísimos cielos que no por inalcanzables no llegan a ser parte de tu ánimo y de tu carne.[58]
>
> (In that house of Nelson's, like in Pedro's (Lastra), intrinsically normalized, my body moved with a liberty that I had never known before in cities; everything was at my disposition, especially the air that we breathe. Because it is a lie that that air is so free and so much the pure property of the whole world. The air inside an unknown fence, of an unknown house, even in those of many friends, it's strange; the chest can't take it in with the same happiness or unconsciousness with which we breathe it in the countryside, even if on plots with owners, but where if you are alone, the air, there, yes, it is yours, just like the highest skies are; even though they are so far out of reach, that doesn't mean they don't become part of your energy and your flesh.)

In this passage, we see that Arguedas feels a stimulating liberty when he experiences the lightness of being in his body, outside of the city. When he describes the ease of having "everything . . . at my disposition, especially the air" it not only symbolizes a sensation of well-being for Arguedas but also his ability to reconnect with the word, given that his struggle to breathe was his struggle to write, and the struggle to write, a fight between living and dying. The air that comes from these "highest skies" above, that only the giant pine tree of Arequipa seems able to touch, links Arguedas's chest to the terrestrial tree, to the celestial sky. When he is reoriented with and by nature, he is able to continue living. Through this passage, he reorients the human in nature, enabling the power of the natural world to almost overtake the consciousness of the human. In signaling this inextricability, he humbles the human before the universe by demonstrating the impact the natural world has on the human.

As the novel unfolds, the *huayronqo*, a Quechua word for a bluebottle fly, is a constant harbinger of Arguedas's death and subsequent transformation into an object—specifically, a cadaver—as well as the partial stagnation of his poetic language. This is of particular note because in many of his other books his language moves seamlessly from Quechua to Spanish. In this last book, however, a particular image of a *huayronqo* becomes the central motif for the way that his own writing is crashing, as many others have already argued. While Arguedas talks about his desire to make the word itself vibrate through his writing, in this last novel the word operates like the *huayronqo*, becoming metaphorically stuck in a consumptive cycle of capitalism. The image of the *huayronqo*, "azulada de puro negra," interrupts the novel on numerous occasions. But the "ron" sound lends the word an onomatopoeic aspect, the "ron" resembling the buzzing of a fly, while the hard "qo" sound would seem to counter the fly's buzzing movement with the hard "k" sounding end, despite the open "o" vowel. The "qo" sound also lends a sonorous heaviness to the word. The word itself both vibrates and gets in the way of itself.

In *The Emergence of the Latin American Novel*, Gordon Brotherston reads the *huayronqo* as a cross between a fly and a hummingbird, that "hovers . . . as the unmistakable omen of death in the Quechua-speaking world Arguedas grew up in, and as a self-incarnation whose separate identity is nevertheless wholly respected." Brotherston's description of the "inebriation" of the fly also draws attention to the paralyzing effect that capitalism has not just on the Quechua culture but in the novel on the global spread of pollution as a result of the industrialization of the city.[59] Throughout the novel, the *huayronqo* is a masculine subject within the story, with agency to consume and rest within the *ayaq sapatillan*, or "corpse-slipper," a small white lily commonly used at funerals. Arguedas's knowledge of the *huayronqo* and the *ayaq sapatillan* is a traumatic experience for him because it comes to symbolize his confrontation not only of his death but of a more symbolic death of the notion of community as a whole.

Throughout the novel, Arguedas describes countless displaced flies, stuck in a consumptive cycle, that find themselves in the *ayaq sapitillan* of Chimbote. Metaphorically, the flower captures the author and his characters. The novel begins with this ominous image that then haunts the rest of the novel, reappearing periodically throughout the text. As the text advances, Arguedas's cadaver, as well as that of the *huayronqo*, work together to continually infect the bodies and the prose of the novel proper. The confrontation with this image that Arguedas provokes can cause restlessness in readers because it haunts the text. Such a haunting is interruptive to the surface of the novel and causes readers to pause before language. The *huayronqo* serves as a warning sign in the novel that speaks to the potential future of a society which represses that which (and those whom) it does not wish to see.

By the epilogue of the novel, dated August 29, 1969, Arguedas describes the *huayco*, or mudslide, that has now buried him: "Pero me cayó un repentino *huayco* que enterró el camino y no pude levantar, por mucho que hice, el lodo y las piedras que forman esas avalanchas que son más pesadas cuando caen dentro del pecho. Quiero dejar constancia que el *huayco* fue repentino pero no completamente inesperado"[60] (But a sudden mudslide that buried the path fell onto me and I couldn't lift it, no matter how I tried, the mud and the rocks that form part of those avalanches, are much heavier when they land inside your chest. I want to make it clear this mudslide was quick, but not completely unexpected). Via the natural phenomenon and metaphor of the mudslide, Arguedas captures the materiality of his world—*el lodo y las piedras* (the mud and the rocks) and carries it with him to the interior of his body, *dentro del pecho* (into my chest). However, unlike the air that ought to vitally fill his lungs, here the author drowns due to the weight of the mixing of the territorial and the corporeal. While in Alberto Moreiras's reading, Arguedas's suicide and the fragmented text symbolize the "end" of a transcultural product, the *huayco* to which Arguedas (and later Moreiras) makes reference is haunted by the *ron* of the *huay*(ron)*qo*, the fly of death and of life that fills the space of death. The sound of the *ron* produced via the contact between the fly and the air is what echoes and reverberates among the materials of the mudslide. There is a persistent living sound that vibrates in the novel, even among death's rubble.

In the postanthropocene turn that has emerged in Western thought today, animate or vibrant materialisms are at the center of the discussion. However, Arguedas was already well down the pathway of such thinking in the 1960s, based on his knowledge and access to indigenous perspectives on nature, and his articulation of his own body as intimately linked to both terrestrial and celestial life and forces.[61] In their sum total, the diaries of *Los zorros* attest to Arguedas's striving to reconnect with his own vitality via the "vibrations of the wor(l)d": "Qué débil es la palabra cuando el ánimo anda mal! Cuando el ánimo está cargado de todo lo que aprendimos a través de todos nuestros sentidos, la palabra también se carga de esas materias. ¡Y cómo vibra!"[62] (How weak is the word when one's energy is low. When one's energy is charged with all that we learn through our senses, the word is also charged with those materials. And oh, how it vibrates!) The exchange between the material world outside of his own body and "the word" is more primordial in Arguedas than orality alone. And this is the same for Vallejo. The material world does not just orally "sound" in their poetry, but it infiltrates their body so that the mixing between forms of life comes through in writing, not just "orally" but as an orientation in the world that sees life *as* relationality, not as a set of static relationships.

It is not surprising that in his most critical novels of capitalism, Arguedas still draws attention to the healing power of his own body in dialogue with nature. His novels are more than stories that entertain, but rather, gateways into another way of perceiving the ecosystem of the Andes, and expanding it to other geographies. Thinking about ecology is not just thinking or writing about nature but thinking and writing as oriented in, by, and alongside other natures than the human alone. Jorge Marcone has recently argued that "the current pattern in Hispanic studies of not engaging enough with the reflection between society and nature and the human and the nonhuman in the history of Latin American literature and the arts projects the false image to our students, South and North, that these topics have been totally secondary in this tradition and that literature and the arts have nothing to say regarding current environmental issues and conflicts in the region." As Marcone demonstrates, in *Los zorros*, Arguedas has to find a way of "reworking his lost connection with all things."[63] One such way is the incorporation of physical motion: the foxes that remain dancing overcome the cerebral and the emotional through their embodied movement, and as Arguedas says, they "run away" with the novel, in the end. Arguedas dispels his energy into more energy, human or fox or river or flower, because, as he said, and as is quoted in the introduction to this book, "there's not much difference between a mountain, an insect, an immense rock, and a human being."[64] His avant-garde ontology is more relevant than ever in the contemporary era of ecological decay.

"La Agonía de Rasu-Ñiti": An Elegy of Rebirth

Continuing with dance, we will conclude with a scene of material rebirth via physical transformation. With uncharacteristic optimism, Arguedas writes to John Murra, in 1961, "He escrito también un cuento, 'La agonía de Rasu Ñiti.' Estoy feliz con este relato porque lo venía madurando desde hace unos ocho años y lo escribí en dos días. Te enviaré una copia. . . . Rasu-Ñiti era un bailarín legendario de Puquio"[65] (I have also written a story, "The Agony of Rasu Ñiti." I am happy with this story because it has been gestating for about eight years, and I wrote it in two days. I'll send you a copy. Rasu-Ñiti was a legendary dancer from Puquio). This succinct and masterful short story, published in 1962, is one of the few literary pieces about which Arguedas actually expresses fleeting satisfaction: he is happy. This story relates the death of a prestigious *dansak'*, Rasu-Ñiti (snow stomper) and his immediate successor, Atoq' Sayku (fox chaser). This story captures the vital connection between the human body and nature and marks a return to Puquio, the setting for "Agua" as well. Written before *Los zorros*, we can see the fox entering Arguedas's imaginary here, too.

In the story, a central *dansak'* (dancer), Pedro Huancayre, receives a sign from Wamani, the mountain god, warning him that his death is approaching. He senses this forthcoming shift inside his body and, specifically, inside his heart, "El corazón está listo. El mundo avisa. Estoy oyendo la cascada de Saño. ¡Estoy listo!—dijo el dansak' "Rasu-Ñiti"[66] (My heart is ready. The world advises me. I am hearing the Saño cascade. I am ready!—said the dancer Rasu-Ñiti). The *dansak'* then prepares himself for death. He explains to his wife, "¡Wamani está hablando!—dijo él—Tú no puedes oír. Me habla directo al pecho"[67] (Wamani is talking!—he said—You cannot hear it. He speaks directly to my chest). The connection that Rasu-Ñiti has with this Wamani is not just imagined spiritually but also experienced corporeally, as the mountain god communicates to him physically. This description enables readers to access an indigenous way of perceiving the world. Wamani descends from the mountain, passes through the sky, and moves through the body of the *dansak'*. The air is the invisible backdrop to the exchange, that which facilitates the contact between the Wamani and the body of the original *dansak'*, Pedro Huancayre.

After the principal *dansak'* begins his dance, Wamani arrives in the form of a condor, his terrestrial form, to accompany Rasu-Ñiti from the terrestrial plane to the cosmos. Birds continuously appear in Arguedas's stories because they connect *Hanan pacha* (the world up above) to *Kay pacha* (the world here on earth), and this story is no exception. In fact, birds appear multiple times in the story: "Las palomas y otros pájaros que dormían en el gran eucalipto, recuerdo que cantaron mientras el padre 'Untu' se balanceaba en el aire"[68] (The doves and other birds that slept in the great eucalyptus tree, I remember that they sang while the father "Untu" balanced himself in the air). As the *dansak'* moves, the birds' chirping sounds permeate the air and, therefore, his body. This connection is made via the air, as the sound connects the two species: the human and the birds. The air is also the backdrop to Wamani's arrival to the *dansak*'s body. Once he arrives, he "aletea sobre [la] frente"[69] (flaps around his forehead) of the dying Rasu-Ñiti. The air is cut by the "flapping" motion, as the wings push against it to create movement. Once the *dansak'* dies, the Wamani settles in to the body of the new dancer, "¡El Wamani aquí! ¡En mi cabeza! ¡En mi pecho, aleteando!—dijo el nuevo dansak'"[70] (The Wamani is here! In my head, in my chest, flapping!—said the new dancer). The use of the verb *aletear* again, as we saw earlier with the quinoa in the wind, animates the image of the moving bird for the reader. The death of one dancer is revitalized in the new one via this flapping bird's transference. The passage from one body to another is indicative of the spiral notion of *ñawpapacha* as it relates to space: the dancers are in the same space, and time is moving cyclically, repeating while changing simultaneously.

When the principal *dansak'* dies, his disciple, Atoq' Sayku, continues the dance, representing the material passing on of life. Once the Wamani enters the new *dansak*'s body, he too begins to dance, just like Rasu-Ñiti, as if the original had not died. In fact, Arguedas describes the new dancer as "Rasu-Ñiti, renacido" (Rasu-Ñiti, reborn), emphasizing the passage of life from one body to another. The dance is now a vital link that unites generations, as the original *dansak*'s daughter exclaims, "No muerto. ¡El mismo! ¡Bailando!"[71] (Not dead. He himself! Dancing!). Even though the new dancer is not her father, his vitality leaves from his body, passes through the air, and is transformed through the continued dance of Atoq' Sayku. The "magic" of the scene is affected by the wind, "La sombra del cuarto comenzó a henchirse como una cargazón de viento"[72] (The shadow of the room began to swell like an accumulation of wind). In this room, the shadow of the sun and the movement of the air combine to alter the material view of the room, linking natureculture together; humans, birds, mountains, sun, and the natureculture structures through which they relate. In this story, as we saw in Vallejo, the cosmic, the territorial, and the human body, and the heart inside are all linked via the passage of the bird into and out of the scene. When the story concludes, Rasu-Ñiti continues to dance via the movement of the next generation. The artistic ritual of the dance is a space of vital renewal that reflects and fosters the continuance of community.

The air also serves as essential backdrop to the scissors of the *dansak'* as they move and cut through it. Wamani takes on the physical form of a condor swooping down from the air to connect the god of the mountain (the cosmos) to the terrestrial humans on earth. Without the movement of the dancer Rasu-Ñiti, the god-bird would not be summoned. And without the ritualistic spirit of the dance, life as presented in the story would not necessarily continue. The Quechua word for death is *wañuy*, but this word also means "to desire in excess," as well as "eclipse."[73] While there is material loss in the story, there is a communication of the ongoing desire for community and connection within the narrative frame through the condor's power, and the mediation of the human and the bird via the dance. Desire is less in the body of one, but emanates from the collective scene, that reveals the process of becoming with other lives.

To conclude, if we read Arguedas with the element of the air in mind instead of land, we can see that it is part of the common base of his project, and a substance that enables relationships between living beings, as well as the interaction between animate and inanimate materials. Air is a consummate plural space in its movement and encompassing nature. To think from and through the lens of the air permits us not only to understand Arguedas's work within a new frame but also to articulate the relations between fields of knowledge by seeing their instability, not as an obstacle to different modes of knowing but as an opening toward acknowledging the plural communities of life that inhabit our world. In Gamaliel Churata's *El pez de oro*, written in 1957 and where this chapter began, part of the multigenred text is written in the form of a play. In addition to the "Pez de Oro" (Golden Fish), mother earth, the mountains, clouds, and the wind are all part of the "Dramatic Actors." The wind is an agent in the play. Writes Churata, "Hay que estar en soledad de paja, de roca, de viento, para sentir la primogenitura de la tierra"[74] (One has to be in the loneliness of the straw, of the rock, of the wind, to feel the birthright of the land). At the conclusion of a conference celebrating the centennial anniversary of Arguedas's life in Lima, Peru, in 2011, a group of dancers performed the traditional scissors dance at the inauguration of a museum exhibit in his honor. The sound of the metal scissors cut through the nighttime air, and the movement of the dancers animated the crowd gathered around to observe them. The event concluded, and the community dispersed. The air was filled with a formidable hope from the performance, and the loneliness I felt walking home late in the Lima night was tempered by the damp wind that accompanied me.

4

Mujeres Creando Comunidad

Communitarian Feminisms from the Bolivian Soil

The principal urban artery of La Paz, El Prado, or *la Avenida 16 de julio,* is the lowest point of elevation in the dramatically convex city of just under a million inhabitants. The hills that fan upward toward El Alto, a city inhabited largely by Aymara indigenous migrants, overflow with boxlike houses built tightly around each other. From the city center, as one's eyes gaze upward, the houses' beige mud brick walls give the appearance of a city built of cardboard. One sloping side of the crater houses the neighborhood of Villa Fátima, a working-class community in the appropriately named *zona periférica* (peripheral zone) that rings the entire downtown area of La Paz. This "villa" sprouts straight out of the side of the bowl, seemingly defying gravity. It is composed of a jumble of small markets and winding streets, in an organizational form that makes embodied sense to the people that move in and out of the bustling neighborhood. Villa Fátima is home to mestizo and indigenous populations alike, with about 12,500 inhabitants total, and is a gateway to the Beni Department and the Amazon region, just to the north of La Paz. It is in Villa Fátima where I came closest to experiencing Julieta Paredes's work because I was able to, albeit briefly, pass through one of multiple material spaces that shape and reflect her work.[1]

The first time I went to visit Paredes—a feminist activist, writer, and organizer from La Paz—I had a difficult time locating her house. Someone who is not intimate with La Paz's hillside neighborhoods cannot expect to simply tell a cab driver to head up to Villa Fátima, with a certain address, and assume the driver will know how to get there. And arriving by bus is also slightly complicated if you have not done it at least a few times before and memorized the contextual clues that indicate where to get off. Having ascended to Paredes's house both ways, I found the communal bus was much more precise once practiced. This defies the rules of Western transport, where a car tends to be the most exact mode of arrival. In Paredes's humble and colorful house, I was affected by what she had told me more than once: that her poetry is practice, that the laundry on her line is similar to the words in a book, and that ideas often originate in a kitchen as much as in a formal meeting.[2] She had recently been in the United States, and we shared dinner at my apartment. This time, she cooked for me: spaghetti and tomato sauce. But before Paredes and I had shared meals in our homes, I had met her elsewhere.

I met Paredes at the interdisciplinary Bolivian Studies Association Conference in Sucre, Bolivia, in June 2006. Paredes, a feminist, lesbian, and Aymara community activist, was attending and presenting at the conference as part of a panel on contemporary feminisms in the Andes. I remember Paredes's presentation because it was distinct from any other that I had heard at that particular conference, or at many others. She sang part of her talk, in both Aymara and Spanish, jumped down into the front row of chairs in the auditorium from the table on stage, and walked among the aisles where a captivated audience, whether critical of her work or not, listened to her contestation of neoliberal feminism and "la misma mierda," (the same old bs) of North American–produced feminism that wished to explain to the South what "it" ought to do and what problems "it" had.[3] Paredes disregarded standard conference decorum by embodying what she was saying as much as speaking the words.[4] She cut through the measured academic air and interrupted the space of the beautiful but formal National Archives facilities in Sucre with the type of engaged, informal style she would use if she were running a community workshop. It was impossible to discern where her body stopped and her ideas started: the two were one in the same. It was performance, and pedagogy, feminism, and a conference "paper" at once.[5]

In what follows, I trace the work of Bolivian feminist and activist Paredes and her work with two activist groups, Mujeres Creando and, later, Mujeres Creando Comunidad. The concrete activities in which Paredes and these two groups have participated include street performances, graffiti art, and writing, among other activities.[6] In her work, Paredes rejects North American neoliberal feminism that does not reflect the material and discursive reality of the majority of the women, men, and queer persons in and from Bolivia. Whereas neoliberal feminism has historically operated under the false assumption that every woman is somehow like, or wants to be like, a North American white woman of European descent, Paredes's feminism attempts to build South–South alliances based on partially shared and partially different material conditions. In her work in Bolivia over the past three decades, she has consistently challenged a global economic system that privileges some Western women as the active thinkers *of* or *for* other women, both in the North and the South. As Paredes demonstrates, "other women" have bodies, minds, and—go figure—problems of their own that materialize in and with their environments. As I elaborate, her work ranges from thinking the "beyond human" from material bodies beyond the white, male subject. From a materialist perspective that starts from her bodymind, she extends her work later to think about feminism from the perspective of a vital community, orientated by and toward the matter of the ecosystem.

A cornerstone to Paredes's and Mujeres Creando Comunidad's community-based feminism is a belief that the community, not the differentiated individual, is the central agent of feminism. A "community" is not formed only out of living human subjects today who differ in degrees but not kind, but hinges upon a more inclusive notion of life that includes the cosmos and its earthly materials. Individuality becomes secondary to a core belief in a community as the central subject.[7] In this sense, as we have seen in the other chapters of the book, relationships among people and things are the fabric of their work. The feminist community for Mujeres Creando Comunidad is not only made up of self-identifying women, but all gender nonconforming, or cis-gender parties in a community, as well as the other natural and material forms that contribute to the constitution of the same. In the model of communitarian feminism that Paredes puts forward she says, "Communitarian feminism speaks from the community as an inclusive principle that cares for life."[8] Life is not, as my close readings will make evident, exclusive to an idealized human, nor to humans alone.

In this chapter, I expand the analysis I have undertaken so far in the book to incorporate the genres of public performance and graffiti while continuing to undertake close poetic analysis. The work in this chapter opens the book's analytic scope because, while Paredes, like Magda Portal and Alejandra Dorado, is a South American feminist, and like José María Arguedas and César Vallejo, was influenced by Marxism, Paredes's lesbian identity has been and continues to be a defining characteristic of her material orientation in the world. Additionally, her Aymara ancestors influence her orientation as well. In what follows, I outline Paredes's early engagement with Mujeres Creando, and discuss the group's early performance and graffiti projects that were conducted before Paredes split from the group. I draw attention to the rose as a natural gift in this section, that catalyzes connections between community members. Second,

I look at a sampling of her poetry, which serves as a site for the reconfiguration of the subject as bound up in the natural and cultural environment of the subject's own surroundings. Third I look at her most important theoretical work to date, *Hilando fino: Desde el feminismo comunitario* (Sewing fine thread: Perspectives from communitarian feminism) (2010) as a contribution that opens up new avenues of conceptualizing feminism in the Andes and beyond.

Before turning to Paredes's and Mujeres Creando and Mujeres Creando Comunidad's work, I want to briefly acknowledge that, since meeting Paredes, I have tried to think about what it is to work *with* her, not *on* or *about* her. The work of relational thinking could be said to manifest itself linguistically as a prepositional predicament. How is it that we move from thinking *about* or *on* toward thinking *with* two or more viewpoints in mind? And what are the implications of that shift? I am acutely aware of my epistemological privileges and geopolitical location as I talk *about* Paredes, and I include myself in the chapter to be equally opaque: I am neither objective nor detachable from this work. I am a white, North American, female academic. And Paredes is a mestiza South American activist with her own set of privileges, from which and with which, I have humbly tried to learn and relate.[9] Through working with Paredes, I have thought a lot about what it means to *corazonar* (co-reason; this word plays on the fact that *corazón* means heart in Spanish, implying that reasoning incorporates the body, not just the mind, and emotion, as is associated with the heart). Ecuadorian scholar Patricio Guerrero Arias has described *corazonar* as "una respuesta política insurgente frente a la colonialidad del poder, del saber, y del ser, pues desplaza la hegemonía de la razón y muestra que nuestra humanidad se erige a partir de la interrelación entre la afectividad y la razón, y que tiene como horizonte la existencia"[10] (an insurgent political response to the coloniality of power, knowledge and being, well, because it displaces the hegemony of reason and demonstrates that our humanity is constructed on the basis of the interrelation between affect and reason, and that existence is the horizon line to both). Paredes's focus on the mindbody as integrated challenges the Western epistemological tendency to consider women as closer to the material, and therefore less capable of producing knowledge. Because she emphasizes their inseparability, she reconfigures the starting point for ways of being in the material world.

Mujeres Creando's Vital Gift Exchange

In 1990, Paredes and fellow Bolivian María Galindo—at the time, a couple—cofounded the anarchist feminist group that continues to be known as Mujeres Creando.[11] They had recently returned to La Paz, Bolivia, from Italy, where they lived in exile for several years, and were determined to take action to raise awareness around gender dynamics in La Paz and beyond.[12] Although never officially exiled by the state, the couple suffered what they described as "un exilio sexual, humano y político"[13] (a sexual, human, and political exile) due to their lesbian identity and outspoken radical politics. From their geographically alienated vantage point, their desire to live openly as lesbians came into stark focus, and they returned to Bolivia prepared and committed to educating those around them about social prejudice, particularly as it relates to gender, sexuality, and class. "Julieta y María regresaron a Bolivia en 1990 convencidas de que debían construir un espacio de mujeres en el país . . . así fue como nació la comunidad Creando, en una casa ubicada en las laderas de Villa Fátima, en las Delicias"[14] (Julieta and María returned to Bolivia in 1990 convinced that they had to construct a space for women in the country . . . that is how the Creando community was born, in a house on the hillsides of Villa Fátima). Paredes and Galindo, along with Mónica Mendoza, a university student in La Paz at the time, officially formed Mujeres Creando in 1991, and shortly thereafter, published their first book, *¿Y si fuésemos una espejo de la otra? Por un feminismo no racista* (As if we were a mirror of the other? Toward a nonracist feminism) (1992). This book argued that North American brands of feminism did not adequately capture women's experiences in Bolivia. Like Vallejo, Portal, and Arguedas argue in their own works and at different historical moments, Mujeres Creando outwardly rejects mimicry as the privileged model for cultural production during late twentieth-century Bolivia.[15]

Mujeres Creando wanted to initiate dialogue on women's rights and issues in La Paz, but they needed a concrete space from which to build their organic movement. Therefore, they opened up the "Centro Cultural Feminista Café Carcajada" in July 1992. They described this café in the early years of its formation as "un lugar adonde confluyen las utopías intuitivas de mujeres campesinas, cocaleras, lesbianas, universitarias, madres"[16] (a place of confluence for the intuitive utopias of peasants, coca growers, lesbians, university students, mothers), underscoring the heterogeneous people around whom the group coalesced. With a space of their own, they developed strategies aimed at raising social awareness around the intersections between gender, sexual, and racial inequalities as they play out within capitalism. Their early work was ambitiously diverse: they produced a newspaper, created a public access television program, performed in the streets, organized women's conferences, operated their small café, and began to spray-paint graffiti around La Paz, an act that would become an ongoing provocation tactic of the group.[17]

Over the course of their first decade of their work, they independently published a range of books, including, *Seamos creativas, hagamos lo imposible, un mundo no machista y sin opresiones* (1992), *Sexo, placer y sexualidad* (1996), a sexual-education handbook for Bolivian women, *Porque la memoria no es puro cuento* (2002), a book that came out of their participation in an international women's conference in Argentina, *Mujeres grafiteando* (2003), a collection of their graffiti and *La virgen de los deseos* (2005), an invaluable research source that provides a historical overview of their work. The only book-length scholarship on Mujeres Creando to date is an edited volume by Elizabeth Monasterios titled *No pudieron con nosotras* (2006), which includes chapters by Paredes and María Galindo as well as Monasterios, Ana Rebeca Prada M., Mónica X. Delgado, and Freya Schiwy; an introduction by John Beverley; and an epilogue by Norma Klahn. This book explores the creation of an autonomous feminism in Bolivia from various disciplinary perspectives. Because the group's early history has been thoroughly researched, I dedicate the rest of this chapter to critical analysis with the goal of manifesting the evolution of the group since their beginnings.[18]

I start with three performances that exemplify the ways that members of Mujeres Creando assert their humanity without compromising their own material orientation in the world, one that is distinct from the ideal disembodied one that has predominated in the West. The first performance I analyze is most directly related to their public demonstration of their sexual identity. Despite the self-exile mentioned earlier, it was not until 1994 when María Galindo, in an interview with the newspaper *La razón*, declared herself a lesbian that Mujeres Creando came to be publically associated with sexual rights as well as women's rights. Prior to this interview, Galindo and Paredes's sexuality was rumored in La Paz, but they were not publically out as a couple. Remaining silent meant that Paredes and Galindo could be further objectified in the eyes of the public instead of act as agents of their own desires. And so, instead of letting their lives become objects of speculation, they designed street actions that served a dual purpose: (1) to create common affective alliances in their community; and (2) to draw attention to the simultaneous difference and similarity of their same-sex desire to other expressions of love around them.

As a first example, in the late 1990s Paredes and Galindo painted an approximately eight- by eight-foot heart in the middle of la Plaza Murillo—the government's center that houses the Presidential Palace, the national Congress of Bolivia, and the Cathedral of La Paz. The deep crimson red color of the heart recalls blood and conjures up a sacrificial scene in the collective imaginary. This symbol implies that they are offering something of themselves to the public by taking the risk of putting themselves on display. But the sacrifice of blood in the name of love jogs a collective memory and loss as well, as the Plaza Murillo was, and continues to be, a site of political strife and protest.[19] The heart shape affirms the positive emotion of love as an offset to a negative one of loss and suffering. Even though Galindo and Paredes had experienced social rejection for years in the city, even being physically attacked one evening, their gift back to their community is one based on love.

In the video of the event, passers-by in La Paz are shown as they gather around while Paredes and Galindo paint. The people in the crowd either nod in tacit approval or, in the case of others, give the "thumbs-down" sign. After they finish painting the heart, but before continuing with their public act, Galindo and Paredes pick up approximately a dozen red roses each, which they begin offering to audience members. Some of the onlookers accept the roses, smelling them or holding them in their hands, others accept them but their body language is noticeably withdrawn, and still others outwardly refuse them. I argue that this act of sharing creates a physical bond between the diverse citizens of La Paz that is mediated through the rose. It is significant that Galindo and Paredes's "gift" is an ephemeral flower. Ralph Waldo Emerson has written, "Flowers and fruits are always fit presents; flowers, because they are a proud assertion that a ray of beauty out values all the utilities of the world."[20] The bestowing of the roses is significant not only because the rose is fleetingly alive but also because the exchange takes place between strangers. Paredes and Galindo do not have any direct affiliation with the recipients of their flowers but create one through the act of gift giving. In his book *Gifts and Commodities*, C. A. Gregory writes, "Commodity exchange establishes objective quantitative relationships between the objects transacted while gift exchange establishes personal qualitative relationships between the subjects transacting."[21] While there is no measurement of the "qualitative" relationships forged by Mujeres Creando, the gesture of offering the roses creates the potential for an affective relationship between themselves and the larger community of which they are a part as mediated via the exchange of the natural object.

The roses imply that those who accept the gift also accept Paredes and Galindo's partial similarity and partial differing from themselves. As Emerson further elaborates, "Gifts challenge the autonomy of the receiver, but the true gift nevertheless unites the giver and the receiver." For this reason, in Emerson's interpretation, "the only gift is a portion of thyself. Thou must bleed for me."[22] The heart painted on the ground implies that Galindo and Paredes have offered up a part of themselves to their community, but also makes the basis of being a human something more common than the differences in sexual desire: the organic blood that runs through the body. They have given something that has the potential to be given again: the affect of love, which functions here as a form of resistance to disembodied forms of capitalism. The performance is based on an affirmative relationship rather than a negative differentiation. Their message departs not from the desire to assert, in my words, "we are lesbians and are so different from you," but rather to beg the question, "if this is a shared communal space, what is it that partially aligns us?" These partial alliances, even if a temporary experience, have an effect on the network of "life," through material exchange.

After they distribute the roses, Paredes and Galindo lay down a blanket and pillows on top of the spray-painted sheet and climb into their makeshift public bed together. Each has a pillow under her head, and each is covered in a wool

Andean blanket typically found in households in the region. This utilitarian blanket might also partially link them to audience members who most likely have one of these ubiquitous materials in their houses, creating a common point of entry into the experience. Galindo and Paredes clasp hands tightly in their shared bed on the exposed street of La Paz. The camera continually pans to the crowd as Paredes and Galindo speak in a complementary form from the microphone. They say: "Estamos aquí vulnerables a sus críticas, su morbosidad, sus condenas y sus juicios, pero ninguna puede negar que nuestro amor es un amor valiente que construye, que crea, que hace una nueva sociedad"[23] (We're here, vulnerable to your criticisms, your morbidity, your condemnation, and your judgments, but no one can deny that our love is a valiant one that constructs, creates, and makes a new society). Through the combination of the exposure of their physical and emotional vulnerability as they lie down on the ground, they open themselves to potential criticism of their differing orientation in the world. However, while acknowledging the possibility of critique, they also point to the underlying love that defines their relationship together. As they describe it, their love is a constructive love that creates space for "a new society": one based in part on a reciprocal acceptance of the simultaneous conditions of difference and similarity at once, in this context.

The gift giving Paredes and Galindo perform demonstrates an embodied, physically present approach to exchange that also has particular salience in the Andes because of the indigenous communities' practice of the system of *ayni*, based on reciprocal exchange. Historically, the Quechua and Aymara indigenous communities related to each other without direct monetary exchange, as part of a broader Andean philosophy of reciprocity. As Josef Estermann has described it: "el principio de reciprocidad dice que diferentes actos se condicionan mutuamente (inter-acción) de tal manera que el esfuerzo o la 'inversión' en una acción por un actor será 'recompensado' por un esfuerzo o una 'inversión de la misma magnitud por el receptor.' En el fondo, se trata de una 'justicia' (meta-ética) del 'intercambio'"[24] (the principle of reciprocity says that different acts mutually condition each other [interaction] in such a way that the effort or inversion of one actor during an action will be recompensed by an effort or an inversion of the same magnitude by the receptor. At base, it has to do with the justice [meta-ethics] of exchange). The exchange of the roses with the audience members begs the question as to what the audience might offer in exchange to Paredes and Galindo as part of the construction of a collective community ethic.

By purposely turning themselves into what their critics might label a "public spectacle," Galindo and Paredes draw attention to their peaceful choice to love each other, and to express their sexuality, in the same space as heterosexual citizens. In the video version of this performance, they move from being seen as partially passive objects of societal critique to partially active ones as they put the viewers themselves under the microscope—those *in* the performance as well as those witnessing it on video. The effect of filming the performance enables television viewers, as well as anyone who was filmed, to look at a sampling of public reactions to Paredes and Galindo, potentially catalyzing reflection. The performance as a whole includes the audience and serves, beyond the surface of what is represented, to critique the ways that sexual desire is policed in public and private spaces. The video makes sensible the ways in which material exchange in the name of an ethical respect for the coexistence of difference and similarity at the same time can make sensible the partial alliances within that contextual community.

Around the time that they carried out this first public action, Mujeres Creando undertook another public intervention that also made visible the neocolonial intersections of capitalism, race, and social prejudice. As part of an episode that they taped for their program "Creando Mujeres" (Creating Women), which ran every Thursday night during primetime on a public access station for three months in 1999, members of Mujeres Creando went to a wealthy area of Cala-Coto in the Zona Sur (southern zone) of La Paz, about twenty minutes by bus from the city center. Paredes and a group of other members of the group stood in front of the large chain grocery store, Ketal, a somewhat obvious symbol of class and racial division in and around La Paz.[25] While the majority of the urban population continues to shop at open-air markets or small stores, the "suburban" population, especially that of the "Zona Sur" (more affluent suburbs) of La Paz frequents supermarkets like Ketal, primarily stocked with imported foods and transnational labels. Indigenous and *criolla* women alike from Mujeres Creando as well as Paredes herself dressed in a *pollera* (traditional indigenous skirt) and traditional Aymara hat stood in front of Ketal to raise awareness on racism in Bolivia. Their goal, as Paredes relates it, was to create community alliances, particularly between women of different class and racial backgrounds.

As women went into and out of the large store, members of Mujeres Creando offered them small pins in the shape of woven hats that were adorned with a ribbon that read, "Un país feliz es un país sin racismos" (A happy country is one without racisms). The hats were representative of the bowler hats that Aymara indigenous women in and around La Paz and El Alto frequently wear. Upon being greeted by Mujeres Creando members, the primarily white, female clientele walking in and out of the store displayed a range of responses: suspicious, dismissive, or receptive to the group's gift. Because traditionally dressed indigenous women are not frequent customers at this store, some of the predominantly white women reacted negatively to them. A few even assumed that they were there begging for money, as captured in the video.[26] Others responded positively, pinning the hat to their lapel or shirt, in a show of solidarity with the antiracist message. But still others, one woman in particular, seemed to think that putting the hat on her lapel was more of a nuisance than anything. She climbed into her car with the delicate pin in her hand. But, encountering difficulty in affixing it to her shirt, she tossed it out the passenger seat's window into a shallow puddle on the road.

The video, which runs only about fifteen minutes, makes sensible the ease with which the women walking in and out of the grocery store will spend money, as juxtaposed with the discomfort that comes with accepting generosity from women visually marked as indigenous and assumed to be of lower economic status. The action attests to the clients' impatience as well, as they prefer to quite literally "move through" the issue of racism than to stop, see it, and reflect upon it, even in its, ironically, antiracist "gift" form. This simultaneously speaks to the speed of capitalism that deems activities that do not involve the exchange of money, or the potential for profit in the long term, as a "waste of [my] time." Paredes's role in deconstructing the racist hypocrisy is pivotal to the action's effect. As she speaks into a microphone at the end of the video, she explains that, in a word, the day's activity was about hypocrisy. She comments that "de chola, nadie me acerca a hablar" (as a chola, no one comes up to me to talk). However, Paredes clarifies, that when she is dressed as "herself," people often stop to say hello or comment on her work. The passive decision of some of the clients to refuse communication with someone "de pollera" (a common shorthand for an indigenous woman) is made evident in the video.

By filming the Ketal encounters, Mujeres Creando confronts its viewers with one of the primary challenges to forming feminist alliances between women of different classes and races. But simultaneously, the group's members demonstrate the possibilities for community building in their portrayal of the women who accept their small pins in a show of solidarity. Because the pins are affixed directly to the body of the recipient, they emphasize, like the roses earlier, the affective alliance created between the women around, theoretically, a somewhat similar physical materiality at base. These bonds are essential to revitalizing a community-based feminism that sees different races and classes not as threats but as potential sites of partial alliance. Without this public performance, the simultaneous existence of difference and similarity between women as well as the exchanges that could facilitate them would not be as publically sensible.

Lastly, Mujeres Creando critiques the absurdity of many images of women that circulate in Bolivia to further critique the capitalist commodification of women, particularly as it flows from North to South America. In this third and last performance, Mujeres Creando publically deconstructs the idealized representation of the North American female body through a street action produced with mirrors, Barbie dolls, and the active participation of members of the group. At the beginning of the action, two middle-aged women and members of Mujeres Creando walk along the street of La Paz, holding a full-length mirror on its side, with Barbie dolls perched precariously along its upper edge. As the women walk along the street, the mirror reflects the racially diverse population of the dynamic La Paz street culture, very few (if any) who look remotely like the blonde, twiglike Barbies. The performance draws attention to the vast abyss between material representation and "real life" as it plays out in the mirror. If the Barbie doll stands in for an idealized female form as produced in the United States (and yet, totally misrepresentative of any woman in any country on the planet), then the motile images of the indigenous and mestiza women reflected in the mirror operate in glaring contrast to the disproportionate plastic dolls.

The mirror adorned with the Barbie dolls manifests the reality that Bolivian women look in the mirror of capitalism and see all that they are materially *not* reflected back to them, instead of all that they materially are. The visual disjuncture makes evident the symbolic violence that results from the circulation of unattainable representations of physical and gendered ideals. As Paredes writes later in *Hilando fino*, "estamos hartas de una estética colonial de lo blanco como bello, cansadas del espectáculo frívolo de cuerpos que se exhiben para el consumo machista, elementos que son parte del culto a la apariencia que el neoliberalismo implanta"[27] (We are fed up with the colonial aesthetic of whiteness as what is beautiful, tired of the frivolous spectacles of bodies exhibited for *machista* consumption, elements that are part of the cult to appearances that neoliberalism plants). Any attempt to live up to the image of the Barbie doll would require the tacit acceptance of an imported model of beauty, unattainable as much at its point of origin as at its destination.[28] Critiques have been leveled at the racist, classist, and corporeal dysmorphia that Barbie has come to symbolize, both in North America and elsewhere.[29] Mujeres Creando's intervention, therefore, not only resonates locally in Bolivia but also demonstrates the abyss between the representation of capitalism's bodies and the materials of vital living bodies, moving in La Paz and elsewhere.

As the video advances, the women of Mujeres Creando are shown wound with white rope, loosely draped around them, with the dolls now adorning them. The rope implies that when women's forms do not correspond to those of the idealized heterosexual white woman, their vitality—their movement and ability to express the affective experience within them to others—is restricted. However, as the video progresses, these same women begin to dance, slowly losing metaphoric control over their bodies. They and their friends tear the Barbie dolls from the rope. Then, they rip or cut the rope that was binding their bodies, shedding it onto the ground. As the women pull the string off of each other, they gift each other movement and freedom from unachievable ideals. At the same time, they make sensible the force of the market and its imposition of idealized images on real, live bodies. The making sensible of the ways that material culture, like these dolls, influences their lives helps to draw attention to the way materials affect the human and not just the reverse; likewise, the video empowers the human to transform the material world.

Guy Debord explains the alienation and loss of spiritual capacity that modernization brought upon both the public and the private sphere ever since the inception of market capitalism, specifically, after the Second World War. Debord's interpretation of this effect is that the sense of alienation we feel from each other, and a certain lack of spirituality, have to do with the invasive presence of "spectacle," one of capitalism's most convincing forms of persuasion: "the spectacle corresponds to the historical moment at which the commodity completes its colonization of social life. It is not just that the relationship to commodities is now plain to see—commodities are now *all* that there is to see; the world we see is the world of the commodity."[30] While Paredes and Galindo use their performances to resist aspects of the symbolic import of North American feminism, we also must be wary of their work's role in contributing to the same capitalist spectacle that it sets out to critique. It is a tricky task to remain in a creative, vital space of "becoming" something new without actually transforming into an image that circulates: "The spectacle is *capital* accumulated to the point where it becomes image."[31] One of Mujeres Creando's challenges has been to maintain a space of resistance to capital without the group itself becoming reified into a fetishized name, or turning into what Freya Schiwy aptly calls "a shock value," instead of resisting incorporation to the very system the group sets out to critique.[32] In the next section, we will see how Mujeres Creando moves from being a group of activists to one of unwitting artists, and tease apart the complexities of this partial transformation.

Graffiti as (Ir)reproducible Movement

Performance art relies on the physical body as the principal conduit for its message. Likewise, graffiti art also relies on the body's movement through space for its creation, but its message comes from the juxtaposition of spray paint and the symbolically invisible public spaces it subsequently makes sensible. Graffiti artists bring often overlooked urban and rural backgrounds to the fore of a collective imagination as much as the content of their words or symbols. The surface and graffiti layer work together to both represent and speak to unseen groups of the population who are underrepresented in the mainstream media and commercial representations of cities, neighborhoods, and cultures. These overlooked populations often pass under the radar of the official lettered culture. Historically, these groups have used graffiti to indirectly or directly critique society while retaining a degree of anonymity; whether partial or complete, this is an important component to the medium. Regardless of whether it is officially tagged or not, graffiti make sensible the abstracted notion of exclusion as it operates within a given community. It disrupts the naturalized environment, drawing attention to those people, things, and ideas that are frequently insensible in a given public space.

The Prado of La Paz (and many North and South American cities) greets the citizen and tourist alike with countless male ghosts turned into looming iron statues. The majority of the men represented, as well as for whom the streets and plazas are named, are of Spanish origin. Simón Bolívar (1783–1800) and Pedro Domingo Murillo (1759–1810) are just two examples. They represent war heroes of the Republic and symbolize a male ethos of war that passively pervades the city, whether it comes from the political left or the right, the present or the past. One of the few female-inspired plazas in La Paz, "Isabel la Católica" is named for the Queen of the Old World, a Spanish import who never set foot in the city. The gap between the types of physical bodies one finds in La Paz in static aestheticized form and the reality of the dynamic social bodies as they move through the streets is notable, just like the example of the Barbie doll described earlier. Keenly aware of the divide between the architectural image of the city and the racial, sexual, and gendered citizens who roam within it, Mujeres Creando members insert their graffiti into the falsely neutral space of the city to grab the attention of complacent citizens and make the walls and buildings newly visible.

In *La ciudad letrada* (1984) (The lettered city), Angel Rama traces the historical coincidence of the physical rise of the Latin American urban space and the symbolic emergence of the lettered, governing class. This synchronicity resulted in an epistemology based on the privilege of written thought and the grid of a city as well as the subordination of other ways of knowing and inhabiting space. Rama notes the importance of graffiti in the intellectual space of Latin America and the way that it represents the peripheral communities of the metropolitan imaginary. I quote from *La ciudad letrada*: "Por la pared en que se inscriben, por su frecuente anonimato, por sus habituales faltas ortográficas, por el tipo de mensaje que transmiten, los graffiti atestiguan autores marginados de las vías letradas, muchas veces ajeno al cultivo de la escritura, habitualmente recusadores, protestatarios e incluso desesperados"[33] (Due to the walls on which they are inscribed, their frequent anonymity, their habitual spelling errors, and the type of messages they transmit, graffiti attest to authors marginalized from writing protocols, many times alien to writing culture and practice, and habitually disregarded, contrarian, and even desperate). Mujeres Creando's graffiti are new in their context because they come from feminist and queer bodies, thereby presenting a new orientation vis-à-vis the public walls and spaces of the city. In their own words, members of Mujeres Creando describe their graffiti as follows: "Grafitear así es pues algo muy serio, es una acción donde ponemos nuestro cuerpo en la lucha histórica para transformar nuestra sociedad. No ponemos un cuerpo heroico, no un cuerpo militarizado, ponemos un cuerpo vulnerable, sensible, sensual, creativo, desarmado y no violento"[34] (Graffiti writing is something really serious, an action where we insert our body into the historic fight to transform our society. We don't bring forth a heroic body, or a militarized body, we offer a vulnerable, sensitive, sensual, creative, disarmed and nonviolent body). Through their insertion of their bodies into an ongoing struggle, Mujeres Creando's members draw attention to the colonial and neocolonial wounds that represent the symbolic and physical violence that they continue to experience, and that we saw earlier in Dorado's work. They act from the body that hurts of Gamaliel Churata, who wrote, in a revision of Descartes, "Yo no soy porque pienso, soy porque duelo"[35] (I am not because I think, I am because I hurt). The affective orientation of their bodies is named as important in Mujeres Creando's work as members contrast their peaceful bodies from those that participated, or continue to participate, in forms of physical violence, like the military bodies represented and discussed previously in Dorado's work in Cochabamba.

As just one example of many, they spray-painted "hombres necios que acusais a la mujer sin razón"[36] (foolish men, you accuse women for no reason), on a wall between two colonial-style windows partially covered by iron grating in La Paz. "Hombres necios," the opening phrase of Sor Juana's most well-known and taught poems, employs the *vosotros* (you, inclusive) form of *acusáis* (you accuse). The use of this form is additional evidence of the direct reference to this past era, even grammatically, in the present. Although it may have been coincidental, these particular graffiti are doubly effective because they are framed by the colonial-style windows that contribute to their message. The architecture links the present verse to the past, visually. Sor Juana used her creative agency in seventeenth-century Mexico to critique the claustrophobic society within which she lived, particularly in relation to the rights of women to access, pursue, and produce knowledge. The ghost of Sor Juana's spirit might be thought to lean out from behind the bars of one of these windows, as if she herself had reached around and spray-painted the graffiti on the wall. In this sense, the context of the graffiti is as important as the more literal message that they contains. It brings to life the inanimate background and flat letters of the words through the hint of the body/bodies that was/were "just there." By conflating their own authorship (the graffiti are signed by Mujeres Creando, despite having borrowed the graffiti from Sor Juana) with that of Sor Juana, members of Mujeres Creando create a community of alliances with women who went before them, while transforming the message into a contemporary time/space via its placement on the public wall.[37]

Due to the graffiti, the city wall becomes a palimpsest: a bulletin board of sorts that serves as a counter space of cultural production for anyone with access to a spray can and the initiative. In addition to the feminist genealogy they create, Mujeres Creando members "sign" their graffiti with their symbol, a combination of the symbol for a woman and an anarchist "A." By signing the graffiti with a symbol, they make their collective presence known, but obviously the individual responsible for the graffiti cannot be identified by name, an evasive tactic to avoid interpellation by the state. While the graffiti may seem to reinstate the human as center to the project of social transformation, the built environment itself—the buildings, walls, design of the city—is a partial agent in the process because it is materially present before the action and affects those who interact with it.

Returning to the concept of the "gift," whereas published books are costly and consequently imply limited access, Mujeres Creando's utilization of public space for some of its "poetry" reminds passers-by of the potential for collective creative work. The graffiti are free, hypothetically accessible to anyone, and a public "gift" (depending on one's perspective, of course). The images continue to be given to others through their public placement and have an effect on those who respond to their message, whether in internal or external ways. Yet the graffiti are not like most other public propaganda that is either an advertisement connected to the production of capital or some form of political propaganda in the name of an electable official. Their graffiti are, in this sense, disinterested in any one single outcome, and instead invested in critiquing the invisible barriers of the systems that they expose. The informal writing makes the material environment sensible, reengaging passers-by with the built and natural environment to which they may have become immune, as well as drawing attention to the potential for their transformation of it and the transformation that "it" can catalyze or inhibit within them. The material environment is no longer neutral but charged with a vibrancy, much like Arguedas's words.

The transformative power of graffiti more so than other media is contingent on their contextual setting and their spontaneous mode of production. Graffiti are not an edited genre, rather, in theory, a spontaneous event. To this extent, duplicating their form is arguably contrary to the original intent of the genre. And yet duplication serves the purpose of bringing more potential alliances and international community support into the fold of the organic feminist movement Mujeres Creando initiated, and recognizes the shared innovation of both formal painting and informal street art. Thinking about the active and unique act of graffiti writing, comparative literature and philosophy scholar Carrie Noland has written, "It was while watching a graffiti writer that I first began to perceive how agency might work. As I observed the writer, his gestures revealed themselves to be simultaneously a repetitive routine and an improvisational dance; a script was obviously at the root of the performance and a script was its ultimate, durable product, but in between, as I could plainly see, a body was afforded a chance to feel itself moving through space."[38] The more I have thought about Mujeres Creando's graffiti and the ways they have traveled, I think it is essential to hold the planned and spontaneous aspects of graffiti, as repetitive motion and an improvisational activity. The wall itself will impact the way a script comes out as will the human hand. It is not entirely passive in the process.

In 1999, the Museum of Contemporary Art in Madrid, the *Reina Sofía* invited María Galindo, who had increasingly become the more public face of Mujeres Creando, to participate in an international exhibit titled *Utopías*. Galindo assembled an installation she called "Así como tú me quieres, yo no quiero ser de ti" (Just like you want me, I don't want to be yours). As part of her performance she called herself an "impostora" (imposter) because she considered herself an outlier to the aesthetic circle of those participating in the exhibit who considered themselves "artists." By calling herself an impostor, Galindo entered into the paradoxical situation of "becoming" an artist at once, the challenge of maintaining difference when entering a space where similarity is a tacit requirement. What's more, placing Mujeres Creando's "art" within an exhibit called *Utopías* in the space of a museum is precisely the reason that Bürger argued that the original goal of merging art and "life" failed due to the great success of avant-garde art in the institution.

The transformation from activists into "artists" continued a year later. Mujeres Creando received another invitation from the *Reina Sofía*, this time to participate in the largest exhibit of contemporary Latin American art the museum had shown to date. Five prestigious art critics from Cuba, Argentina, Mexico, and Spain, all of whom had diverse curatorial tendencies and interpretations, organized the exhibit. A discussion broke out among them when one of the critics, Rafael Doctor, proposed that Mujeres Creando exclusively occupy a coveted space in the museum's exhibit space for one month. His suggestion was met with skepticism because Mujeres Creando's work—performance and graffiti art—was not readily classifiable and did not originate from formal arts training. It more predominantly grew from a dedicated commitment to sociopolitical change.[39] In the end, Mujeres Creando occupied the aforementioned coveted space in the museum for over a month, during which time Galindo, Paredes, and Florentina Alegre (another participant and member of the group) interacted with over seventy thousand visitors.

Through its participation in this second exhibit, Mujeres Creando again indirectly confronted the dissenting critics as well as visitors with what the limits of their conception of "art" might have previously been. However, in terms of the embeddedness of the group's project within its society, the decision to engage in the space of the museum betrayed the commitment to doing on-the-ground, grassroots community organizing work, and the difference between these two modes of engagement would increasingly divide the group. Paredes has been consistently more interested in enacting informal social change from a community base rather than producing aesthetic projects that do not stem from or speak back, necessarily, to market trends in "popular art." The first installation in the Reina Sofía only initiated their exhibits in museums and is indicative of part of a gradual process of incorporation into a system of aestheticized art to which Paredes has remained consistently opposed. After this exhibit in Madrid, Mujeres Creando, without Paredes, received invitations to represent members' work from art centers in Zaragoza, Barcelona, and Valencia, as well as Germany. Most recently, Galindo exhibited her newest work *Ninguna mujer nace para puta* (No woman is born a whore) in Bilbao, Vitoria, Zarauz, and Zaragoza. This exhibit and accompanying book—coauthored with another South American feminist activist named Sonia Sánchez—aimed to draw attention to the exploitation of sex workers and the exploitation of women's bodies in Bolivia and beyond.[40]

I draw attention to these exhibits to make the point that, while Mujeres Creando's graffiti originally emerged as a result of local context, these same graffiti have been reproduced various times. By displacing the graffiti and its articulation in a specific geographic context, Mujeres Creando moves from the public space of the street to the private space of the museum. In the process of their transference, do the graffiti lose some of their subversive power? The graffiti might represent the ability of Mujeres Creando to move in and out of coexisting worlds. The agonic tension between the public and the private spaces, as well as with different communities, puts their transformative capacities at center. They can be partially artists and partially activists, partially against capitalism, but embedded within it regardless. In their displacement from their original material context the interpretable, readable message of the graffiti art becomes its principal point; that is to say, the words alone contain the message, not necessarily their placement, or their disruptive appearance of the environment from one day to another. During the process of displacing the graffiti from their original time-space, the spontaneity of the gesture—the vital movement of the hand—is lost. And with it, the essential social risk factor that seems to be a key component to the act of artistic transgression. And yet, what is gained is international recognition, beyond Bolivia, of important work being done on non-Western feminisms.

As an indirect but nonetheless important result of the group's entrance into the official space of the Reina Sofia, "Mujeres Creando" also, however, crystallized as a proper name. Instead of remaining as "women [who are] creating"—that is, creating a something unnamed but immanent—they became internationally identifiable as a branded proper name. While individualism is "the unquestionably desirable standard" of capitalism, it is also so easily conflated with a brand name or a logo as to become disembodied.[41] If "Mujeres Creando" becomes a marketable "brand," then how does it help or hinder the group's local social movement? The group was originally a group of women who were continuously creating—moving bodies catalyzing actions in progress in their material setting. The sense of the ongoing provocation of their work is symbolized by the gerund, ending in "-ando." However, this transition from a subject and an action into a proper noun is the result of not just a selling-out process that converts the diverse movement into a nameable, locatable, and commodified group, but also an inevitable result of the agency of the market itself. Whereas before, Mujeres Creando were the subjects and actors of their own movement, they solidified their conversion into a partial object of capital by entering into the formal museum space and thereby gaining "recognition within the institution."

What has been vital to this group's success is actually their participation in a capitalist economy as well as their refusal of it. They move in and out of different spaces in a chameleon-like, strategic way. Their own insistence to differ without difference and to simultaneously point out the common without absorption into a false whole or unity, is a vital space of potential micromovements. It is that same contradiction—Vallejo, we recall, both is and is not Vallejo in his speaking of hope—that underscores the other chapters of the book as well: the coexistence and irresolution of a will to differentiate and to simultaneously be common.

Paredes's Vital Community-Based Feminism: Poetry and Practice

María Galindo and Paredes co-led Mujeres Creando for close to ten years, but in 2002 Paredes split left the original group to turn her attention to what she would come to refer to as community-based feminisms in and around La Paz. As Elizabeth Monasterios and Paredes herself relate it in *No pudieron con nosotras* (They sure could not with us), Paredes began to define herself from an Andean feminist position that privileged the anarchist traditions of the anticolonial feminist fights, like that of Bartolina Sisa, and an Andean form of political organization based on a communal-democracy, whereby political action would be initiated from a Feminist Assembly.[42] With a commitment to activism at the grassroots level, Paredes spearheaded community-building activities for the La Paz members of the Asamblea Feminista, a diverse group of women who have worked to promote women's needs to the Morales government. The Asamblea Feminista also has members in all nine provinces of Bolivia, attesting to the scope of its reach.

Paredes maintains the original Café Carcajada for Asamblea Feminista meetings as well as a site for hosting educational programs and social outreach activities. She and her Mujeres Creando Comunidad colleagues have developed a conceptual framework for community-based feminisms that was published under the title *Hilando fino: Desde el feminismo comunitario* (2008; translated into English by Margaret Cerullo and Antonia Carcelén in 2015 as *Hilando fino: Perspectives from Communitarian Feminism*), as I explore following here. Galindo, on the other hand, opened a new café called La Virgen de los deseos (the virgin of desires), in 2005 and has maintained the group's original name, Mujeres Creando. Galindo is more heavily involved in the international arts and performance arts worlds. Whereas Paredes continues to shun traditional aesthetic categories like "performance," "artist," and "poet," Galindo's work continues to be more publically performative and provocative.

Throughout the production of all of the work just discussed, Paredes consistently wrote poetry and continues to do so. This quieter work, behind the scenes, begins to plant some of the seeds that become the framework that Mujeres Creando Comunidad lays out in *Hilando fino*. For instance, in her published book of poetry *Con un montón de palabras* (2000), Paredes begins with "Cuando el suelo que nos sostenía / se diluye/desmayado / enfermo / cansado de tanta pobreza"[43] (When the soil that used to sustain us / is diluted / faint / sick / tired of so much poverty). and goes on to describe the disillusionment of the soil, soil that "no entiende / porque el capital se dedica a hacer más capital / más capital para el Banco mundial / y el Fondo Monetario Internacional"[44] (doesn't understand/why capital is dedicated to make more capital / more capital for the World Bank / and the International Monetary Fund [IMF]). In this poem, the soil is what sustains Mujeres Creando, who "return" via song and dance the vitality to this "naked soil," that brightens up to the colors of the rainbow, metaphorically, after the group performs their offering. The soil sustains the life of the community in the poem, and is made sensible as part of the poetic ecosystem. The incorporation of the natural environment into her poetry comes back up later in the community-based feminisms platform, as we will see.

Another untitled poem in the collection conveys the submersion of the subject in the material world.

> Entre este cielo, esta tierra
> entre océanos, mares y dos polos
> que me envuelven
> desgrano mi existencia
> sorbo mis penas
> hundo mis manos
> entre los sudores, risas y dolores
> de cuerpos y cuerpos
> contemporaneidad mágica
> que me conmueve y me mueve
>
> Soy.[45]
>
> (In the midst of this sky, this earth
> Among the oceans, seas and two poles
> That surround me

I peel back my existence
I soak up my difficulties
I bury my hands
Among the sweat, laughter and pain
Of bodies and bodies
Contemporary magic
That overwhelms me and moves me

I am.)

In this poem, simple in its language and message, the poetic voice emphasizes her embedded location in the broader universe that envelops her existence. The experience of coming into a consciousness of being is contained in the materiality of experiences as well and their physical effects on the voice of *Soy* (I am). The act of "burying" her hands in another material body is the relationship that "moves" and even "overwhelms" the subject. In fact, the *Soy* (I am) that breaks apart from the first stanza is the after effect of the rest of the relationships laid out in the poem. Like Portal describes her poetry as made of *linfas humorales* (lymphatic substances), Paredes draws in the sweat and dampness of physical existence, the bare materiality to the experience of being alive with the world. Paredes's final *Soy* (I am) is a result in the poem of her existence within the matter of the cosmos, not her mastery over it. She consequently places the "soy" at the end of the poem, after naming the rest of the materials before the subject.

Paredes's consistent recognition of material existence and her animation of the natural environment of Bolivia contribute to and show up in new ways in her most significant theoretical and methodological production to date, the short manual/manifesto *Hilando fino: Desde el feminismo comunitario*.[46] In this short but impactful book, Paredes and her colleagues (re)orient feminism in Bolivia by posing a dual critique of both neoliberal *and* indigenous perspectives concerning gender. This transcritical approach expresses the richness of Paredes's project because she addresses both the internal and the external power dynamics that contribute to gender oppression, strengthening the complexity of the project.

At its base, the book proposes a new way conceptualizing feminism from the perspective of a community that exists in and with time and space. The initial part of the book provides an overview of neoliberalism in Bolivia, and particularly, the ways that only a small part of the population historically benefited from neoliberal restructuring: "Bolivia, como el resto de Latinoamérica, entra en 1985 en un ajuste estructural cuyas bases político-económicas están en los ajustes estructurales impuestos por el imperialismo, en el interés de garantizar sus enormes tasas de acumulación y apropiación usurera de los excedentes económicos y los recursos naturales de los países del llamado tercer mundo"[47] (Bolivia, like the rest of Latin America, enters into a structural adjustment phase in 1985, whose political economic bases are the structural changes imposed by imperialism, in the interest of guaranteeing enormous rates of accumulation and usurious appropriation of the economic excesses and natural resources of the countries of the so-called third world). Paredes traces this economic history because it is relevant to acknowledge and understand what the conditions were that have led to her theorization of a communitarian feminism in the first place. Via her critique of neoliberalism, she also makes her more radical community-based feminism differ from the institutional feminism run by nongovernmental organizations in La Paz. This is the same critique we saw manifested earlier via the early performance work. The critique here, though, also places more direct attention on natural resource exploitation, not just the exclusionary discourses of neoliberal feminism.

Paredes criticizes neoliberal individualism, writing "no todo empieza y termina con tu ombligo y existen otras personas más allá de ti"[48] (not everything begins and ends with your belly button, and other people exist beyond you). Accepting alterity in someone else equates to recognizing others in the world neither as a threat to our personhood nor as an amorphous extension of self, but a reaffirmation of a relational community made of differings in degree, not categorical binaries. According to Paredes, at least up until now, *la comunidad boliviana* in the political and social imaginary refers mainly to men and not women as currently used in discourse: "Se percibe a las mujeres detrás de los hombres o debajo de los hombres o lo que es lo mismo subordinadas a los hombres"[49] (Women are perceived as "behind" men or "below" them which is to say, they are subordinated to men). This perspective echoes Silvia Rivera Cusicanqui's observation that, "la noción de identidad como territorio es propia de los varones, y las formas organizativas que han adoptado los pueblos indígenas de Bolivia están todavía marcados por el sello colonial de la exclusión de las mujeres"[50] (the notion of identity as territory is based on men, and the organizational forms that Bolivian indigenous populations have adopted are still marked by a colonial trademark, the exclusion of women). Both Paredes and Cusicanqui signal that internal colonization is as much of a threat to women's inclusion in community as the continual legacies of what Cusicanqui names "the colonial condition," and that she expands on in many of her writings.[51]

As an alternative to theorizing feminism from the individual, *Hilando fino* emphasizes the complementariness between male and femaleness (not as individualized and sexualized bodies but rather as energies within the broader community). From the perspective of indigenous communities, historically the male (*chacha*, in Aymara) has been metaphorically placed hierarchically above the female (*warmi*, in Aymara). However, in her reconceptualization of what she perceives as the hierarchy, Paredes places *chacha* and *warmi* next to each other, horizontally, rather than in a vertical layout. If the female and the male side of the community are not both actively participating in the functioning of their social body, then the entire body cannot function well. In order to experience *suma qamaña* or *buen vivir* (the complete life, in Aymara; the plentiful life, or the good life, in Spanish), all portions of a given body must operate together in dialogue with time and space.[52] It is only then that a community can participate in rethinking and reshaping society. Intercultural philosopher Josef Estermann has argued, "Para la filosofía andina, el individuo como tal no es 'nada' (un 'no-ente'), es algo totalmente perdido, si no se halla dentro de una red de múltiples relaciones"[53] (In Andean philosophy, the individual as such is not anything [a nonentity], it's something totally lost if it is not located within the network of multiple relationships).

While on the one hand the relationships among a plurality of subjects are vital to a sustainable community that is in harmony not only as an entity but in relationship to the material environment, on the other hand, the idea that the *ayllu* is a utopic fix to neoliberal individualism is also problematic. The idea that the *ayllu* is "el verdadero sujeto en los Andes"[54] (the real subject in the Andes), as expressed by intercultural philosopher Javier Medina, has been a problematic principle for Paredes because it occludes the diversity of the *ayllu* itself. Even though there is, in theory, a "complementary" gender structure, it is also riddled with power dynamics—like those of the hierarchical ordering discussed earlier.[55] As a response, Paredes argues that the term "gender," has been used to stand in for "women" of late by indigenous communities who claim a model of "gender complementarity," as if women were the "gender problem" that needed to be tacked onto an existent community. But this perspective of complementarity often results in an additive model wherein the female is the *yapa* or "extra" to the dominant male subject.[56] In order to reclaim agency and gain political traction, Paredes reconceptualizes gender so that it is no longer just a category that privileges men but is instead a category that comes to mean only relative to a diverse community base. She dismantles the notion of complementarity as it is commonly conflated with "heterosexual pair" in favor of what she calls a *par político*, or political pair. This reconfiguration enables her to think beyond a male/female binary, in theory: "No queremos pensarnos frente a los hombres sino pensarnos mujeres y hombres en relación a la comunidad"[57] (We don't want to think about ourselves in distinction with men but rather think about women and men in relationship to the community). "Complementary" therefore means only in relationship to a community that is more than an idealized group of heterosexual pairs. In the sense of a political pair, complementariness is related more to what people do in context than what they "are" biologically. This antiessentialist stance enables more flexibility within the category of "human" as well as material contextualization as the starting point. In sum, instead of proposing a counterhierarchy, responding to colonial difference with a direct inversion of a power dynamic, Paredes creates an affirmative politics based on differings within a broader community context and without taking the heterosexual pair as the basis for complementariness.

In her book, Paredes defines "community" as composed of five central components: the body, time, space, movement, and memory. In her approach to the material body, Paredes argues that we have to decolonize "esa concepción escindida y esquizofrénica del alma por un lado y cuerpo por otro; eso es lo que ha planteado la colonia"[58] (that divided and schizophrenic conception that would have the soul as one side and the body as another; that is what the colony has proposed). Instead, Paredes goes on to say that she understands the body "from the point of view of biogenetics to energy, from the sphere of affectivity, passing onto sensibility, and feelings, eroticism, spirituality, arriving to creativity."[59] The diverse components of any physical body only thrive in a corresponding space and time. And so, Paredes argues in the name of understanding space as a VITAL FIELD [capitalization in the original] in which the body develops, "Space is where life moves and continues to reproduce itself."[60] She refers to the vertical and horizontal axes of space, one axis that includes what is up above, here, and below, and the other axis that includes past, present, and future. Time and space together create the vital present. Paredes's consideration of space instead of place enables a more inclusive, expansive notion of not just territorial location but the cosmos, as it envelops and constitutes "the community." Space is a "vital field" that extends beyond the geographic coordinates of earth, encapsulating matter that the human eye cannot see. This reconceptualization of community within a cosmological space enables Paredes to trouble the notion that a community exists on its own, with autonomy over space or time. Instead, the three are interwoven.

Paredes further elaborates the idea of vital spatiality when she names the space below, *manqha pacha*, where ancestors, seeds, roots, natural resources, thermal gases, the heat of the rock, minerals and underground animals as well as the energy and knowledge that Pacha Mama offers, dwell. This space is in complementary relationship with the materials up above, *alax pacha*, of the sky and stars, that represent air space, the space of communications, telecommunications, satellite communications, and where the ozone hole and contamination dwell. Here, on earth, is a middle space that connects both the below and the above.[61] The idea that humans are alive not by themselves alone, rather, via their complementarity to, and reciprocity with, the materials around them manifests a relational approach to community that considers natureculture as a continuum. The middle space is just one and, in the configuration that Paredes lays out, is downplayed because of its existence as only relative to the other spaces.

The title of Paredes's book illustrates the ways that she draws attention to the body and memory in her conception of community. And it captures the way that her gift—the thinking behind the book she writes—continues to be passed on to other people: "We call on all of you together to weave bridges and spool thread, in this case, through the theoretical reconceptualization of us as feminist women; a framework of actions that might enable us to discover others through ourselves, and ourselves through others. We propose a practice of alterity, reciprocity, complementariness, and autonomy."[62] When Paredes invokes the daily practice of weaving, which has gone on since the precolonial period, and that of spooling thread, she connects the present generation of women to those from the past, by means of the important tradition of weaving in the Andes. The act of weaving, while it results in a beautiful product, is more than just art. It is a ritual celebration of the community, the construction of a spiral history that is still becoming again in the present, and the visual archive of the memories of ancestors. Therefore, Paredes's metaphor reminds women of an important historical and aesthetic contribution to their indigenous communities: a daily vital practice. Weaving, intimately connected to the body, which touches each thread directly and leaves its active imprint in the form of a pulled stitch or an irregular mark, also connects community to the memory of its past. It is an archive that is not written, and not fully performed, but that symbolizes a vital encounter between the body and the artistic object as they are oriented toward each other via the act of *hilando*.

Lastly, Paredes argues that the five components of the body, time, space, movement, and memory are necessary for the achievement of *sumaq q'amaña* (also appears as *suma qamaña* elsewhere), or *buen vivir*. This expression directly contrasts with notions of *bienestar* (well-being) that originate in neoliberal development discourse and operate from the perspective of the individual at the center of capitalism. *Suma qamaña*, outlined by Medina in his book *Suma qamaña: por una convivialidad posindustrial* (2006), means to live well in Aymara, but to live well as a person in a community, not just as an isolated individual.[63] It also means to live well, both materially and spiritually. David Choquehuanca, Bolivia's chancellor of the exterior until January 2017 and an Aymara intellectual, has contrasted living well to both capitalism and socialism, and talked about the primacy not of money (as in capitalism) nor of man (as in socialism), but rather of "rivers, air, mountains, stars, ants [and] butterflies—along with consensus decision-making, living in complementarity, defending identity, finding unity with other peoples, accepting differences, prioritizing cosmic rights, knowing how to eat, knowing how to drink in moderation, knowing how to dance in the ritual rather than merely folkloric sense; knowing how to work; knowing how to protect seeds."[64] As her own introduction to her book, Paredes writes: "It only remains to say many thanks sisters, thanks to life and to the struggle and to the Pachamama." In Quechua, *Mama* translates to "Mother" and *Pacha* to "world" or "land," later widened to mean cosmos or universe.[65] Paredes's community-based feminism is situated in the broader philosophic project of *buen vivir*, bringing the materiality of women's bodies and experiences in its local setting to the forefront of conversations around not development as the individual gaining mastery over his or her environment but rather the development of a healthy, life-sustaining community, and the ecosystem. As the introduction to the Spanish version notes, "Some of the tools Julieta has provided permit us today to keep working the earth in this process of change, to plant, care for, harvest and live in community, thinking and making a path to keep dreaming, having learned from our sister that dreams are constructed in daily life with the body."[66] The book plants seeds for a consciousness toward the environment as well as the care for the earth as enmeshed with human endeavors.

In conclusion, while Paredes and Mujeres Creando worked in a performative mode early in their activist careers to draw attention to their right to difference and their common humanity, Mujeres Creando Comunidad has turned to the quieter project of working at a grassroots level that aims to change the way communities think about themselves within the multiple local and cosmological spatial enfoldings that they are a part of. These spaces include them already; they are not spaces that they control. Paredes's poetry, as well as her work in *Hilando fino*, speaks to the importance of material relationality as a site of vital potential for new conceptions of life that include more than what the human alone can see. We will end with Paredes's poem, "Laga Titicaca," (*Laga* is purposefully spelled with the "-a,") in which she directs herself to the "Hermosa Laga Titicaca" as a source of energy and strength to the rebellious women of the region. Along the lake's shore, Paredes says, "y al fin podamos / levantarnos unidas en wiphalas / reventar las piedras en la madrugada / y rescatar la fuerza y la ternura de nuestra subversiva Pachamama"[67] (and at the end / we may lift ourselves up, united in our *wiphalas* / to rile up the rocks in the early dawn / and to restore the force and the tenderness of our subversive Mother Earth). The poem calls for the uniting of a community based on the *wiphala*, a symbol of indigenous unity, and on the call to the earth as an ally in restoring nature. Our human impact on materials, and unique ability to partially rescue or partially aid in destroying the force and the tenderness of nature, is a community's greatest risk and greatest strength in sustaining and perpetuating life.

5

Magda Portal's Bare Life in the Sea

Similar to the way that Julieta Paredes addresses Lake Titikaka at the end of the previous chapter, in her poem "Song to Lima," poet Magda Portal (Lima, Peru 1901–1989) directs herself to an informal "you" representative of the personified capital city of Peru. She writes, "you woke up one day, resting on the coast," and elaborates that "a talking river . . . gave you the name Rímac Lima!"[1] Rímac, which comes from the verb *rimay* (to talk), in Quechua, is animate in the Quechua language and here, further enlivened by Portal, as the river poetically names the city.[2] Throughout her poetic corpus, spanning over sixty years, Portal brings the material environment of which she is a part to life, making sensible the inseparability of natureculture in Lima and the Andes. In this chapter, I complement criticism that primarily reads and frames Portal as a feminist subject to argue that simultaneously her poetry is embodied by a nomadic, partial subject intertwined with nature and the material environment. Portal's poetry evolves from expressing individual concerns of her own voice to presenting a philosophy of life that moves beyond the human in its concern for life as a cosmological and connected ecosystem. I read her poetry as mobilizing a sense of community based on *zoë*, a bare potential for life, in order to expand readings that focus on Portal's work as an avant-garde feminist. I additionally mine her work for the philosophy of life it presents, beyond biopolitical identity.

Zoë stands for the mindless vitality of life carrying on independently and regardless of rational control, while *bios* is the political, intelligent, discursive side of (human) life.[3] *Zoë* refers to what the human shares with other forms of life, particularly as mediated through natural materials like land, water, light, and air: common planes of contact between humans, other species, and natural substances. In this chapter, I use *zoë* to encompass those lives left out of the category of "human," relative to their time, but whose vitality continued to influence Portal after their physical death.[4] *Zoë* represents the potential for partial alliances among differing bodies in an ecosystem based not on what separates them but on what they have in common: their materiality. Portal's poetry, as it evolves over the course of her life from the 1920s through the 1980s, illuminates that because any subject is an embedded subject—that is, already part of the environment the subject critiques—the human's sustainability depends on an ethic that thinks with *zoë*, and not just *bios*, at its center. Therefore, I ask what Portal's poetry contributes to our understanding of a recognizable human subject (namely, the female poetic and politically activist voice for which she is known and the frame within which she has been studied) and the subject's accompanying and lesser (i.e., according to the perspective of a Western humanistic tradition) half, *zoë*.[5] Portal's poetry emphasizes a "vital life" as one that is able to be transformed by, and to transform, other materials. She unearths the shared energy in excess to the categorical human, the bare potential for life, that actively resists political incorporation by shirking classification and location, like the avant-gardes themselves.[6]

In this chapter, I return to the historical avant-garde in Peru. In this way, the last chapter serves as a bookend to the first on César Vallejo as I circle back to the "beginning," but work from another angle. To make manifest the ways that Portal's poetry centers around *zoë* as a source for ongoing social change as it evolves from the 1920s onward, I focus on four attributes of Portal's 1920s essays on aesthetics and on a range of selections of her poetry. First, I make manifest Portal's vital materialist aesthetic, as she presents it in two of her key essays on art, much as we saw in the first chapter on Vallejo. In this first section, I look at "Andamios de vida" (1926) (Scaffolding of life), published in the journal *Amauta* and "El nuevo poema y su orientación hacia una estética económica" (1928) (The new poem and its orientation toward an economic aesthetic), published during her political exile in Mexico.[7] Both essays attest to the ways in which, during the revolutionary milieu of mid-1920s Peru, Portal cultivated an aesthetic that valued national materials as something common to life in the Americas and a starting point for their own revolutionary thinking. In both these essays, Portal equates art and the physical body as a first step in unhooking from the position of disembodied universal male subject, whose body has historically been invisible as the default reference for "the human."[8] The assertion of the body represents an emergent feminist materiality that serves as a common thread throughout Portal's work and the critical works about her. The material bases of her art anticipate a feminist community yet to come, relative to her present, and contribute to the contemporary relevance of her work today.

Second, I look at the early years of Portal's biography and consider the concept of misrecognition or anonymity—not recognition—as a defining attribute to her self-(un)fashioning, particularly during the early years of her career. I draw on Horacio Legrás's work on literature and subjection to analyze Portal's strategic evasion of state recognition. Portal partially challenges the principles upon which the liberal and capital-driven state operate: the incorporation of subjects who seek to live "better" within a nascent capitalist economy. I argue that Portal cohabits partial subject and partial object positions, depending on the context in which we visit her. This oscillation, not necessarily by choice, makes sensible the ways in which the symbolic "less than" position granted the female resonates with the ways in which nature is objectified as well within Western humanism. In her navigation of the society of her day, she holds onto part of her life as what is beyond the recognizable or legible text. I read this refusal of one's own interpellation as a manifestation of *zoë*, a bare life that simply *is*, but does not need to, and demands not to, be represented in official language to matter.[9] This resistance to incorporation is redolent of an avant-garde rejection of the status quo and institutionalization.

In the third section, I look at the way that a sampling of her elegies, which appeared in various poetry collections throughout her long career, serve as poems addressed to lives that will never read them but yet are the very exigency for their creation. In this sense, her elegies are another indication of *zoë*, not *bios,* as the catalyst for a potential community yet to come. In addressing herself to lives gone by, Portal calls on lives that are now gone but still present via their transformation into nature. Such lives include indigenous and nonindigenous persons alike. Through the calling forward of these lives gone by, Portal opens up the potential for an imagined community to come but that nonetheless might spark vital change in the current moment as it becomes sensible via art.[10] In a sense, Portal's elegies speak to those lives that were left outside the protective apparatus of the state, but that are evidence of the continuum of life as *zoë* as it is materially transformed.[11] While these elegies are directed to named lives, they are motivated by an exigency in the present for material transformation that Portal makes sensible through her writing.

Lastly, as I demonstrated through the materials of rock, water, air, and soil in previous chapters, I look at the way Portal invokes the sea and the air as natural materials that envelop and intermingle with the human subject. In all the sections, Portal opens up a biological, political human toward *zoë*—life as becoming in all its forms. This is a necessary step in the consideration of a network-based approach to subjectivity in which natural and cultural materials are not passive onlookers but partially active subjects that *differ* but are not entirely *different from* the human. Portal's own decision to go back to the ocean after her own death might be seen as her belief in a philosophy of immanence in nature which those that survive her celebrated via her transformation into ashes, then water, and ultimately, the air.[12]

In sum, the readings I provide are ultimately driven by what I see as a necessary reconsideration of the relevance of Portal's work given the ways she participated in the 1920s, the 1960s, and up until the end of her life in 1989 in challenging the principles of capitalism and liberalism. Now, in a new era of environmental and social changes in Latin America, what life forms does her work anticipate, relative to its time? While the rise of technology in Peru was a hallmark of the 1916–1930 avant-gardes and present in much of the Peruvian avant-garde poetry of the era (Oquendo de Amat as perhaps the most obvious example), the natural materials of the environment are likewise embedded in these poems but have passed by less noticed. Like the rocks and stones that appear in Vallejo's poetry and the air and birds in José María Arguedas's, Portal's poetry weaves in witnesses to life beyond the human. Approaching Portal's poetry from the vantage point of an ecosystem, wherein each component is dependent on each of the others, enables us to partially glimpse the vitality of the bare materials of which we, as part of such a system, are made. In looking at Portal in this light, we might consider that which is "new" about the Andean avant-gardes as continuously relevant in the region today as postanthropocene perspectives that no longer separate the human from the rest of nature increasingly gain traction.[13]

Historical Background

Daniel R. Reedy and Kathleen Weaver, among others, have researched and published biographies on Portal, but I will summarize a few facts to orient readers before my analysis of her work.[14] She was born in 1900 in the El Barranco section of Lima, an area of the city that abuts the Pacific and is known for its bohemian and literary vibe. Socially and politically engaged throughout her entire life, she continued to write well into her eighties, composing her last poem in 1988, the year before she died. In her lifetime, she published five books and myriad essays. Her books include the poetry collections, *Una esperanza y el mar* (A hope and the sea), first published in 1927, by José Carlos Mariátegui's Minerva Press; *Costa sur* (South coast) (1945); and *Constancia del ser* (Constancy of being) (1955). She also published a book titled *Flora Tristán, precursora* (Flora Tristán, precursor) in 1944, and a novel loosely based on her own life, *La trampa* (The trap) in 1957.[15] The evolution of Portal's work reflects the shifts in her political alliances and allegiances. Prior to publishing her first collection of poetry in 1927, Portal was active in a range of different newspaper projects in and around Lima. During the 1920s, she published politically oriented essays in journals, all in line with her Alianza Popular Revolucionaria Americana (APRA) party politics.

Despite a lengthy career, Portal is most commonly identified as one of Peru's earliest avant-garde feminists and an active participant in the socialist movement that spread across much of Peru, primarily from 1916 to 1930.[16] Her literary evolution is unique compared to many of her contemporaries. She survived many of her earliest avant-garde allies, including Serafín Delmar, alias Reynaldo Bolaños, fellow author and father to her only daughter. She also outlived her daughter, Gloria, who died tragically in her early twenties. During this early era, she was accompanied in her work by fellow feminist artists María Wiesse, Dora Mayer de Zulen, Carmen Saco, Julia Codesio, Ángela Ramos, and Miguelina Acosta Cárdenas, among others.[17] The tight economic straits at the turn of the century in Peru as well as her family's poverty—her father's early death led to financial woes—contributed to Portal's formation as a writer and political activist.[18] She came of age when Peru was regaining footing after the destabilizing War of the Pacific (1879–1883), a war that was initiated due to jockeying between Bolivia, Peru, and Chile over mineral deposits along their borders. After Peru nationalized their nitrate mines, asserting their control over their resources, Chile feared for the future of its business interests in the Tarapacá Province in southern Peru as well as in Tacna and Arica, and mounted an attack. Bolivia and Peru were aligned in their front against Chile, but despite their best collective efforts, Peru ultimately had to cede the Tarapacá Province to Chile. Reedy describes that this war, "not only left painful scars on the national psyche and pride, but also brought to ruin one of the most robust economies of nineteenth-century South America."[19] Subsequent agrarian reforms that resulted from the war led to cracks in the long-standing system of hacienda-generated wealth, and corporate development began to take hold, especially along the coast north of Lima. Peter F. Klarén summarizes: "these changes in the national economy, in turn, were part of a much wider process of economic transformation that saw the Peruvian economy . . . pulled increasingly into the broader economic structure of the industrializing nations of Europe and the United States."[20] The economic uncertainty due to shifting geopolitical relationships continued to influence Peru and Bolivia for much of the first half of the twentieth century. Likewise, the exploitation of natural resources that shaped the early twentieth century has continued in the Andes, despite the progressive language of the Ecuadorian (2008) and Bolivian constitutions (2009).

With respect to national political party formation in Peru, the Partido Civil formed in 1871, just prior to the War of the Pacific, and continued as the dominant party up until 1919. They were known for their conservatism and gradual alliance with the military, despite antimilitary beginnings. However, due to growing unrest with the increasingly sinking economy, two-time president

José Pardo (1905–1908; 1915–1919) was ousted in 1919 by Augusto B. Leguía, under the military leadership of Andrés A. Cáceres. The Mexican and the Russian revolutions influenced Peru in the early twentieth century, making the ruling class increasingly anxious about potential workers' rebellions; subsequently, they instituted cautionary measures to avoid strike conditions. The conservative Leguía established a rigid government focused on solidifying an autocratic approach to managing the state. For instance, under his rule, municipal elections were suspended, a new constitution was developed, and university students and dissidents were either exiled or imprisoned if they did not perform the role of the acquiescent national subject that Leguía wished to cultivate. Leguía would remain in power for eleven years, until 1930, when Luis M. Sánchez Cerro overthrew him.

The political context between 1919 and 1930 is particularly relevant because it was during Leguía's "Oncenio," or eleven-year rule, that Portal began publishing. Because she did not have the financial resources to officially enroll in university classes, she informally found her way into La Universidad de San Marcos (the oldest university in Peru, chartered in 1551, and where Arguedas taught). She recounts this experience to Weaver: "Every day as I walked home from the office where I worked I passed its [the university's] imposing entry and glanced in at the interior gardens and patios. One day on impulse I crossed the threshold."[21] Crossing this threshold impacted Portal significantly as she became connected to the very people who would help her to become more publically recognized among Peru's intellectual circles. In 1922, she began regularly attending gatherings organized by several bohemian groups and became close with Vallejo. She gradually became an outspoken supporter and cofounder of the growing leftist APRA party.[22]

In the early days of the APRA party's solidification, Portal was a central ally to Haya del Torre: "Durante casi setenta años, [ella] fue una tenaz luchadora a favor de las causas políticas y sociales de su país y de las Américas. En México en 1928, era la única mujer entre los fundadores del APRA"[23] (For nearly seventy years, she was a tenacious fighter in favor of political and social causes in her country and the Americas. In Mexico, 1928, she was the only woman among the founders of the APRA party). As Reedy also confirms: "Magda no se arredraba ante las causas justas y revolucionarias y se comprometía sin temor. Se vio marginada y despreciada al ejercer su libertad y al rebelarse en un ambiente donde la mujer debía ser más bien ama de casa y no militante política"[24] (Magda was not intimated in the face of just and revolutionary causes, and she committed herself without fear. She was seen as marginalized and underappreciated because she exercised her liberty and rebelled in an environment where women had ought to be housewives, not political militants). Portal's familiarity with transgressing spaces previously closed to her afforded her a keen awareness of what it was like to be an outsider. Her precariousness as a subject afforded her the awareness of the exclusionary climate in which she found herself, and from which she would be exiled. Portal's humble upbringing and precocious personality combined to positon her as an advocate not only for herself but for a community that could begin anew, "de la semilla"[25] (from the seed).

Portal's Orientation toward Art

Turning to the literary milieu during the period just outlined, José Carlos Mariátegui's arts and political journal *Amauta* (1926–1930) made sensible a local and international network of thinkers that wished to stimulate political transformation during the Leguía era. Under his leadership, the journal brought disparate voices together to catalyze aesthetic-political change, from a socialist position, which in Peru largely consisted of land reform that would redistribute wealth and address "the indian problem."[26] Portal came to know Mariátegui and Haya de la Torre indirectly in part through student-worker movements of the era. APRA had decided to open a local branch of the Universidad Popular González Prada as part of its movement, in order to bridge students and politics.[27] As part of its efforts, the university hosted the "Fiesta anual de la planta de árboles" (Annual Tree Planting Festival), relying on the metaphor of the seeds to activate new political life and to make obvious the material link between the socialist cause and the autochtonous Peruvian and indigenous soils.[28] Through such events, Portal became part of a budding avant-garde network of authors, including Mariátegui.

Portal was invited to contribute on numerous occasions to his monthly journal, *Amauta*, and wrote either poetry or essays. Portal presented her take on the art of the era in the essay "Andamios de vida," which ran in issue 5 of *Amauta*. In this, her first contribution of many to the journal, Portal describes the magazine as a vanguard "organ," drawing attention to the ways in which it served as one material component of an assemblage of parts that made up avant-garde events occurring in Peru during the 1920s and 1930s.[29] In this same essay, Portal critiques a European-derived approach to the avant-garde, emphasizing America's material environment as relevant to the construction of an avant-garde (in her words) distinct from Europe's. According to Portal, the infinite "*-ismos*" of Europe represent only the first step in processes of transforming the social system in Peru.

> Pero *Amauta*, revista de avanzada, tiene el deber como dice Haya de la Torre, de revisar valores e inclinar toda su estructura moral hacia los vientos de renovación estética e ideológica, para afianzar bien su cartel de órgano de vanguardia—De ahí que el arte nuevo—tal como lo entendemos los jóvenes de América, para quienes—es necesario decirlo una vez más—los *-ismos* fenecidos en Europa no significan sino la primera voz de alerta en la revolución del Arte.[30]

> (But *Amauta*, a journal that promotes the advancement of the party, has the responsibility, as Haya de la Torre says, of revising values and inclining all moral structures toward the winds of aesthetic and ideological renovation, to effectively reinforce its role as vanguard organ—From there, new art—as the youth of America understand it—it's necessary to say it one more time—the dying *-ismos* of Europe don't signify anything but the voice of the first alert in the name of the revolution of Art.)

Portal downplays the *-ismos* of Europe that she and Vallejo described as contributing to José Ortega y Gasset's concept of the *deshumanización del arte* and the sclerotization of "schools" instead of to the advancement of material relativity, adaptability, and action. She calls for a new assemblage of artists, the "youth of America," thereby moving the focus of the social revolution away from Europe and toward a continental or hemispheric model via the "winds of aesthetic renovation." The "new artist" isn't separate from the wind but in relationship to it, as it moves particles throughout the air. The material conditions of the Americas—the nations' collective "youth," for instance—afford them a different perspective than that of Europe's leaders. Portal creates a need, therefore, for the artists of the Americas, and particularly Peru, to vitalize a socialist revolution based on the continent's material resources and the potential of transforming the same.

In the third section of the same piece, "El sentido vital de las nuevas estéticas" (The vital sense of the new aesthetic), Portal incorporates biological metaphors to make the case that art, too, is metaphorically alive and to draw attention to embodied affective experiences of the world beyond the intellectual sphere. She argues that the generation anterior to her own received and experienced scientific, sociological, and philosophic advances "epidermically," but, arguably, that these changes did not sink into the deeper recesses of the body. They were expressed at a surface level through "las ondas concéntricas del radio" (concentric radio waves) or in the "cabina de un aeroplano" (airplane cabin). With the technological advances of wartime Europe and the industrialization leading up to World War I, art was separated from life and transformed into just another technology like radio waves or an airplane cabin. But Portal argues that her generation needs to reject the "placas instantáneas de la comprensión rápida y la creación sintética"[31] (the instantaneous allure of quick comprehension and synthetic creation). Instead, the luxury of receiving a synthetic artistic object passively and "instantaneously" is countered by Portal with the possibility of a more lasting impact felt deeply in the body facilitated by the slowing down of the artistic encounter.

By extension, like the motors that spin outside the body, Portal describes art's most formidable aspect as its dynamism and borrows from the vocabulary of machines to explain the role that "new art" has in jump starting the nerve centers of the people. Art is an actant in this reading and has agency ascribed to it via the poet. It performs a role in society, both impelling action, singing, and even "undressing"; as she writes, "El Arte nuevo canta siempre la realidad de ACCION sea pensamiento, sea movimiento—Y para nuestros pueblos latinos, soñadores e inactivos, demasiada falta hace un propulsor de energías que despierte las fuerzas creadoras de un gran futuro próximo"[32] (New Art always sings the reality of ACTION: be it thinking, be it movement—And for our Latin American peoples, dreamers and inactive, we need a propeller of energies that awakens the creative forces of the great near-future). In this description, Portal uses capital letters to signal the action-oriented purpose of "new" art, and proposes that art will catalyze and propel "our peoples" toward the future by impacting the body. I interpret her description of art as a "generator of energy" as part of the vital materiality of Portal's definition of the vanguard art project. The "energy" is created in the relationship between the body and the object of art. "El Arte nuevo" is not a material object that exists as separate from the bodies that produce it, but it is also not the same as the creator's body. It is a partially active agent that has the propensity to instigate human action: the intellectual and the material are inseparable, not only from each other but from the actions they inspire. While industrialization and its frenetic production of energy outside the human body were increasingly visible in the form of machines, Portal reminds that art, too, "impele a la aclaración del motor cerebral"[33] (may impel the cerebral motor toward clarity). Portal makes visible the mutually animating effects of human bodies and artistic bodies in terms of the energy that their encounters creates. If art is made of "nerves," then it is not an object over which humans have unchallenged power, but a material force that can—and in Portal's revolutionary definition, must—stimulate movement in others.

The title of Portal's essay also speaks to her approach to art: "Andamios de vida" (Scaffolding of life). The word *andamios* lends itself to multiple interpretations. It refers to a structure, a framework, and to corporeal movement, all of which Portal links together in her writing. The word *andamio* primarily refers to scaffolding around which or upon which to construct something. However, it also refers to the movement or action of walking or the mode or manner in which one walks (*modo o aire de andar*). Because *andamio* has multiple meanings, signifying scaffolding and the "movement" or "air" with which one walks, the connection between the form and structure of art and literature and the vital movement that it animates is insinuated. One cannot separate, for Portal, the energy that art instigates inside the human from the materiality of the object. The material structures of a society, and through the metaphor, artistic forms, are only as valuable as the movements they facilitate. When utilized pompously as decoration or artifice alone, their vitality is lost. They become closed structures, disconnected from the reality around them. The reference to scaffolding is future oriented; it anticipates life to come, given its incomplete material form.

Because Portal collaborated so closely with Haya del Torre, the founder of the APRA socialist political party, she was forced into exile, arriving to Mexico via Cuba in the late 1920s (having already been exiled to Bolivia for a year in 1925).[34] From Mexico, and influenced by fellow material feminist Alexandra Kollantai, who served in Mexico as Russian ambassador, she wrote another important piece on aesthetics titled "El nuevo poema y su orientación hacia una estética económica" (The new poem and its orientation toward an economic aesthetic). In this essay, published in 1928, Portal writes about the ways in which the War (World War I) gave way to a new vital modality, "una ideología mundial procreada por la Guerra—i la revolución—dieron un arte disímil a todas las formulas preestablecidas. Era indudable que la técnica tenía que removerse en sus cimientos"[35] (a worldwide ideology that grew out of the War—and the revolution—gave rise to an art unlike all the preestablished formulas. It was undoubtable that techniques had to be pulled up from their foundation). In her version of poetry oriented from and toward America, she describes the new poet as "receptor de una emoción cósmica, es el trasmisor de esa emoción de múltiples matices en la manera más humana. I cuando lo sea más aún, al llegar al eje ideal de la despersonalización, plena I absoluta, habrá surgido el poeta de la multitud"[36] ([the] receptor of a cosmic emotion, the transmitter of that emotion of multiple shades in the most human manner, upon arriving to the ideal axis of depersonalization, full and absolute, the poet of the multitude will have emerged). Portal argues against a poetry that only produces aesthetic pleasure, referring to a movement that must come forth from all the angles of the earth—the mines, the countryside, the factories, the warehouses, and the herds—that will give rise to a central energy. The "central energy" of Portal's movement comes from the relationship between different materials that, in the socialist discourse of the era, was representative of the overcoming of the personal for a common cause bigger than the self. The idea that a central energy directs the liberatory fight deemphasizes the energy of one subject and diffuses that energy as something coming from not a collective community of people but material factors that impact the revolution: the multitude. While Portal's vision of the new aesthetic is cultivated in "la manera más humana" (the most humane manner), it is also determined by "una emoción cósmica" (a cosmic emotion), that encompasses what, as we also saw in Vallejo, is beyond human comprehension. This cosmos envelops and dwarfs the human and the terrestrial.

Portal's equation of art to a living being was not limited to her work during the 1920s and 1930s. She continued to describe aesthetic objects from a materialist point of view, even after her disavowal of APRA party politics.[37] In a piece written in the 1960s, Portal's personal biology enters into her poetry in a way that prefigures the work of material feminists. In her short essay "Mensaje"

(Message), which served as the opening to the collection *Constancia de Ser* (The constancy of being) (1965), Portal inscribes her body directly to her poetic output through the following words: "Algo de mí, del oculto rebullir de mi sangre en lo hondo del pecho, de su llama vibrante / Algo que diga cómo amaneció la vida en mi camino, las palabras, el canto. Porque a fin de cuentas la poesía es un manar de linfas humorales—sangre, lágrimas—que le brotan a uno de la carne como de herida recién abierta, de los ojos, de los costados."[38] (Something of me, of the hidden bubbling of my blood in the depths of my chest, from its vibrant flame / Something that might say how life awoke in me along my journey, the words, the song. Because at the end of the day poetry is a stream of lymphatic humors—blood, tears—that sprout from the body like a recently opened wound, from the eyes, from the sides).

The "vibrant flame" inside her chest to which Portal refers is the energy contained in her material body life made manifest through her art. But it is not her body in its wholeness that is comparable to the poem, but the raw materials that both are and are not "the body": the tears, the blood, and also the "something," the "*algo*," that awakened life in her. Portal experiences and translates her body not as a contained structure but an open organism in touch with the other material bodies around her: poetry among them. The idea that poetry is made of living substances draws attention to the liveliness of the poem. It is not so much an inert object but an extension of the materials required for a sustainable life. Art serves, in this sense, as a prosthetic tool to supplement the blind spots of the rational human, and to provoke vital movement in readers' mindbodies. By emphasizing the connection between body and artistic object, Portal presents her belief that art is not autonomous from the body but an extension of the materials that make up biological form: liquids, cells, and the materiality of the brain. Her poems are initiated from the specifics of her own biological life but are metaphoric containers of life: bare life that enables them to live beyond the host of the body of the artist, making them links to the common materials that unite generations and bodies.[39]

Portal's Self-Distancing

Portal's life and work also showcase her at times partially hidden identity during her lifetime as an advantage, not a disadvantage. The shirking of nameable, identifiable self connects Portal to a community of indistinguishable *zoë*, that is differentiated from countable and classifiable subjects. First, she published her first poems in the Lima-based magazine *Mundial* in 1920 under a pseudonym, Tula Soavani, protecting herself from public visibility and recognition. Second, she refused to accept official state recognition in 1923, when she won, under her own name, the lyric poetry category in the "Juegos Florales" literary competition at the University of San Marcos. She refused to attend the ceremony and to accept the prize because that would have required her to address President Leguía. The disavowal of nameable subjectivity in relationship to the political structure of the state is an inverse phenomenon to the assumed goal of positive recognition upon which literature as assertion of biopolitical identity operates.

Portal's refusal to be recognized is ironic because many of Portal's allies, most likely with the best of intentions, were quick to depict her as a recognizable subject, differentiated from others. For instance, her very close comrade and ally Mariátegui writes of the poet: "con su advenimiento le ha nacido al Perú su primera poetisa"[40] (with her arrival, Peru's first poetess has been born). Performing an inaugural birth for Portal in language, Mariátegui creates a new label—*poetisa* (poetess)—and names Peru as her owner. "Su primera poetisa," ultimately objectifies Portal and places her in direct relationship to the state, her literary proprietor. Mariátegui's, and by extension, Peru's ownership of Portal converts her into an object before she has even been able to step into a subject position of her own. I am not refuting the dearth of known female poets in nineteenth-century Peru, one that Mariátegui is innocently naming, but Portal writes precisely to those *poetisas*—of whatever race—who could not read or write poetry, but that demand the possibility of the same after the fact. The "addressees" of poetry from a century before very well might have been the *poetisas* that are now "born" into the nameable existence. Their previous absence and unrecognizability necessitate Portal's poetry, and it is those lives that Portal invokes. She does not speak *for* them, but rather *to* them, revitalizing their memory for a perpetually new audience in the present.

Portal biographer Kathleen Weaver begins her book with an anecdote that highlights Portal's misrecognition. As a representative of APRA, Portal traveled with her then five-year-old daughter Gloria to Puerto Rico on the steamship *Guantánamo* in 1929. Weaver describes Portal's physical appearance, "Five foot two, slender, her chestnut hair in a stylish bob . . . also on the steamship was a troupe of dancers. . . . Eventually she [Portal] made her way to the offices of a newspaper whose editors she had thought would be meeting her at the landing."[41] The newspaper editors went on to say, incredulously: "You? Magda Portal?" and explained that they thought she was one of the dancers who happened to be arriving at the same time. This case of misrecognition of Portal as writing-subject—makes sensible the precariousness in the sense of fragility, of the individual as underwritten by the misrecognition of what an outspoken woman in politics looked like at the time. However, these mistakes also open up a creative freedom that is impossible to duplicate once one is recognized and assigned expectations as well as pinned down to a certain degree as a proper noun, with a proper body: Magda Portal. In her unrecognition, she eludes life as it was seen in her historical moment, anticipating "new life forms to come," even in her own era.

Latin American literary critic Horacio Legrás interrogates the concept of recognition, explaining that he sees it inextricably tied to the formation of a subject, in his book *Literature and Subjection* (2008). He inquires as to why the topic of recognition has not been taken up more in philosophy, given that recognition is one of the key components to subjection, "there is a certain agreement that in being recognized, our freedom and individuality shine forth, unbound of all the chains that history, violence, and culture weaved around us."[42] However, he goes on to demonstrate that recognition is connected to property, and therefore, directly contingent on its relationship to national economies. He warns, within the broader topic of the recognition of the Latin American literary subject, and moreover Latin American literature *as* subject, that "although recognition seems to advocate the cause of the underdog . . . we must confront the fact that recognition is above all a strategy through which power reasserts itself in the minute details of the everyday." By extension, when a state "recognizes" literature, that literature then becomes indebted in some way to the state.[43] Conversely, in the examples I provide above of Portal, she navigates the advantages of misrecognition. In passing under the radar or choosing to remain unrecognized, comes an indecipherability that keeps "Magda Portal" protean, "caracterizada por su inconformismo, y que rechaza las reglas sociales establecidas y un comportamiento femenino determinado"[44] (characterized by her noncomformity, and that rejects established social rules and any predetermined feminine behavior). Going unrecognized can be a form of protest before the state and the institution of literature. These moments of misrecognition are a positive instance of being able to move within the category of bare life through keeping "her life" and "her literature" to herself/itself, thereby freeing her to move outside of institutional confines.

This is not to say that Portal was not determined to speak and to write. Attesting to the silence that is part of female subjectivity during Portal's era, she writes to an unknown interlocutor, "Nunca me has preguntado quién soy yo. Te basta lo que dicen los demás de mí"[45] (You have never asked me who I am. It's sufficient for you just to know what others say about me). These lines, cited from Portal's "Identidad" (Identity), capture the fact that Portal is explained by others, while not expected to explain herself. In other words, she is an object of discourse, not a discursive subject in her own right. Despite the feminist work that Portal promotes, directly and indirectly, her work does not just speak to her gendered difference but also speaks from a locus of colonized subjectivity in general. As a primary example of the way that Portal was objectified, Mariátegui praised both Vallejo and Portal as two inimitable literary voices of their era.[46] However, if we look at the different ways in which Mariátegui describes the two poets' "contributions" to the world, we gain access to the burden that being female carried during the era. Vallejo contributed a new poetic epistemology, while Portal was simply "la primera poetisa." This is not to say that the difference between the two poets is not important, nor to equate Vallejo's poetic to Portal's. In his now famous *Siete ensayos*, Mariátegui explains that prior to Portal women writers either wrote like men or wrote with a neutral, "asexual" tone. However, for Mariátegui, "La poetisa es ahora aquella que crea una poesía femenina. Y desde que la poesía de la mujer se ha emancipado y diferenciado espiritualmente de la del hombre, las poetisas tienen una alta categoría en el elenco de todas las literaturas"[47] (The poetess is now she that creates a feminine poetry. And ever since poetry by women has been emancipated and spiritually differentiated from that of men, poetesses occupy a high category in the lineup of literatures). While Portal's gendered difference is what makes her "la primera poetisa," it is not what makes her a "poet," or a "unisex politician," as she would have had it (as quoted earlier in "Hacia la mujer la nueva"). Mariátegui uses words like "ternura" (tenderness) and "caridad" (charity) to describe her writing, thereby essentializing the poetry that one would "expect," according to him, from a female "spirit," as differentiated from the male.

The attention that Mariátegui bestows on her is fraught because he takes her up as an object of study just as she is articulating female subjects (herself, and her predecessors) as historical agents in their own right. Unlike Portal or her other female contemporaries, the default white male subject does not have to become an object of study immediately upon producing thought or prove that he is a subject while writing. Mariátegui does what is expected of him from his locus of enunciation, while Portal fights to occupy a position that, at the same time she acquires it, is just as quickly reincorporated into the dominant male discourse. Portal is simply one example of the reality that nondominant subjects must pass through a two-step process during the historical avant-garde era. First, they often have to align themselves with other dominant subjects and their discourses to access a public forum. Second, to be heard and sustained as a subject, they need the recognition of precisely the silencing subject for their own emergence to become solidified. This recognition of the other runs the risk of negating the very "becoming subject" it can so quickly objectify. Arguably, this subject–object predicament continues until there are too many female "subjects" to keep track of, and therefore, enough traction to avoid falling—the one for the group—into the object position.

While the Portal–Mariátegui relationship is contradictory, one appreciates Mariátegui's refusal to group Portal with other "feminist" poets of her era, because it attests to his ability to differentiate her from just "any woman" and to instead see her as a person with her own attributes: "Esta poetisa nuestra . . . no desciende de la Agustini. No desciende siquiera de la Mistral, de quien, sin embargo, por cierta afinidad de acento, se le siente más próxima que de ninguna. Tiene un temperamento original y autónomo. Su secreto, su palabra, su fuerza, nacieron con ella y están en ella"[48] (This poetess of ours . . . she does not descend from Agustini. She doesn't even descend from Mistral, however, because of a certain affinity of accent, she is closer (to Mistral) than to any other. She has an original and autonomous temperament. Her secret, her word, her strength, were born with her and are in her). Mariátegui places Portal on a pedestal as (autonomous) national muse but then undoes her agency by employing the possessive, "Esta poetisa *nuestra*" (This, our, poetess). Here, Mariátegui not only speaks for an unidentified "we," but one that is hypermasculine since she is supposedly "la primera poetisa," as interpellated by men. Therefore, Mariátegui reinforces his privileged position relative to Portal, but at the same time, articulates her strength as well as her autonomy as compared to other *poetisas* of her generation. Portal consistently accepted Mariátegui's help with her career, and in many ways, if not for his visibility and early praise, perhaps she would not have attained such visibility; and, of course, it was Portal who requested that his essay on her be used as the prologue to her collection *Constancia del ser*.[49]

In the same essay, Mariátegui references "un escritor de brillantes intuiciones, Félix del Valle, me decía un día constatando la multiplicidad de poetisas de mérito en el mundo, que el cetro de la poesía había pasado a la mujer"[50] (a writer of brilliant intuition, Félix del Valle, mentioned to me one day when talking about the multiplicity of poets of merit in the world, that the scepter of poetry had passed to women). This statement, again, while it attests to the emergence of female poets in society, also locates women's agency in a male-centric dialogue because Mariátegui calls del Valle brilliant first before naming women as noble poets. Mariátegui forges a bond with another male writer at the same time as he speaks of Portal. The paragraph continues with an essentialist take on what, exactly, constitutes feminist poetry: del Valle believes that "La poesía deviene un oficio de mujeres" (Poetry has become a women's trade). Mariátegui admits that this may be extreme but adds that "Pero lo cierto es que la poesía que, en los poetas, tiende a una actitud nihilista, deportiva, escéptica, en las poetisas tiene frescas raíces y cándidas flores. Su acento acusa más élan vital, más fuerza biológica"[51] (But what is certain is that the poetry that, in male poets, tends toward a nihilistic, sporty, skeptical, attitude, in the female poets has fresh roots and a candid flourish. Its flavor has a more vital attitude, a biological force). While naming a female difference may seem positive, Mariátegui's take on feminist thinking implies that women (as well as indigenous peoples) are somehow more connected to an abstract spirituality that would define women by their essence instead of their agency and self-invention. This is an example of the way that the politics of gender were complicated in the avant-gardes and echoes Javier Sanjinés's argument in the Bolivian context: that ultimately vitalist discourse was used to reappropriate the indigenous (and in Mariátegui's case, the female) into the dominant state discourse.

Despite Mariátegui and Félix del Valle's intentions, their interventions attest to the precarious political position that Portal occupied during her era. Both authors essentialize what constitutes poetry and, moreover, women. Vicky Unruh explains that although Mariátegui labeled "dilettante feminism" a product of bourgeois liberalism, he argued that as a "pure idea" feminism was "essentially revolutionary."[52] However, Mariátegui's naming of that which is emerging negates the power of the emergent subject to speak or evolve for herself because she is mediated so quickly through a dominant, masculinist lens. In light of all of this, Portal inhabits the role of an emergent subject because she represents a wounded and vulnerable being deeply concerned with the themes of suffering and pain as they shape what it is to be an invisible subject in her society. Based on her unique approach to subjectivity, she does present something we might liken to her own philosophy of a subject. Or as Gonzales Smith says, "podemos deducir que Portal pone en práctica una propuesta 'original' que caracteriza toda su obra vanguardista"[53] (we can deduce that Portal puts an original proposal in practice that characterizes all her vanguardist work), and that moves beyond a simple aesthetic renovation.

In the poem "Un pálido reflejo" (A pale reflection), the oscillation between the poetic voice as subject and object is made evident. This poem is the first of two in the section of *Una esperanza i el mar*, titled "poemas claroscuros" (chiaroscuro poems). The sharp contrast between light and dark as well as the contours between presence and absence are established via the tension embedded in the title of the short section. In the poem, the poetic voice is haunted by death, "i tuve así un color llama de cirio / a la luz clara / un color de muerto"[54] (And like that I had a color of a wax flame, a clear light / the color of death). Here, the poetic voice refers to the "color de muerto," an imposible "color" to name, but that contrasts with the "luz clara," that rests right before it. At the same time, she contrasts the sensation of the hot flame with death, which is more readily associated with cold. Attesting to her romantic view of life, Portal says that "Después de pasar por la vida / llevando prendidas / todas las garras en la carne. . . . Más junto de mi alma esta Noche / he querido g r i t a r"[55] (After passing through life / visibly carrying / all of the scratches on your flesh. . . . Closer to my soul is Night / I have wanted to s c r e a m).

The idea that one's life is narrated via the words and perspective of another has perhaps never been captured more poignantly than by Frantz Fanon (1921–1961): "I came into the world imbued with the will to find a meaning in things, my spirit filled with the desire to attain to the source of the world, and then I found I was an object in the midst of other objects."[56] Throughout *Black Skin, White Masks*, Fanon struggles to arrive to black consciousness: not the consciousness that he is interpellated, as evinced in the expression "Look, a Negro!" but rather someone who possesses and thinks from his own embodied sense of being in the world. He speaks about the "nonbeing" that determined his existence as he was interpellated again and again by others.[57] As he asks, how was he to compose his body in the world? And how was he to compose his *self*? While the historical context is different, as well as their races and genders, the anticolonial philosophic work that Fanon does resonates in the context of Portal. This is to say that much as for Fanon, "black is a white construction," in Portal's era, "female," is a male construction. The return to a primal scream recalls Frantz Fanon's spiral into nothingness in order to enter into a new consciousness in *Black Skin, White Masks.* Portal's poetic voice returns to a prelinguistic space of the scream: the first noise a baby makes to acknowledge the existence of another. This vital form of communication cuts across questions of race, gender, sexuality, and class and returns the subject to a bare material form as that which is common.

To the Bare Life of the Addressee

In his one-page essay, "To Whom Is Poetry Addressed?" Giorgio Agamben makes the case that the true addressee of poetry is "not a real person," but an exigency that is neither "necessary nor contingent, neither possible nor impossible."[58] He goes on to write, "insofar as it demands to be read, poetry must remain illegible. Properly speaking, there is no reader of poetry." What does the paradoxical "there is no reader" statement indicate? Agamben writes, "This [the "no reader" mentioned above] is perhaps what Vallejo has in mind when, upon defining the ultimate intention and the dedication of almost all his poetry he found no other words but "por el analfabeto a quien escribo" (for the illiterate person, to whom I write) ("Himno a los voluntarios de la República"). The most antiimperialist position an artist can take, perhaps, is one that speaks not for "el nuevo espíritu de las muchedumbres ciudadanas" (the new spirit of the crowds) as Portal said of her own work, but to them, as in a calling forth of the potential bare life, human or other, left out. This is why Vallejo speaks *to* the illiterate man, not *for* him. And this is what Ortega captures in the case of Vallejo when he says that his poetic language "no es un espacio indagatorio transreferencial: no es la <<casa del ser>> sino su intemperie"[59] (It is not a transreferential investigative space: it is not the "house of being" but rather its outside). The outside is the space of potential life: of zoë, that is the basis of all life, but only included in the biopolitical sphere as an exclusion.

In her recent book on death and elegy, *Dying Modern: A Meditation on Elegy* (2013), Diana Fuss observes that "a dead body and a poetic discourse are mutually incompatible, two formal states each precluding the other. A poem implies subjective depth while a corpse negates interiority. A poem signals presence of voice while a corpse testifies to its absence. A poem quickens language while a corpse stills it."[60] Portal writes poems that are like elegies because they bring the inanimate and sometimes dismembered corpse back together and transform dead material through aesthetic rebirth. Through the liveliness of the artistic object the past, present, and projected future can emerge as a moving relationship, relative to the now.

I argue that Portal's poetry is addressed to a current audience but also, to anyone who cannot read it: an exigency that is beyond her reach. In Portal's elegies, she presents life as something continuous and unbound by historical time, and addresses dead beings as if they still existed even though they are no longer recognizable humans.[61] Elegies might be said to operate like shadows, a recurring trope in Portal from her first collection of poetry in 1920 up until the last poem she wrote in 1985, because they emerge from a threshold that straddles the world of the living and that of the dead; as well as voice and silence.[62] Agamben writes, "beyond believing or fighting for rights and truth, the artist is primarily the one who brings sensitivity—a sharing to dreams and things, and the poet is the one who sings in the muted voice of unknowable beings."[63] Portal aims to bring two such "unknowable beings" into the community: Micaela Bastidas and Flora Tristán, to whom Portal directly addresses her elegies. On the one hand, these elegies on the surface run the risk of representing and speaking for, in the case of Bastidas, indigenous women. On the other hand, they draw attention in my reading to the part of these fallen heroines that is *zoë*: life, as it continues beyond their proper names, as a continual site of transformation for the future. Portal does not so much reanimate these women as "people," but as a bare energy and contagion of revolution that can permeate future generations.

Portal speaks to Bastidas (1745–1781), famous indigenous rebel and political martyr, in the first elegy I will discuss. A smart logistician, Bastidas led the 1780 Túpac Amaru (II) rebellion from behind the scenes, strategizing and plotting the rebels' moves, urging her husband, José Gabriel Condorcanqui (Túpac Amaru II) that he should have attacked Cuzco earlier during the rebellion to avoid the mounting resistance. Ultimately she, her husband, and their children were killed after losing Cuzco, as Charles Walker has recounted in his long study on this rebellion.[64] In her elegy to Bastidas, titled simply "Palabras a Micaela Bastidas," Portal speaks directly to her—a her who is certainly not able to read her poetry now—and names Bastidas's ability to inspire indigenous peoples not as an ephemeral spirit but as active bodies in protest beyond the national project: "Pero estuviste tú para insuflar coraje a tus indios vencidos para imponer el nombre del Perú más allá de los Andes de los llanos de Colombia de los chacos de Bolivia y del Tucumán"[65] (But you were there to breathe courage into your conquered Indians, to impose the name Peru beyond the Andes, and the planes of Colombia, Bolivia, and Tucumán). Portal does not speak *for* Bastidas, but *to* her, moving beyond the politics of representation and reanimating this heroine as materially dead but philosophically alive. Portal testifies to the ways in which the indigenous rebellions of the eighteenth century went beyond the confines of the modern nation-state, as they continue to do today.[66] She writes, "En ti lucharon todas las mujeres todas las madres ultrajadas las muchachas heridas"[67] (In you fought all of the women all of the insulted mothers the injured girls). Portal reanimates Bastidas's single life to stand in for the lives of the women unrecognized biopolitically that Bastidas fought on behalf of, in the name of, and in place of, in the context of the poem. These women—most likely illiterate and probably unable to read this poem—are the addressees of the poem: not (just) the ones who are actually reading it. The poem therefore speaks to a community of *zoë*, of bare life in its raw potential, that exists beyond the confines of historical or even contemporary recognition. Micaela Bastidas is described as a contributing member to the "llamado de la Historia que anunciaba el inicio / de la libertad del Continente Americano"[68] (call of History that announced the initiation of the freedom of the American Continent).

Portal directly negates Bastidas's physical death to draw attention to Bastidas's continued presence in the Andes, asserting, "Tú no has muerto *Micaela Bastidas*"[69] (You have not died, Micaela Bastidas). Here, the poetic voice directs herself to this "tú," that cannot read the poem, but is the equivalent *inalfabeto* for whom Vallejo writes above: the voice that demands the poem but is an impossible reader. Portal also draws attention to the importance of the Andean landscape in her poem by connecting Bastidas's legacy directly to the natural environment: "Alta de pie sobre los Andes / único pedestal para tu estatua / sobre tu tierra india / alta con la mirada al sol que siempre nace / luego de toda noche / por oscura que sea"[70] (High upon the throne of the Andes / the only pedestal for your legacy / upon your indian lands / lifted with your eyes to the sun that always is born / after all nights / no matter how dark they may be). This last stanza represents the nonhuman recipients of the poem as well: the nature to which Bastidas via Portal, looks and in which she resides. Portal highlights the relationality between the fallen heroine and the sun, and places the fallen hero at the base of the omnipresent Andean mountains. Considered as a whole, this elegiac praise of Bastidas revitalizes this impossible subject in the present from the perspective of *zoë*, life in its continual rebirth as it stretches backward in time and unfolds into the potential future, dispersed among the new recipients of the poem and the landscape itself.

Portal's series of cantos offer us access via her own poetic voice to *zoë*. She is able to speak to the unspoken and make visible the unseen in her poem to Bastidas and her writing to Túpac Amaru. Each elegy stands in for more than the name and work, but for the other unnamed or unrecognized potential lives that have disappeared from the biopolitical realm and as both impossible and potential subjects at once. As she will write upon the death of Javier Heraud, fellow poet, in 1963, "Hay palabras / palabras, pero no dicen nada, rubricadas con sangre / suspensas de silencios. . . . Son las palabras del Perú irredentas de los pobre cadáveres sin llanto de la tierra sedienta de las piedras caídas sin destino / son el indio y el cholo el campesino y el minero"[71] (There are words / words, but that don't say anything, reddened with blood / suspended in silences. . . . They are the unrepentent words of the poor cadavers without cries from the dry land of the fallen rocks without destiny / they are the indian and the cholo the country-dweller and the miner). These cadavers "sin llanto" are the recipients of the poem, the bare lives unheard but that nonetheless exist in a vital community here in the poem, un-incorporable, at least in part, to the state. Agamben once remarked that "friends do not share something (a birth, a law, a place, a taste): they are shared by the experience of friendship. Friendship—he asserted—is the non-division that precedes every division, because that which partakes is the very fact that it exists, life itself. The Addressee shows us this very fact: *we exist,* undivided, like the breath that travels through all beings."[72]

Portal's creation of poetic alliances between past and present was not only based on heroes from within the Andes, but also on a desire to forge feminist alliances beyond the region. To this end, Portal dedicated a great deal of time to Tristán, who consistently transgressed the social dictates of her time, despite her short life (1803–1844). Tristán, born to a French mother and a Spanish aristocrat who lived in Peru, left France in 1833 to boldly claim her inheritance from her uncle, who was to become viceroy of Peru. Portal spent about six years between 1939 and 1945 in Chile after being released from almost a year in prison in Lima. It was then that she began to reflect and write about Tristán, as well as to compile the poems that would come to make up the collection *Costa sur* (South Coast). She published her book *Flora Tristán, precursora* (Flora Tristán, precursor) in 1945.[73] Portal begins the book with the following dedication: "Dedico a las Mujeres Peruanas con mi fe en su futuro libre de sumisiones"[74] (I dedicate this book to the Women of Peru with my faith in their future, free of submissions). If we analyze the details of Tristán's life that Portal focuses on, we gain valuable insight into the latter's approximation to the world via what she focuses on about Tristán. For instance, Portal quotes Tristán's belief that "without the liberation of women, man will not be liberated."[75] While from a twenty-first-century perspective the gendered binary expressed in this line seems too simple, this was an iconoclastic statement in its time because women were still primarily relegated to the private sphere in both nineteenth-century France (Tristán's home) and Peru. Tristán and Portal move beyond the specificity of the gendered particularity to the feminist movement and toward the benefits of the liberation of women to "man," used as a placeholder for the human here.

In honor of International Women's Day in 1983, Portal also composed the poem "Himno a Flora Tristán." In this poem, Portal elevates Tristán from mere mortal into secular heroine via the trope of the hymn. The transformation that

Portal undertakes begins as early as the title of her poem. "Himno" originates from the Old French *ymne* and Old English *ymen*, both from Latin *hymnus* (song of praise), and from Greek *hymnos* (song or ode in praise of gods or heroes,) used in the Septuagint (a translation of the Hebrew Bible into Greek) for various Hebrew words meaning "song praising God."[76] In the first two stanzas, Portal explains that Tristán was not born into any fortune, "Ningún hada madrina la visitó en su cuna" (No fairy godmother visited you in your cradle) and that she suffered an arduous existence, "¿por qué el dolor signó su juventud sin gozo?" (why did suffering imprint your joyless youth?). After establishing Tristán's humble beginnings, Portal explains that even in spite of the adversity she faced, Tristán "caminó por la vida / por las dispares rutas / de la lucha y la acción / compartiendo dolores"[77] (walked through life / through its disparate routes / of struggle and action / sharing sufferings). The idea that part of Tristán's actions involved "shared suffering" recalls our previous analysis of Vallejo, who likewise expressed suffering not in terms of his particular experience but as something that originated beyond and in excess of his subjective existence. Portal underscores the way that Tristán's sharing of suffering, or to put it more simply, "empathy," led her to begin "sembrando esperanzas en el alma del pueblo"[78] (planting hopes in the soul of the people). The way that Portal transforms suffering recalls Vallejo's "Voy a hablar de la esperanza" (I am going to speak of hope) in which hope, while only referenced in the title, manages to last as a constant force in the poem, even in spite of and perhaps because of the acute pain named in the poem. Portal's aesthetic works to reveal and inspire a vitality through the resuscitation of Tristán's energy.

As the hymn continues, Portal delineates Tristán's union work: "fundó la UNIÓN OBRERA / para hombres y mujeres / sin razas ni fronteras / solo la Unión Sagrada de los trabajadores" (you founded the UNION OF WORKERS / for men and for women/regardless of race and without borders / only the Sacred Union of the workers). In these lines, Portal's interpretation of Tristán's nondiscriminatory, idealistic mission is highlighted as she is described as if she were gender and race blind and able to unite people based exclusively on class. But, then we read as Portal reanimates a specifically feminist Tristán by visiting her grave, "Pero ya asoma el alba / ya se pronuncia el nombre / de la mujer-destino / sobre su humilde tumba / brotan flores y cantos / ¡y se escucha la marcha / triunfal de las mujeres!"[79] (But the dawn already peeks through / it has already pronounced the name / of the woman-destiny / upon your humble tomb / flowers and songs emerge / and one hears the triumphant march / of women!). In this stanza, Portal demonstrates that new life—here in the form of flowers and sounds (cantos)—as it flourishes from the other side of Tristán's grave. The echoes of history reverberate in the present as a result of the present tense "se escucha," while also potentially extending into the future because of the flexibility of the present. La "marcha triunfal" is not necessarily over; one "hears" it in the present because the implication is that it continues into the future. The present tense is relative to the reader of the poem, and so for each new recipient, there resonates hope of continued resistance class, and gendered, resistance. Finally, in the last stanza of the hymn, Portal concludes by animating a collective "we" to celebrate Tristán via the present subjunctive tense: "Celebremos su nombre." As Portal did in the hymn's opening, she reconnects Tristán to nature via the metaphor of this "flor amanecida" (awakened flower). While the traditional *aubade* or *alborada* is a song sung at dawn, usually about parting lovers and plays on the dawn, Portal transforms the genre from its representation of lovers to a "dawn song" that praises the feminist movement.[80] Tristán's life is commemorated and then resuscitated via the metaphor of the flowers, as they flourish, poetically, around her tomb.

Returning to Diana Fuss, she argues that poetry, in particular in response to the social decline of death, concentrated on reviving the dead through the vitalizing properties of speech. However, she observes that at the very moment in history that death merely appears to vanish from the public stage, the dying start manically versifying and the surviving begin loudly memorializing. Even the dead commence chattering away in poetry, as if to give the lie to "modernity's premature proclamation of death's demise."[81] As she writes, "It is the reemergence in the modern period of the dawn song, one of the most archaic of poetic forms, that helps to revive the elegy, reminding us that, in truth, elegies have never been just about dying and reviving. They have also been powerful mediums of surviving."[82] Portal's series of Cantos to fallen heroes shows that poetry can be a surviving genre for a collective. She is able to speak the unspoken and make visible the unseen in her poem to Bastidas, her works on Flora Tristán, and her writing on Túpac Amaru. She employs personification in all three cases to bring these figures back to life. They all stand in for more than their particular names and work, but for the unnamed potential lives that were not heard in their time.

In addition to women that she reanimates via her poetry, in a slightly earlier poem "Verbo de amor" (Verb of love), from the collection *Costa sur* (1945), Portal directs herself toward an unnamed potential someone who has died, referring to a "silencio tremendo"[83] (tremendous silence) that weighs in the air. The poetic voice beseeches the fallen/lost friend, "¿En qué mar ignorado / naufragará tu sombra?" (In what ignored sea / would your shadow have shipwrecked?). The "sombra" referenced here is the presence of the friend's existence that still lingers, implying that he or she is not completely gone but has left an intangible trace on the poetic voice's life. The description of the dead person's voice is, "Y tu voz, y tu voz / quebrada y como herida, con los ojos cerrados tu voz era mi guía" (And your voice, and your voice / split and like a wound, with your closed eyes, your voice was my guide). At first it sounds like the dead person's voice has completely disappeared, but soon after, a few stanzas later, the poetic voice explains that "todo está lleno / de tu sombra y la mía / tu voz está en el eco / y vibra todavía"[84] (everything is full / of your shadow and mine / your voice is in the echo / and it still vibrates). The poetic voice laments the loss of the loved one, but at the same time, through the poetic elegy, performs her friend's life, as it still vibrates in the poem. While the poetic voice wishes to "forget you," (*Quiero olvidarte*), the elegy is a metonymic representation that reanimates the corporeal materiality of the body transformed through the creation of the poem. This past haunts the present body of Portal, as it reverberates in the sound, the light, and the shadows of the oceans that surround her.

The Sea of Life

Born so close to the Pacific, Portal refers to the sea consistently throughout her career both as a romantic space of freedom, a touchstone for her own understanding of self, and as the source of life, as it extends, unfolds, and returns full circle.[85] Throughout her poetic corpus she demonstrates interest in other natural forms that speak to her partial recognition of other forms of life that share commonalities with her own subjectivity. It is at this interface between her own subjectivity and the recognition of its openness to other materials that she makes evident her humanity in contact with others. In an early prose poem published under the name Tula Soavani, the poetic voice directs herself toward a bird: "lentamente cruzas el cielo como si estuvieras cansado . . . pájaro herido y tembloroso . . . viejo árbol abandonado en el yermo, contra el que se retuerce el viento y te desgaja, impiadoso . . . yo soy como todos vosotros yo os comprendo yo os ayudo a llorar"[86] (slowly you cross the sky as if you were tired . . . injured and trembling bird . . . old abandoned tree in the grass, against which the wind twists and splits you off). The poetic voice moves toward the suffering bird to create an intimate relationship of empathy and closeness as the poetic *yo* is like the *vosotros*, of the birds, even helping the injured bird cry. The poem beseeches recognition not from another human being, necessarily, but directs itself to the birds themselves. The metaphoric displacement of self enables a relational sense of life between the poetic self and other live beings to emerge in the shared body of the poem. The poem is directed to birds, this *vosotros*, that will not ever read the poem, but without whom the poem would not exist.

As her career unfolded, Portal remained consistently open and attuned to the natural environment of the ocean around her. Two poems in Portal's later collection "Costa sur" (1945)—"Clamor" and "Anhelo"—present the friction between a poetic voice that says "I" and the *zoë*, simultaneously present and necessary to the existence of legible subject. In "Clamor" the poetic voice finds herself hovering by the sea—a perpetual fascination and obsession of Portal's—but without a beach. The subject's ungroundedness symbolically negates her locus as subject, and the sea becomes a metaphor for the "oleaje tremendo de mí misma" (the tremendous surf of myself). When she describes herself as *oleaje* (surf), the poetic voice steps outside her subjectivity, displaced momentarily onto the wave. The poetic voice expresses distress over being different, of "no ser como los otros / ¡Angustia de sentirse diferente!" (not being like the others / Anxiety of feeling different!). The identification of "not being like the others" does not lead Portal to seek recognition in the poem from other humans but instead to find solace in the birds and the vast ocean.

The poetic "I" is further entwined with nature in the simply titled "Clamor" of *Costa sur.* The poetic voice turns inward only to return back to the sea: "Tanto mirarse adentro como a un fondo sin fin" (So much looking inside oneself like a bottomless well) she writes, revealing an interior and infinite space. The anxiety—both alienation from her self and others—leaves her with the original beachless sea as solace: "Movible espejo del mar, ancho como la eternidad, paisaje de mi ser" (Moving mirror of the sea, wide like eternity, landscape of my being). She then describes the sea as "my mirror, my shadow, never-doubting lover, faithful lover." The sea becomes an extension of the poetic voice, as she says, "And when you vibrate and you raise your godly choleric voice, I will vibrate with you according to the same violent rhythm." The vibrational pulse of the ocean and the poetic voice are in sync in the poem; even in the violent thrashing, the *yo* inhabits the same rhythm. The poetic voice moves toward and takes solace in an agent such as the "sea" that contains "a todos los seres que se acercaron a mi ver" (all of the beings that approached my line of sight). In the space of the poem, the anxious subject who at times only accesses a primal scream to express herself reveals a desire to let go and hand over the self to a force that is not a Christian god, or the "dios colérico" (choleric deity) of the sea, but the sacred space of the poem, a space that reaches toward *zoë* not as the state of exception of state-imposed violence but of a partially chosen state of exception: of being with other lives, beside and beyond one's self.[87]

In the collection *Una esperanza y el mar* (1927), Portal's "Poema 17," also encapsulates a desire for the loss of self: to escape the containment of recognizable identity. "Quisiera perderme de mí misma . . . de los hilos tensos que el corazón tiende a los cuatro puntos cardinales de la Vida" (I would like to lose my very self . . . from the tense threads the heart tethers to the four cardinal points of Life). Here, Portal writes Life with a capital to express that it encompasses more than her personal experience, by which she feels confined. The poetic voice longs to move beyond the confines of her existence as *bios*, as a particular subject, to get out of the confined form and the city to access a plane of bare life—*zoë*—where life is much vaster than the experience of the single biological subject, and a stronger force.

¡Perderse! Tendido vuelo
por sobre las agujas de las ciudades
más altas por sobre el mar
como un globo cargado de oxígeno
que sueltan a merced de los vientos
L e j o s Más allá de todas las distancias
    L e j o s de M I

(Losing oneself! A stretched-out flight
up above the spires of the cities
most high up above the sea
like a balloon full of oxygen
that moves at the mercy of the winds
F a r Well beyond all distances
    F a r from ME)

The poetic voice desires to lose herself: to escape from her own "me-ness" and to inhabit the air, like a "globo cargado de oxígeno" (a balloon filled with oxygen) that moves at the whims of the wind.[88] The idea of existing "beyond all distances" is to imagine a world where the concept of distance does not matter. This is a concrete impossibility but yet the hope to which the poem is addressed, echoing the erasure of causality named by Vallejo in "Voy a hablar de la epseranza." Portal addresses herself to a future possibility for the experience of life, beyond the singular subject. To address oneself to "Life" is to speak to a generative material vitality that is in the process of being transformed as one speaks; it exemplifies the fact that "[z]oë refers to the endless vitality of life as continuous becoming."[89]

In the self-reflective poem titled "Las palabras oscuras," (The dark words) Portal connects a sense of poetic alienation to an existential rift between self and the natural environment. When the sea with its accompanying rhythms of crashing waves retreats, the screams of the furies within the poetic voice run rampant. The disconnectedness that the poetic voice experiences from the elements of the natural environment that orient her in space alienates her from her self as well as from a source of enchantment that the world, it is implied, used to perform for her. Portal writes in the second half of the poem, therefore, of the distance of the sea.

Está lejos el mar está lejos
lejos está su ritmo su cadencia sonora
y la soleada inmensidad de sus rotas estaturas
que amortiguen los gritos de mis fieras
ya no son mías ni el alba pura ni la estrella de la mañana

ni el polen de la flor ni el canto de los pájaros
ya no se tiende a mí la mano dadivosa del encanto.[90]

(The sea is far it's far away
its rhythm and its sonorous cadence
and the lonely immensity of its broken statures
that numb the screams of my furies
no longer are mine the pure dawn or the morning star,
nor the flower pollen nor the birds' song,
and the open hand of enchantment doesn't reach out to me.)

The tone of the poem is one of loss and remorse, at no longer being able to "possess" (they are no longer mine) the dawn or the morning star, the pollen or the song of birds. While the self-referential possessive pronouns—*mis, mías, mí*—affirm the poetic subject's desire for self-expression, simultaneously the observation that without the natural world her words turn dark, links the poetic voice's vitality to the natural world around her. Without this link, life dims. In the following poem of the same collection, the poetic voice waxes more existential, expressing alienation again, that she is "lejos de la certeza de esta piedra que rueda / inexorablemente hacia la nada"[91] (far from the certainty of this stone that rolls / inexorably toward nothing). The stone that, while it rolls, heads toward "nothing" stands for the constancy of movement regardless of what is coming. However, with the poet's darkness, the idea of a stone that does not move at all is the opposite of being certain in the world. If unable to rely on her material bearings, the poetic voice is quite literally disoriented in the world, and beseeches the materials themselves to hear her anxiety.

In the poem "Dudas," the poetic voice, anticipating her forthcoming death, explains to her sister that "Voy a quedarme para siempre / Y devolverle el aire y el aliento"[92] (I'm going to stay forever / And return the air and the breath to you), referring to the dispersal of her "paso por la tierra" back to the air and the breath back to the collective network of materials that make up the world around her. These materials in relationship to the poetic voice make her own life continue beyond the specificity of her embodied form. In the same vein, but years earlier in "Clamor," she refers to the ocean as the source of everything.

Todo viene de ti, Mar, todo viene,
Toda vida te pertenece y por eso soy tuya,
el cielo que te copia y la tierra que te hurta,
y el hombre que te teme.
....
Un día, ¿qué sé yo cuándo y cómo?
Volveremos a unirnos, a juntar nuestras vidas.[93]

(Everything comes from you, Sea, everything comes,
All of life belongs to you and for that reason I am yours,
the sky that copies you and the earth that steals you,
and the man that fears you
....
One day . . . who knows when and how?
We will return to unite, to merge our lives.)

The ocean is a site of return for Portal, and the source of perpetual Life. In coming face to face with her own death, she describes its arrival as a slow process. Her last poems read as introspective literary preparations for her own passage toward not death, but into another cycle of material transformation. Portal's recurring and intimate connection to nature is restated at the end of her life, as she writes in one of her last poems, "Caminar."

Sigo caminando   ahora
Seguiré caminando
Aún después de dejar
Mi envoltura silvestre
Caminaré en el aire
        en el agua
en la luz derramada
hasta que me disuelva
en el espacio.[94]

(I continue walking   now
I will continue walking
Even after leaving
My sylvan surroundings
I will walk in the air
        In the water
In the spilled light
Until I dissolve
In space.)

This future-oriented poem expresses Portal's belief in life as it continues to unfold after her embodied form has passed. Life, unpossessed, continues: her material form is now transformed back into the water, still present. Rather than succumb to death, Portal continues a vital existence through her transformation into energy that hangs in the air and circulates in the water and the light. Or, as Iñigo García-Bryce cites, "Magda Portal, más que una poetisa del arte revolucionario, más que una ensayista vertebrada, más que un temperamento en tensión emotiva, es una fuerza en acción, un hontanar trémulo de dinamismo, un metal líquido en fusión continua"[95] (Magda Portal, more than a poet of revolutionary art, more than a well-structured essayist, more than a temperament in emotional tension, is a force in action, is a tremulous dynamic spring, a liquid metal in continuous fusion.[96] This sentence captures the transformations she continues to make, even, now in her case, from the other side of the grave. She is a "liquid metal" in ongoing transformation, not a stationary form, a dynamic material that infuses the contemporary age as much as the past.)

Even at the end of her life, Portal was financially insecure and on the margins of society. Two months before Portal's death, in March 1989, Gustavo Valcárcel, one of the chief editorial writers at the Lima paper *La República*, made a public plea in support of Portal's life because it pained him that she was dying a precarious subject, unable to pay for her prescriptions in the hospital.[97] A few months later, the day after her death on May 11, 1989, *La República* published an article titled "Magda Portal, la poetisa de los pobres, ha muerto" (Magda Portal, poetess of the poor, has died). In this two-page article, the authors name her as a role model to generations of women who saw in Portal, "la figura símbolo que señala el norte de su camino" (the symbolic figure who signals the north of their journey).

To embody her spirit and to enact what was Portal's desire to return to the sea, a group of her closest companions performed, essentially, the ideas expressed in her poetry. Graciela and Juana, her sisters, as well as dignitaries, saw the poet off, throwing flowers into the water after her ashes. Through their physical movements, they performed the transformation that Portal had sought in her poetry: a transferral of the individual to the collective and a material mixing between her body and the water. Additionally, a number of feminists who Portal had inspired accompanied her departure.[98] For this poet who believed ardently in the "constancy of being," this fitting end freed her from the confines of being a biopolitical subject and moved her into relationship with the sea, to the degree that neither one was any longer distinguishable from the other. As she had written years earlier, "I am a sea . . . i am a sea . . . i am a Sea."[99] The final transference of self to the life of the ecosystem performed by those Portal most admired was fitting for poetry that subordinated individual concerns for those of a broader community.

Over the past fifteen years, an awareness of the fragility of the natural earth and the interconnectedness between humans and other species has, albeit unevenly, moved to the fore of the global political conscience. In recognizing human lives as one form of life, philosopher Emanuele Coccia writes of the fundamental experience of life: "Breathing is the first and most fundamental rapport that each animal has with the most substantial fluid in the cosmos, the air." For Coccia, being and living in the world are also not dissimilar to the life of fish; "to be immersed," he writes, is life in its full experience. Portal consistently emphasized, as her life and poetry unfolded, that we are living "in the sea of the perceivable world."[100] Her poetry makes material relationality sensible, helping readers see that beyond the confines of our own human form, the other materials around us are the conditions for our existence, and for our experience of this world. As Vallejo writes, "Qué nos buscas, oh mar, con tus volúmenes docentes"[101] (What do you look for in us, oh sea, with your docent volumes!). The sea, a natural and living actor, looks for the *nos*, the undefined object of a "we," with whom assemblages might be formed. Portal, immersed in the sea, is a metaphor for bare life dispersed back into the cosmos; energy transformed into water and breathed in by the *costa verde*, or Vallejo's "greening pebbles," of Lima and the cosmos.

Conclusion

New Material Orientations in the Andes and Beyond

The purpose of this book has been to trace the ways that thinking with Andean avant-garde artists makes manifest a vitalist materialist approach to life that enables us to recognize the embedded nature of the human in the material environment. I revisited different avant-garde productions of the 1920s, the 1960s, and the 2000s to trace an approach to material culture that sees it as partially impacting humans instead of just the reverse. I have taken art and literature from various moments of crises in capitalism as my corpus for demonstrating that the human is as much material as it is a partial subject with critical capacities. I have attempted to demonstrate that each of the artists demonstrates the liveliness of the artistic object itself as metaphor for other "lively bodies," in nature that matter and constitute life.

In organizing the book, I have drawn on a notion of spiral time that comes from Quechua and Aymara cosmovisions and from the avant-gardes themselves to look at resistance to dominating forms of organizing life as ongoing. I have defined resistance as a reorientation of the relationship between humans and the other organic and inorganic materials of their naturalcultural environs. I have provided close readings of the ways in which the material world of things comes to life via artistic production to reorient readers within their own ecosystems, both natural and cultural at once, and to emphasize the bare materials that make up plants, animals, and the natural substances of which we humans are made. I have also drawn together the work that feminist artists both in the historical avant-gardes and today have contributed to the troubling of binaries upon which vital materialist thinking depends, with a view to how the aesthetic realm makes sensible an ecosystems perspective of community. Through an emphasis on the bare body and materiality, the authors ironically at once reinforce an anthropocentric point of view through the collapse and comparison of the body *and* diffuse the primacy of the human subject into a relational network that operates through coexistent differings and similarities.

The contemporary Lima artist Cherman Kino, who I referenced in the first chapter on César Vallejo, included in his Warhol-esque inspired image of the poet in 2011 a quote from "Los nueve monstruos" (The Nine Monsters): "Hay, hermanos, muchísimo que hacer" (There is, brothers and sisters, so very much to do). Via this citation, Cherman Kino invokes the past through its materialization in the image and this quote to reinspire social change in the present but more importantly, future, Andes. This gesture as well speaks to the spiraling backward and forward of the avant-garde projects. In a parallel context, Michelle Clayton pointed to the growing sense of Vallejo's significance in discussions of contemporary relations between poetry and politics as signaled in an October 2007 article by Garrett Keizer. The article ran in *Harper's Magazine*, and Keizer, too, cites the same Vallejo line that Cherman Kino uses in his image.[1] In other words, Vallejo's work has been taken up again in the Andes and beyond very recently as politics continue to shift in ways that challenge the inevitability of global capitalism or communism.

In the Andes, and much of South America, however, the contemporary period has been defined not by a stagnation in politics, but rather a turn to progressivisms, while far from utopic, nonetheless has opened political discussions in ways previously unseen. That said, many of them have also catalyzed a very recent turn to the right as well. While I do not claim that the artists of this project were conscious of where the politics of their own respective eras would lead, the vital material tendencies in their work might be a way of linking different ways of being oriented, as a human and beyond the category, in plural Andean worlds. While Vallejo, Magda Portal, and José María Arguedas were to varying degrees influenced and involved in material revolution informed by Marxist philosophies, they also were disruptors of a one-size-fits-all form of politics. Likewise, Julieta Paredes and Alejandra Dorado perform similar roles in current-day Bolivia. The artists I have analyzed are collectively motivated by a desire to make manifest the shortcomings, without discrediting the strengths, of Western humanism's approach to instead posit Life as a network of animate and inanimate forces—as an agent of sustainability in ways that might move us beyond thinking from the perspective of the contained human being and reorient us not toward nature as an object but as part of what is human.

The 2008 Constitution of Ecuador was the first national constitution to incorporate and recognize enforceable Rights of Nature, or ecosystem rights.

Specifically, chapter 7 of the Constitution is titled "Rights of Nature" and consists of four articles, numbered 71–74. Article 71 stipulates that Mother Nature, or *Pacha Mama*, where life is reproduced, has the right to exist, persist, maintain, and regenerate, its vital cycles, structure, functions, and evolving processes. Every person, people, community or nationality, is able to demand the recognitions of rights for nature before public organisms. Moreover, the State will motivate natural and juridical persons as well as collectives to protect nature; it will promote respect toward all of the elements that form an ecosystem. Additionally, Article 72 elaborates that "Nature has the right to be restored. This integral restoration is independent of the obligation on natural and juridical persons or the State to indemnify the people and the collectives that depend on the natural systems."[2] The recognition of the "rights" of nature, while it does not let humans off the hook, at a minimum gives us insight into an alternative way of conceiving of the language of rights. The artists I have looked at make sensible alternative ways of thinking about materiality in contrast to the predominating models of their relative times. Their art might help affect the sensorial realm of those who are thinking about politics differently, reorienting them before their material world, as materials become "activated." The animate materials of the avant-gardes I have analyzed are partial sites of confluence and overlap with the discourses of *buen vivir* (good living) in ways that could be productive for thinking about partial alliances against dominant forms of organizing life.

Similarly, in the case of the Bolivian Constitution signed into action in 2009, Law No. 071 recognizes the rights of Mother Earth, as well as the obligations and responsibilities of the "plurinational state" and society to guarantee the respect of these rights. Under this law, Mother Earth is defined as "the dynamic living system composed of the indivisible community of all systems of life and living beings, interrelated, interdependent and complementary, that share a common destiny." Furthermore, "Life Systems" are defined as complex and dynamic communities of plants, animals, microorganisms, and other beings in the surroundings where human communities and the rest of nature interact as a functional unit under the influence of climatic, physiographic and geological factors."[3] The point is not that Mother Nature writes the constitution, but that human subjects think with the material world around and beside them as partially participatory and active in the process of determining the conditions for a future that is based on living "well" together instead of "better" as an isolated individual or moreover, species.

The concepts of *vivir bien* (living well) and *buen vivir* (good living) have been proposed, at least in theory, as counter to western nongovernmental organization–dominated development discourse, which assumes a linear path to neoliberal enlightenment. As I mentioned in the introduction, Eduardo Gudynas makes the point that *buen vivir* remains an unfolding philosophy that is not meant primarily as a template for organizing economic affairs. Instead, it describes a way of life and a form of development that sees social, cultural, environmental, and economic issues working together and in balance, not separately and hierarchically as at present. However, the pragmatic problem within well-intentioned philosophies of *buen vivir* is an age-old one. While many of the posed ideas are novel in theory because they open up potential new ways of thinking about the rights of nature and the rights of the indigenous groups that steward much of the land affected by natural resource practice, these new articles are not necessarily instituted in practice. While Evo Morales was elected and initially supported by the majority of Bolivia, despite the polarization that his campaign set off, over his more than ten years in office he has alienated many of his original constituents. In part, the global economy has put outside pressures on Bolivia to support its extractive needs, leading to Morales's inability to stay true to his environmental plans. Just one such example is the nascent relationship Bolivia has forged with China, the latter keen to access lithium deposits in the Salar de Uyuni region. Despite the leftist, progressivist turn on paper, an extractive and externally dependent economy prevails. In this sense, while the philosophies of *buen vivir* inform the constitutions of Bolivia and Ecuador, they run the risk of acting as empty signifiers that have largely shifted since they have been formally instituted in legal documents. Moreover, due to his own unbridled political ambition, Morales has refused to accept the results of the popular vote that declared in a 2017 referendum that he could not stay in office for another term.

Eduardo Gudynas also makes the case in "Más allá del neoliberalismo y el progresismo"[4] (Beyond neoliberalism and progressivism), that the new left governments, while they cite Marx or Lenin in order to attack Imperialism, have not necessarily moved beyond "la obsesión en el crecimiento y el consumo, y la negación de los impactos sociales y ambientales de estos"[5] (the obsession with growth and consumption, and the negation of the social and environmental impacts of the same). The economy of Bolivia has grown significantly under Evo Morales, but it is also still an extractive economy and largely contradictory to the indigenous interests upon which it was purportedly built. Rather than accept *buen vivir* as a strict blueprint for change, Gudynas suggests that it is better to view it as a launching pad for fresh thinking and new perspectives: "It helps us see the limits of current development models and it allows us to dream of alternatives that until now have been difficult to fulfill."[6]

In thinking about the continued role of the arts in making differing orientations toward a common material world sensible, the links between the treatment of nonhumans as well as all types of humans might continue to be made sensible via new materialist critiques of the binaries upon which humanism is built in favor of a more nuanced approach. As Rosi Braidotti has observed, "if the multifaceted critiques and revisions of humanism empowered the sexualized and racialized human others to emancipate themselves from the dialectics of oppositional hierarchical master–slave relations, the crisis of *Anthropos* relinquishes the forces of naturalized others, instituting a zoontological turn. Animals, insects, plants, cells, bacteria—in fact, the planet and the cosmos, as a whole—are called into play in a planetary political arena."[7] The Andean avant-gardes of the past, present, and future are a set of ongoing projects that look outward beyond the human and might serve as a source for our tracing of the limits and potentials of humanistic approaches to material transformation in an era of looming environmental degradation, alongside the indigenous philosophies of *buen vivir* and plurality.

Another inroad into indigenous philosophies of nature is Eduardo Viveiros de Castro's work, based on research in the Brazilian Amazon, which has reinvigorated ontological approaches to anthropology, providing a particularly convincing counterpoint to the foundational binary upon which Western ontology has rested. Viveiros de Castro, in various fora, argues that the very basis of Western anthropology, which has been the assumption of a universal nature–culture divide, and by extension, a belief in nature as what is shared and culture as that which varies, is in fact a false belief.[8] Instead, Viveiros de Castro argues that nature itself is multiple, and culture, that which everyone has, thereby turning the Western paradigm on its head. Based on his research in the Brazilian Amazon, he has theorized indigenous perspectivism; that is, the belief that what matters in the Amazon experience of being is not only what humans see but also how humans are seen. In this framework, a jaguar, for instance, might be seen as a human in certain paradigms in the Amazon, whereas the human is seen as prey to the jaguar. This perspectivism within nature is very different than a Western paradigm toward nature that adopts only one perspective—that of the static human. The indigenous ontologies that Viveiros de Castro outlines in various fora ironically situates the human perhaps even more in the center of the ontological world, in that the human sees the birds as human, at times. However, in this metaphoric collapse between species, life as dynamic and relational is consequently more holistically respected within the community.

The artists I have analyzed here contribute to making sensible the plurality of material orientations and materials that make up the Andes region. While they speak and produce from different embodied orientations, they share points of contact that are mediated via the bare materiality of their bodies and environments. Violence committed against nonhuman agents, as Jorge Marcone argues in his reading of Arguedas's *Los zorros*, partakes of the same logic of exploitation perpetrated against poor, gendered, and racialized human subjects.[9] By recognizing the simultaneously common and differing materiality to bare lives, the life of an ecosystem that is not based on hierarchies but on complementary accompaniment and companionship might become an alternative starting point for thinking about partial points of alliance and contact between species and between ways of being in the world instead of attempting to either eradicate difference or claim complete incommensurability.

I will end with an image of what I see as a symbol of "formidable hope." In January 2017, the artistic collective *Bufeo* (River Dolphin), led by Christian Bendayán and other artists from Iquitos, Peru, and its surrounding areas, organized an exhibition titled, "Del tiempo en que humanos y animales todavía no se distinguían" (From the time when humans and animals still were not distinguished from each other), a quote taken from Claude Lévi-Strauss. The exhibit includes art by ten different artists from this group, named after the real pink dolphins that populate the Amazon river and its tributaries. In their collective statement the artists say that these works "exploren y representen estas estrechas relaciones entre humanidad y naturaleza o cultura y naturaleza, propias de la sociedad amazónica. En estas conexiones se demuestra una capacidad particular de convivir y escuchar a otros seres, un contacto importante que se está perdiendo en la región por la contaminación y destrucción del entorno natural"[10] (may explore and represent these tight relationships between humanity and nature or culture and nature, characteristic of Amazon societies. In these connections, we see the particular capacity to live with and listen to other beings, an important type of contact that is disappearing in the region because of the contamination and destruction of the natural surroundings). One of the paintings included in the exhibit, coproduced by Miguel Vilca Vargas and Graciela Arias, presents sepia-toned figures of indigenous peoples as the background "screen" to vibrantly colored plants, flowers, and animals. The muted and understated humans in the background of the canvas are visually secondary to the rest of the life that frames them. These images make sensible a different way of being oriented by the world: one in which vitality is conveyed via nature with the human in the background, almost fading from the canvas or equated with the canvas itself. Because of the ways in which it facilitates our ability to sense differently, the aesthetic realm can help (re)embed humans back into the web of rivers, rocks, seas, animals, air, trees, and other forms of life without which they could not survive. In this realization, humans might become better advocates for the material surroundings in and of which they are made through the formation of partial alliances with other species and natural materials.

Acknowledgments

The Andes region has fascinated me since I traveled to Cuenca, Ecuador, in 1999, with little idea that the trip would be the first of many. If not for the hospitality and patience of many people in Bolivia, Ecuador, and Peru, this book would not have been possible. Years later, during a summer visit to Bolivia, I had the fortunate experience of meeting Julieta Paredes and Alejandra Dorado. Their ongoing work inspires me daily, and I am grateful for their friendship and collaboration on this project. Additional thanks to Claudia Coca for sharing her beautiful artwork for the cover and for her contributions to other projects. And thanks to Susana Bedoya, who has kept me apprised of so many of Lima's cultural offerings over the years.

I am indebted to the mentors that shaped my thinking, particularly in the Department of Spanish and Portuguese at the University of California, Berkeley. Estelle Tarica imparted knowledge on Quechua, José María Arguedas, and Andean studies to me and offered keen advice long after graduate school. I hope that an ounce of her brilliance and precision shines through my prose. José Rabasa fostered my philosophic tendencies and encouraged me to ask unanswerable questions. Nelson Maldonado-Torres and Richard Rosa both provided criticism and comments on early versions of this project and introduced me to an eclectic group of thinkers and writers. The friends I made in Berkeley continue to be intellectual partners: Heather Bamford, Mónica González, Luis Ramos, and Karen Spira, among many others. I also must acknowledge Christine L. Quinan, whose editing eye influenced the dissertation stage of this project.

More recently, Vicky Unruh and Jorge Coronado read or listened to portions of this book and offered invaluable feedback. Thank you.

I am fortunate to have a supportive department and community at Marquette. Thanks go to my chair, Anne Pasero, and colleagues Eugenia Afinoguénova, Pilar Bellver, Dinorah Cortés-Vélez, and Julia Paulk for their belief in my research. I am grateful to Sally Gendron, Jennifer Vanderheyden, and Michelle Medeiros for their camaraderie, as well as to Sonia Barnes, Jeffrey Coleman, Scott Dale, Bouba Diakite, and Todd Hernández for their friendship. The Klingler College of Arts and Sciences helped fund travel related to the completion of this book; my sincere thanks to Rick Holz, Jeanne Hossenlopp, and James South for their ongoing support.

I also owe thanks to the colleagues I had at Mount Holyoke College: Justin Crumbaugh, Micaela Díaz-Sánchez, Rogelio Miñana, and many others, supported my work. Summer and conference travel grants from Mount Holyoke College aided in the completion of this project. Sonia Alvarez and Heidi Scott at the University of Massachusetts, Amherst also helped me in multiple ways during my time in the Five Colleges area, as did Sara Brenneis and María Elena Cepeda. Silvia Tandeciarz at The College of William and Mary and José Antonio Mazzotti at Tufts University offered helpful comments on a very early book proposal.

This book would also not have been possible without the generous support of Greg Clingham, Aníbal González, and Pam Dailey at Bucknell University Press, as well as the editing team at Rutgers University Press. I thank all of you so much for your guidance throughout the publication process. The review process was immensely helpful, and I am grateful for the generous feedback I received; it has strengthened my project, and any shortcomings of this book are entirely my own.

Juan G. Ramos and Raquel Alfaro were spirited comrades and conspirators on Latin American literature and theory as I wrote this book. Likewise, the whip-smart members of my Milwaukee writing group have helped see this project through its final stages: Sarah Carter, Sarah Schaefer, Katie Vater, and Kay Wells.

Thanks to my fellow Milwaukee dwellers, Jeffrey, Jess, Sarah, Nicole, Elmer, Renee, Travis, and Bryan, for being here at the same time. To Siobhan Walsh and Elizabeth Simmons, my oldest and dearest of friends, thank you for conspiring early on about how to trouble the world; and to Greg, a steady interlocutor and fellow complainer of all things mundane, I am glad you are in my life.

My parents, Mike and Sharon, instilled in me a love of reading, writing, art, and music while I was growing up. They taught me to value diversity and inclusion before I knew what such concepts were and to question the social inequalities around me. They modeled the art of being a welcoming host, a gracious guest, and—if all else fails—an entertaining storyteller. Their lessons, as well as those of my grandparents, are everywhere in this book. Colin,

Kate, and Julia's competitive spirit, hilarious wit, and collective soccer skills are only some of the reasons why I adore them. And to Jasper, my friend, que aprendas español. Te quiero mucho.

Lastly, to Laura, thank you for your infinite patience and magnetic authenticity. You're a shiny compass without direction and an honest smile with no agenda. Your ease in the material world astounds me every day and inspires me to be a more grounded, generous, and reflective human being.

Thank you to the following journals for permission to reprint previously published material: a section of chapter 1 was published as "The Vitalist Aesthetics of Antenor Orrego and César Vallejo," *Chasquí* 43, no. 1 (May 2014): 26–43; an early draft of chapter 3 was published in Spanish as "El aire de Arguedas: una sustancia común y crítica," *Revista de Crítica Literaria Latinoamericana* 39, no. 75 (2012): 51–76. Lastly, the article "Julieta Paredes and Alejandra Dorado: Queer Art and Human Rights in Contemporary Bolivia," *Letras femeninas* 36, no. 1 (Summer 2010): 19–36, informed the beginning of chapter 4.

Notes

Introduction

1 José María Arguedas, *Los ríos profundos*, edited by Ricardo González Vigil, 2nd ed. (Madrid: Catedra, 1998), 11.

2 Unless otherwise noted, all translations are mine.

3 Later in the chapter Ernesto says to his father, "—Papá, —le dije, —cada piedra habla" (Arguedas, *Los ríos profundos*, 146) (—Dad,—I said to him—every stone talks). And shortly after, "—Cada piedra es diferente. No están cortadas. Se están moviendo" (ibid.) (—Every stone is different. They aren't cut. They are moving). Ernesto is contrasted in the chapter with his uncle, "el Viejo," who represents the colonial point of view of nature as that which is to be conquered. In the case of Ernesto, his subjectivity is intertwined with the vital materials of his world. This topic is elaborated in chapter 3 of this book.

4 Carolyn Dean has written a fascinating book from an anthropological point of view on the history of rock and stone in the Incan culture. See *A Culture of Stone: Inka Perspectives on Rock* (Durham, NC: Duke University Press, 2010), where she traces the potentially animate power of rock historically in the region. See also chapters 1 and 2 in this book for additional references to Dean.

5 James Martin Harding's recent work in *The Ghosts of the Avant-Garde(s): Exorcising Experimental Theater and Performance* (Ann Arbor: University of Michigan Press, 2013), is an example of work being done in the growing arena of new avant-garde studies. In the Latin American context, editors Matthew Bush and Luis Hernán Castañeda have recently published a volume on the state of the avant-gardes today, *Un asombro renovado: Vanguardias contemporáneas en América Latina* (Madrid: Iberoamericana; Frankfurt am Main: Vervuert, 2017).

6 Writes Sara Ahmed, "Orientations might shape how matter 'matters.' If matter is affected by orientations, by the ways in which bodies are directed toward things, it follows that matter is dynamic, unstable, and contingent." Orientations matter in two ways: that they are important, and in a second sense, "of being about physical or corporeal substance," Ahmed, "Orientations Matter," in *New Materialisms: Ontology, Agency, and Politics*, ed. Diana H. Coole and Samantha Frost (Durham, NC: Duke University Press, 2010), 234–235.

7 I am using the term "mindbody" to subvert the notion that the two are separate entities. The mind both is and is not the body; the body both is and is not the mind. This is along the lines of Donna Haraway's term "natureculture," which problematizes the oppositional binary between the two. She develops the concept most significantly in *The Companion Species Manifesto: Dogs, People, and Significant Otherness* (Chicago: Prickly Paradigm Press, 2003), 12.

8 See Manuel DeLanda, "Interview with Rick Dolphijn and Iris van der Tuin," in *New Materialisms: Interviews and Cartographies*, ed. Graham Harman and Bruno Latour (Ann Arbor: University of Michigan Library, Open Humanities Press, 2012), 38–47, http://hdl.handle.net/2027/spo.11515701.0001.001 (accessed March 24, 2018).

9 For instance, Jorge Coronado's *The Andes Imagined: Indigenismo, Society, and Modernity* (Pittsburgh: University of Pittsburgh Press, 2009), takes the starting point of *indigenismo* in Peru as an entry point into the twentieth-century turn toward a regional approach to identity.

10 As Mabel Moraña argues in relationship to Gamaliel Churata's humanism, in my readings here, the authors do not negate or deny the agency of the human but temper a predominating occidental approach to the same from a distinct material orientation. See Moraña, *Churata Postcolonial* (Lima: Latinoamericana Editores, 2015), 69.

11 Vicky Unruh writes, "Luis Valcárcel declared in Peru's *Amauta* that 'just as the mountain range running from South to North gives unity because it serves as column and axis, so is there a common desire among youth: create American culture'" "Hay varias Americas," as cited in Unruh, *Latin American Vanguards: The Art of Contentious Encounters* (Berkeley: University of California Press, 1994), 131.

12 In Peru, the most current census available is from 2007, in which 13 percent of the population was identified as indigenous. The results of the 2017 Census have not yet been published. See: https://revistaideele.com/ideele/content/%C2%BFsabemos-cu%C3%A1nta-poblaci%C3%B3n-ind%C3%ADgena-hay-en-el-per%C3%BA (accessed March 30, 2018). In Bolivia, thirty-six different indigenous languages are identified as official in the Constitution: http://www.comunicacion.gob.bo/?q=20130725/nueva-constitucion-politica-del-estado-boliviano (accessed March 30, 2018). In Ecuador, the Instituto Nacional de Estadísticas y Censo (The National Institute of Statistics and the Census), lists that 6.8 percent of the population identifies as indigenous in the most recent census of 2010: http://www.ecuadorencifras.gob.ec/resultados/ (accessed March 30, 2018).

13 The European avant-gardes' emphasis on primitivist aesthetics and the search for a "pure" origin as expressed in books like Alejo Carpentier's *Los pasos perdidos* (La Habana: Consejo nacional de cultura, 1953), hinges upon the concept of indigenous cultures as existing "backwards" in time, behind the modern (European) cultures.

14 Jorge Coronado is the scholar that has worked most directly on defining "lo andino" in the last decade. His work in *The Andes Imagined* as well as forthcoming projects are directly concerned with this topic.

15 Alcides Arguedas captures the "degeneracy" of the Bolivian nation perhaps most succinctly in the line, "Todo es inmenso en Bolivia, todo, menos el hombre," *Pueblo enfermo* (1909; Chile: Ediciones Ercilla, 1937), 109 (Everything is immense in Bolivia, everything, except man).

16 The topic of *indigenismo* is vast and beyond the scope of this book. For a nuanced argument on the contradictions within the discourse itself, read as both emancipatory and colonizing, see Estelle Tarica's *Intimate Indigenismo: The Inner Life of Mestizo Nationalism* (Minneapolis: University of Minnesota Press, 2008), which studies authors Rosario Castellanos, José María Arguedas, and Jesús Lara.

17 Javier Medina speaks to the continual orientalization of parts of society in Bolivia: "A nivel de sociedad, digamos que la humanidad colapsa en la civilización occidental: el lóbulo izquierdo, y en la civilización oriental: el lóbulo derecho, del cual forma parte la Indianidad," Medina, *Vivir bien: ¿Paradigma no capitalista?*, ed. Ivonne Farah H. and Luciano Vasapoll (La Paz, Bolivia: CIDEM-UMSA, 2011), 40 (At the societal level, let's say, humanity collapses into Western civilization: the left brain, and Eastern civilization: the right brain, of which Indianness forms a part). This continued duality operates at the base of divisions between Occidental and Oriental within Bolivia and beyond.

18 Eduardo Gudynas, "Los progresismos sudamericanos: Ideas y prácticas, avances y límites," in *Rescatar la esperanza: Más allá del neoliberalismo y el progresismo* (Barcelona: EntrePueblos, 2016), 28–29.

19 For a synopsis of *Buen vivir* and *plurinacionalidad* from Bolivian and Ecuadorian perspectives, I refer readers to Salvador Schavelzon's *Plurinacionalidad y Vivir Bien/Buen Vivir: Dos conceptos leídos desde Bolivia y Ecuador post-constituyentes* (Quito, Ecuador: Abya-Yala; Buenos Aires: CLACSO: 2015). Schavelzon provides thorough discussions of the two concepts as they have evolved in both countries in the last decade.

20 Eduardo Gudynas has written extensively on the new left turn in Latin America. He uses the umbrella term "Los progresismos" to refer to a process that was initiated with the election of Hugo Chávez in Venezuela in 1998 (who assumed the government in 1999), and reached its apogee around 2010. The "progresistas" are diverse, but in the case of Bolivia and Ecuador, they are described by Gudynas as citizen sectors that had been historically marginalized but then became protagonists of the elections. The indigenous population in Bolivia was particularly key in the momentum of the MAS party (Movimiento al socialismo) "Los progresismos sudamericanos," 28–9.

21 Schavelzon, *Plurinacionalidad y Vivir Bien/Buen Vivir*, 71.

22 Eduardo Gudynas and Oliver Balch, "Buen vivir: The Social Philosophy Inspiring Movements in South America." February 4, 2013, n.p., https://www.theguardian.com/sustainable-business/blog/buen-vivir-philosophy-south-america-eduardo-gudynas (accessed July 4, 2017).

23 Marisol de la Cadena observes, "Taking my cue from Stengers [Elizabeth], I intend this . . . essay . . . as an invitation to take seriously the presence in politics of those actors, which, being other than human, the dominant disciplines assigned either to the sphere of nature . . . or to the metaphysical and symbolic fields of knowledge," de la Cadena, "Indigenous Cosmopolitics in the Andes: Conceptual Reflection beyond 'Politics,'" *Cultural Anthropology* 25, no. 2 (2010): 336.

24 The legislation to incorporate nature into the 2009 Plurinational Constitution of Bolivia came in 2011, after pressure from indigenous groups. Commenting on this, Vice-President Alvaro García Linera said, "it makes world history. Earth is the mother of all, [i]t establishes a new relationship between man and nature, the harmony of which must be preserved as a guarantee of its regeneration," García Linera, "Bolivia Enshrines Natural World's Rights with Equal Status for Mother

Earth," *Guardian*, April 10, 2011, n.p., https://www.theguardian.com/environment/2011/apr/10/bolivia-enshrines-natural-worlds-rights (accessed March 12, 2018).

25 DeLanda, "Interview with Rick Dolphijn and Iris van der Tuin," 18.

26 For William Rowe's readings on the influence of Quechua and its knowledge system on Arguedas, see his book *Mito e ideología en la obra de José María Arguedas* (Lima: Instituto nacional de cultura, 1979).

27 See the chapter "Pachasofía: Cosmología andina" in Josef Estermann's book *Filosofía andina: Estudio intercultural de la sabiduría autóctona andina* (Quito: Abya Yala, 1998): 179–181, for an elaborated discussion on cyclical time.

28 In Peru, Spanish is the official language, but so are Quechua and Aymara in areas where there are a substantial number of speakers, per article 48 of the Constitution; Article 5 of the 2009 *Constitución política del estado plurinacional de Bolivia* names as official *castellano* and thirty-six official indigenous languages. See Constitución Política del Estado Plurinacional de Bolivia, 2009, http://www.ftierra.org/index.php/generales/14-constitucion-politica-del-estado (accessed March 24, 2018).

29 Jacques Rancière, *The Politics of Aesthetics: The Distribution of the Sensible* (London: Continuum, 2004), 30.

30 Peter Bürger, "Avant-Garde and Neo-Avant-Garde: An Attempt to Answer Certain Critics of *Theory of the Avant-Garde*," trans. Bettina Brandt and Daniel Purdy, *New Literary History* 41, no. 4 (Autumn 2010): 705.

31 See Rancière, *The Politics of Aesthetics*, 30, where he talks about the potential "community to come" of the aesthetic realm of the avant-gardes versus the avant-garde as political party. For recent revisionist Marxist work in the context of the Andes, see Irina Alexandra Feldman, *Rethinking Community from Peru: The Political Philosophy of José María Arguedas* (Pittsburgh: University of Pittsburgh Press, 2014); and Juan G. Ramos's recent chapter, "Disruptive Capital in Andean/World Literature: A Decolonial Reading of Enrique Gil Gilbert's *Nuestro Pan*," in *Decolonial Approaches to Latin American Literatures and Cultures*, ed. Juan G. Ramos and Tara Daly (New York: Palgrave Macmillan, 2016), 141–160.

32 José Ortega y Gasset, *La deshumanización del arte y otros ensayos de estética* (Madrid: Revista de Occidente en Alianza Editorial, 2006), 35. According to Unruh, the words "human" and "humanized" became veritable buzzwords in Latin American vanguard discourse. Vicente Huidobro, in the 1916 poem "Arte poética," urged poets to create their own roses rather than celebrate nature's, and spoke of art's humanizing effects. He argued that art should "humanize things" and that poets must have a certain dose of singular "humanity" with which to imbue their work (Unruh, *Latin American Vanguards*, 25–26).

33 Vicente Huidobro, "Arte poética," in *Las vanguardias latinoamericanas: Textos programáticos y críticos*, ed. Jorge Schwartz (Mexico City: Fondo Cultural Económico de México, 2002): 100–101. Ortega y Gasset also opines, "El poeta empieza donde el hombre acaba" ("Deshumanización del arte," 35) (The poet begins where the human ends), emphasizing a creative sphere that is materially detached from the human.

34 Unruh, *Latin American Vanguards*, 21.

35 Ibid., 24.

36 Coronado, *Andes Imagined*, 1.

37 Ibid., 15.

38 "El problema del indio" is the second essay in José Carlos Mariátegui's *Siete ensayos de interpretación de la realidad peruana* (México City: Ediciones Era, 2002), 35–45.

39 Mariátegui, "Presentación de *Amauta*," ed. José Carlos Mariátegui, Ricardo Martinez de Torre, and Alberto Tauro, *Amauta* 1, no 1. (1926): 1.

40 Antonio Cornejo Polar, *Escribir en el aire: Ensayos sobre la heterogeneidad socio-cultural en las literaturas andinas* (Lima: Editorial Horizonte, 1994), 146.

41 Writes Javier Sanjinés, "Viscerality is the extreme position of looking at reality with 'both eyes,' to use the term first promoted by indigenous groups in the late 1970s." The idea of both eyes was in response to (just) "the eye of reason" of Cartesian perspectivalism, Sanjinés, *Mestizaje Upside-Down: Aesthetic Politics in Modern Bolivia* (Pittsburgh, PA: University of Pittsburgh Press, 2004), 11.

42 At various times in *El zorro de arriba y el zorro de abajo*, José María Arguedas refers to his disidentification with other authors of his era. For instance, when he writes, "de Cortázar sólo he leído cuentos. Me asustaron las instrucciones que pone para leer *Rayuela*," Arguedas, *El zorro de arriba y el zorro de abajo*, ed. Eve-Marie Fell, Edición Crítica (Paris: ALLCA XX, 1996), 12 (by Cortázar, I have only read short stories. The instructions for reading *Rayuela* scared me); and with regard to Alejo Carpentier, "En cambio, a don Alejo Carpentier, lo veía como a muy superior. . . . ¡Es bien distinto a nosotros!" (ibid.) (On the other hand, don Alejo Carpentier, he seemed very superior. . . . He's very distinct from us!). He later self-deprecatingly opines "Con razón los cortázares nos creen tan microbianos," Arguedas, *Obras completas* (Lima: Editorial Horizonte, 1983), 5:146 (No wonder why the Cortazars of the world think we are so microbial), differentiating himself from these two icons of the Latin American Boom.

43 Arguedas, *Zorros*, 9.

44 Julio Premat, "Los relatos de la vanguardia o el retorno de lo nuevo," *Cuadernos de literatura* 17, no. 34 (July–December 2013): 51.

45 Here, I align myself with Cary Wolfe's work on posthumanism and the definitions he provides. As he writes, "posthumanism in my sense isn't posthuman at all—in the sense of being 'after' our embodiment has been transcended—but is only posthuman*ist*, in the sense that it opposes the fantasies of disembodiment and autonomy, inherited from humanism itself, that [Katherine] Hayles rightly criticizes," Wolfe, *What Is Posthumanism?* (Minneapolis: University of Minnesota Press, 2010), xv.

46 Vicky Unruh's second book, *Performing Women and Modern Literary Culture in Latin America: Intervening Acts* (Austin: University of Texas Press, 2006) and Susan Rubin Suleiman's work *Subversive Intent: Gender, Politics and the Avant-Garde* (Cambridge, MA: Harvard University Press, 2012) are two examples of work that speaks to the central role of women in Europe and Latin America during the avant-gardes. However, on the whole, the movements of the 1920s and 1930s were dominated by men, again, why the "humanizing" aspect to the projects is limited to a certain "type" of human, with some exceptions.

47 Aníbal Quijano, "Coloniality of Power, Eurocentrism, and Latin America," *Nepantla: Views from South* 1, no. 3 (2000): 536.

48 Santiago Castro-Gómez, "(Post)Coloniality for Dummies: Latin American Perspectives on Modernity, Coloniality, and the Geopolitics of Knowledge," in *Coloniality at Large: Latin America and the Postcolonial Debate*, ed. Mabel Moraña, Enrique Dussel, and Carlos A. Jáuregui (Durham, NC: Duke University Press, 2008), 263.

49 Luis Tapia's *La invención del núcleo común: ciudadanía y gobierno multisocietal* (La Paz: Muela del diablo, 2012) and Juan Duchesne Winter's *Comunismo literario y teorías deseantes* (La Paz, Bolivia: Plural Editores; Pittsburgh; PA University of Pittsburgh Press, 2009) are two examples of work done in the Bolivian context on new forms of community. Julieta Paredes's work on community-based feminism is another example of reconfigurations of the concept of community based on the contemporary Bolivian context.

50 Silvia Rivera Cusicanqui, "La noción de "derecho" o las paradojas de la modernidad postcolonial: indígenas y mujeres en Bolivia," *Revista Aportes Andinos* 11 (2004): 1–15.

51 Mabel Moraña, *Inscripciones críticas. Ensayos sobre cultura latinoamericana* (Santiago: Editorial Cuatro Propio, 2014), 93.

52 Rancière, *Politics of Aesthetics*, 29–30.

53 Ibid., 19.

54 Evan Mauro, "The Death and Life of the Avant-Garde: Or, Modernism and Biopolitics," *Mediations* 26, nos. 1–2 (Fall 2012–Spring 2013): 120.

55 Ibid., 120.

56 Ibid., 123.

57 Bürger, "Avant-Garde and Neo-Avant-Garde," 714 and 694, respectively.

58 José Muñoz's *Cruising Utopia: The Then and There of Queer Futurity* (London and New York: New York University Press, 2009) also looks at avant-garde art, such as that of Andy Warhol, as opening up to a horizon line of hope via his readings of Ernst Bloch. He calls for the "revivification" of the queer political imagination; here, it is the revitalization of avant-garde critiques of humanism.

59 Ibid., 1.

60 I revisit "buen vivir" in the conclusion, naming some of the problems that have been signaled around the application of this term already.

61 Marco Thomas Bosshard has also been a key figure in promoting the recognition of Churata's work. Bosshard's book on Churata, and *El pez de oro (Retablos del Laykhakuy)*, ed. José Luis Ayala (Puno: Corpuno, 1987), titled *Ästhetik Der Andinen Avantgarde: Gamaliel Churata Zwischen Indigenismus Und Surrealismus* was recently translated into Spanish by Helena Usandizaga, 2014. Additionally, attesting to a renewed interest in Churata, Usandizaga also edited a critical edition of *El pez de oro* (Madrid: Cátedra, 2012).

62 Moraña's and Elizabeth Monasterios's recent works on Churata (*Churata Postcolonial*, 2015; and *Vanguardia plebeya del Titikaka: Gamaliel Churata y otras beligerancias estéticas en los Andes*, 2015, respectively) expand earlier scholarship undertaken by Cynthia Vich on *Boletín Titikaka*, as elaborated in her book *Indigenismo de vanguardia en el Perú* (Lima: Fondo Editorial de la Pontificia Universidad Católicia del Perú, 2000) and by Yazmín López Lenci in *El laboratorio de la vanguardia en el Perú: Trayectoria de una génesis a través de las revistas culturales de los años veinte* (Lima: Editorial Horizonte, 1999), both with foci on the Puno-based avant-gardes.

63 The quote in the body of the introduction is from Yazmín López Lenci, *El laboratorio de la vanguardia en el Perú* (Lima: Editorial Horizonte, 1999), 22. José Carlos Mariátegui's "El problema del indio" lays out his land-based solutions to the social inequities of early twentieth-century Peru. Elizabeth Monasterios's ongoing work on the Andean avant-gardes illuminates some of the lesser-known artists from the Lake Titicaca region of Bolivia and Peru, especially those involved

in the production of *Boletín Titikaka*, again, like Gamaliel Churata, his brother Alejandro Peralta, and the group *Gesta Bárbara*. Monasterios refers to the "poco estudiado fenómeno que fue la vanguardia andina" ("Poéticas del conflicto," 544) (little-studied phenomenon that was the Andean vanguard) emphasizing that the region has been overlooked. In recent years, this has changed substantially as much new scholarship by Monasterios herself and others has addressed these legacies.

64 Alejandro Peralta, *Ande; El Kollao*, ed. Luis F. Chueca and Domingo Pantigoso (Lima: Pontificia Universidad Católica del Perú, 2006).

65 *Boletín Titikaka* 16 (1927): 13.

66 Ibid.

67 Alejandro Peralta, "La pastora florida," in *Ande; El Kollao*, ed. Chueca and Pantigoso, 3.

68 Ibid.

69 María del Mar, "Estética andina," *Boletín Titikaka* 16 (1927): 13.

70 Sara Ahmed, *Queer Phenomenology: Orientations, Objects, Others* (Durham, NC: Duke University Press, 2006), 110.

71 "Hallazgo de la vida", lines 1–2, in César Vallejo, *Obras completas / The Complete Poetry: A Bilingual Edition*, trans. Clayton Eshleman (Berkeley: University of California Press, 2008).

72 Ibid.

73 Julieta Paredes, *Hilando fino*: *Desde el feminismo comunitario* (La Paz, Bolivia: CEDEC, 2008), 12.

74 José María Arguedas, quoted in Ariel Dorfman, "Arguedas y la epopeya americana," in *Recopilación de textos sobre José María Arguedas*, ed. Juan Larco (La Habana: Centro de Investigaciones Literarias, Casa de las Americas, 1976), 28.

75 Churata, *El pez de oro*, 13.

76 Ibid., 34.

77 Ibid., 40.

78 Differing vs. difference is an important distinction. To say something "differs" enables a mutation that is slight or significant, but that does not lose the matter in common. If we start with the idea that there are ways to differ without being different *from* a presumed or implicit center, then relationality is the basis for ontology, not difference.

79 Vicky Unruh provides a prescient reading of Churata and other avant-garde artists along these lines, "[a] striking feature of this Americanist language is the penchant for organicist metaphors, telluric and anatomical, through which America, portrayed as the earth or as a living, breathing human body, would engender the new American art." *The Art of Contentious Encounters*, 131.

80 Antero Peralta, "El uno y vario del arte vanguardista," *Chirapu*, Arequipa 1, no. 2 (1928): 2.

81 Jane Bennett, *Vibrant Matter: A Political Ecology of Things* (Durham, NC: Duke University Press, 2010), 23. Likewise, Jorge Marcone writes, "an actant is something that acts or to which activity is granted by others. It implies no special intention or motivation. The nonhuman actant (an animal, a plant, or a thing) is neither an object nor a subject but an "intervener." Thinking about actants as "inverveners" is particularly helpful, as Marcone applies it, to José María Arguedas's work in "Latin American Literature at the Rise of Environmentalism: Urban Ecological Thinking in José María Arguedas's *The Foxes*," *Comparative Literature Studies* 50, no. 1 (November 2013): 80.

82 Bennett, *Vibrant Matter*, 2–3.

83 This is summarized in Bennett's chapter "Vitality and Self-interest": "If environmentalism leads to the call for the protection and wise management of an ecosystem that surrounds us, a vital materialism suggests that the task is to engage more strategically with a trenchant materiality that is us as it vies with us in agentic assemblages" (*Vibrant Matter*, 111).

84 Matthew Bush and Luis Hernán Castañeda delineate the return to the avant-gardes, particularly in the prose of late twentieth- and early twenty-first-century Latin America, and question the divergences and convergences that authors like Marío Bellatín or César Aira, for instance, show with the "-ismos" of the historical vanguards in their edited volume, "Introduction: Un asombro reonovado," in *Un asombro renovado: Vanguardias contemporáneas en América Latina*, ed. Matthew Bush and Luis Hernán Castañeda (Madrid: Iberoamericana; Frankfurt am Main: Vervuert, 2017), 9.

85 Julio Premat, "Los tiempos insólitos de Mario Bellatin: notas sobre *El Gran Vidrio* y las radicalidades actuales," in *Un asombro renovado: Vanguardias contemporáneas en América Latina*, ed. Matthew Bush and Luis Hernán Castañeda (Madrid: Iberoamericana; Frankfurt am Main: Vervuert, 2017), 149.

86 Bush and Castañeda, "Introducción: Un asombro renovado," 10.

87 Premat, "Los relatos de la vanguardia o el retorno de lo nuevo," 52.

88 In José Carlos Mariátegui's "El proceso de literatura" (The process of literature), essay 7 in *Siete ensayos* (Lima: Ediciones Era, 2002): 294; he describes Magda Portal as "la primera poetisa" (the first poetess) discussed in more detail in chapter 5, 261–265.

89 The original October 1922 version of Antenor Orrego's "Palabras prologales," in *Trilce*, by César Vallejo (Lima: Talleres Tipográficos de la penitenciaria, 1922), xvi, was published with errors that were fixed years later.

90 Prosthetics have been in existence since Egyptian times. In fact, in 424 B.C., Herodotus wrote of a Persian seer who was condemned to death but escaped by amputating his own foot and making a wooden filler to walk thirty miles to the next town, and Pliny the Elder (A.D. 23–79) wrote about a Roman general in the Second Punic War (218–210 B.C.) who had a right arm amputated, see Kim M. Norton, "A Brief History of Prosthetics." *Amputee Coalition* 17, no. 7 (2007): 11, https://www.amputee-coalition.org/resources/a-brief-history-of-prosthetics/ (accessed March 25, 2018).

91 I am using the word *chakana* to mean the "meeting point" or the "crossing point" of the book, as it is defined in Quechua.

92 Portal, quoted in Daniel R. Reedy, *Magda Portal, la pasionaria peruana: biografía intelectual* (Lima: Ediciones Flora Tristán, 2000), 7.

93 Jane Bennett, in "Encounters with an Art Thing" talks about the concept of animacy in art, and particularly in "broken art," *Evental Aesthetics* 3, no. 3 (2015): 91–110.

94 It is interesting that Portal uses the verb *vibrar* because the Vibrationist movement of art in Europe, led by Uruguayans Rafael Barradas and Joaquín Torres García, was characterized by a merging of subject and object. Vibrationism captured the idea that "in the paradigm of modernity, the observer is no longer distanced from the object of observation and the relation between the two becomes unclearly demarcated or as Einstein would say, it becomes viscous." This viscosity is present in Portal's description. See Candelas Gala, *Poetry, Physics, and Painting in Twentieth-Century Spain* (New York: Palgrave, 2011), 15.

Chapter 1 César Vallejo's Lithic Poetry: Stones as Material Guides

1 Julio Ortega refers to the virtual subject that César Vallejo creates in his Introduction to the Catédra version of *Trilce*: "Habla, por todo ello, el sujeto virtual, la hipótesis de un sujeto hecho en el diálogo desigual, en la agonía de sus incumplimientos y desamparos; pero también en la promesa de estos ceros a la izquierda," Ortega, "Introducción," in *Trilce*, by Vallejo (Madrid: Cátedra, 1991), 16–17 (The virtual subject speaks, throughout all of that, the hypothesis of a subject made in unequal dialogue, in the agony of his defaults and abandonments; but also in the promise of these zeros to the left).

2 *Entrambos* comes from the poem "XVII" of *Trilce* and emphasizes the merging of the "2" of the first line of the poem through the truncation of the "e" and the merging of the two words (entre + ambos). "Su cadáver estaba lleno de mundo" (His cadaver was full of world) is the last line of the poem "Pedro Rojas" from the collection *España aparta de mí este caliz* (1937).

3 The graphic artist Cherman Kino is one of those who has recently revisited Vallejo (and nine other poet/writers) in his 2011 exhibit, "De verso en verso, 10 poetas 10" (Lima, Perú: Inauguration, Bookstore El Virrey, December 5, 2011). In his depiction of Vallejo he includes the citation, "Hay hermanos, muchísimo que hacer," by Vallejo, "Los nueve monstrous," in *Poemas humanos*, ed. Julio Vélez (Madrid: Cátedra, 1991), 146. (There is, brothers and sisters, so very much to do) but then adds, "y no has hecho ni mierda" (and you haven't done shit). An article on the exhibit is found at http://archivo.elcomercio.pe/luces/arte/diez-poetas-peruanos-inspiran-nueva-muestra-cherman-noticia-1339646 (accessed March 31, 2018).

4 Jane Bennett, in explaining her political concept of vibrant materiality, writes, "there is also public value in following the scent of a nonhuman, thingly power, the material agency of natural bodies and technological artifacts. Here I mean 'to follow' in the sense in which Jacques Derrida develops it in the context of his mediation on animals. Derrida points to the intimacy between being and following (something, someone), always to be in response to call from something, however nonhuman it may be." The idea of being "called to" Vallejo's gravesite or called to Machu Picchu is what I am thinking of here; a call from a technological artifact that draws us near to our material environment. The stone is not the *same degree* of agent as the human, but affects us emotionally or vitally through initiating our move toward it. See Bennett, *Vibrant Matter: A Political Ecology of Things* (Durham, NC: Duke University Press, 2010), xiii.

5 Ibid., viii.

6 Sara Ahmed, *Queer Phenomenology: Orientations, Objects, Others* (Durham, NC: Duke University Press, 2006), 157.

7 Bennett, *Vibrant Matter*, ix.

8 Stephen M. Hart recently writes, "Whereas the political poetry of other Latin American poets has a dated feel about it for readers of our post-communist world Vallejo's verse—precisely because of its moral ambiguity and its refusal to separate the personal (including his own body) from the political—has a contemporary feel about it which strikes a chord for readers of poetry in the twenty-first century," Hart, Prologue, in *Politics, Poetics, Affect: Re-visioning César Vallejo*, ed. Stephen M. Hart (Cambridge: Cambridge Scholars, 2013), x.

9 "*Trilce* es el libro más complejo de la poesía escrita en lengua castellana" (*Trilce* is the most complex book of poetry written in the Spanish language) according to

Julio Ortega, and "Depués del radicalismo de *Trilce*, la poesía tendrá otras medidas," *César Vallejo: La escritura del devenir* (Lima: Taurus, 2014), 85–86 (After the radicalism of *Trilce*, poetry has new measures).

10 Manuel DeLanda, "Interview with Rick Dolphijn and Iris van der Tuin," in *New Materialism: Interviews and Cartographies*, ed. Graham Harman and Bruno Latour (Ann Arbor: University of Michigan Library, Open Humanities Press, 2012), 46, http://hdl.handle.net/2027/spo.11515701.0001.001 (accessed March 24, 2018).

11 Julio Ortega observes that Vallejo "no está buscando decir mejor, sino decir menos" (*César Vallejo: La escritura del devenir*, 45) (He is not looking to say things better, rather to say less).

12 The original October 1922 version was published while Vallejo was in prison, referred to in the introduction. Antenor Orrego, "Palabras prologales," in *Trilce*, by César Vallejo (Lima: Talleres, Tipográficos de la penitenciaría, 1922), xvi. These "Palabras prologales" are also available in César Vallejo's *Trilce*, ed. Julio Ortega (Madrid: Cátedra, 1993), 365–376.

13 Vallejo, "XX," in *Trilce*, ed. Julio Ortega (1993), 116.

14 Julio Ortega, *César Vallejo: La escritura del devenir*, 21

15 Prosthetics have been in existence since Egyptian times. In fact, in 424 B.C., Herodotus wrote of a Persian seer who was condemned to death but escaped by amputating his own foot and making a wooden filler to walk thirty miles to the next town. See Kim M. Norton, "A Brief History of Prosthetics," *Amputee Coalition* 17, no. 7 (2007): 11, https://www.amputee-coalition.org/resources/a-brief-history-of-prosthetics/ (accessed March 25, 2018).

16 The first line cited in this paragraph comes from Vallejo, "XXVI," in *Trilce* (1993), 142; and the second line from "XLVII," in ibid., 221. The text following the portion cited from "XLVII," in ibid., 221, reads, "según refieren cronicones y pliegos / de labios familiares historiados / en segunda gracia" (as the short chronicles and papers refer to/from historied family lips / in a second grace). This stanza juxtaposes the ciliated reef with historical documents that are equated to the body via the "labios familiares" (familiar lips). Jean Franco observed this phenomenon as "the process of humanizing the species is reversed," because the "species drive" eclipses the articulation of the individual voice. Jean Franco, *César Vallejo: The Dialectics of Poetry and Silence* (Cambridge: Cambridge University Press, 1976), 72.

17 I recognize that poems and prostheses are human creations, and therefore, recenter the human as perceiver of the universe. However, thinking "beyond" human is not necessarily the denial of the critical thinking skills and extraordinary capabilities of the human, but rather, an acknowledgment of the limitations of any individual in mastering his or her universe. Therefore, the need for enhancements to human functioning is another place where the limit to the human is, albeit ironically, manifested.

18 In an article I will discuss again later in this work, Christiane von Buelow describes that "Vallejo's poems fervently question the nature of language, effectively undermining any self-enclosed or self-enclosing notion of the aesthetic object." The poems, in their openness, act like affective prosthetics to the human body too. Christiane von Buelow, "Vallejo's Venus de Milo and the Ruins of Language," *PMLA* 104, no. 1 (January 1989): 41.

19 New materialist philosophy has been criticized for being apolitical because of its

arguments against the subject; however, the intention of the work as I understand it is to make more nuanced the Marxist idea that revolution is a macropolitical project.

20 As I will make the case in chapter 5, the addressee of the poem is an exigency, that is, a future-located need or desire for something that is not yet present in the contemporary.

21 Luis Alva Castro reminds: "No olvidemos que con él se había cometido una de las más grandes injusticias, pues habiendo sido convocado por el propio César Vallejo para escribir el prólogo de *Trilce*, manos enemigas, envidiosas de Antenor Orrego, en las ediciones siguientes eliminaron dicho prólogo. Haya de la Torre siempre le decía que debía hacer justicia con lo que fue voluntad expresa escrita de Vallejo: que ese prólogo estuviera siempre unido a su obra," *Antenor Orrego: la unidad continental y los orígenes de la modernidad en el Perú*, ed. Alva Castro (Lima: Fondo Editorial del Congreso del Perú, 2009), 16 (Let's not forget that one of the greatest injustices was committed with him, considering that he had been called by César Vallejo himself to write the prologue to *Trilce*, and then enemy hands, jealous of Antenor Orrego, eliminated this prologue in the editions that followed. Haya de la Torre used to always say that the work ought to do justice to what was Vallejo's expressed written desire: that *that* [my italics] prologue would always accompany his work).

22 El Grupo Norte was made up of intellectuals, artists, and professionals from the middle class that, at the beginning of the twentieth century, took on the work of fighting for social justice within a three-tier class system, particularly through agrarian and educational reforms. This group was based in Trujillo and included Antenor Orrego, César Vallejo, Haya de la Torre, Alcides Spelucín, and José Eulogio Carrido.

23 Antenor Orrego, *Mi encuentro con César Vallejo* (Bogotá, Colombia: Tercer Mundo Editores, 1989).

24 Luis Alva Castro, "Introduction," in *Antenor Orrego: la unidad continental y los orígenes de la modernidad en el Perú*, ed. Alva Castro (Lima: Fondo Editorial del Congreso del Perú, 2009), 16.

25 Orrego, *Mi encuentro*, 218.

26 Ibid., 218.

27 Ibid., 218–219.

28 See César Vallejo, *Poemas en prosa; Poemas humanos; España, aparta de mí este cáliz*, ed. Julio Veléz (Madrid: Cátedra, 1991).

29 Orrego, *Mi encuentro*, 219.

30 Ibid., 220.

31 Ibid.

32 As Chang-Rodríguez observes of Orrego, "En sus dos primeros libros, *Notas marginales* (1922) y *El monólogo eterno* (1929), Orrego ofrece colecciones de aforismos inspirados en Bergson, Nietzsche y filósofos orientales" [In his first two books, Orrego offers collections of aphorisms inspired in Bergson, Nietzsche and eastern philosophers], 20.

33 Antenor Orrego, "¿Qué es una filosofía?" *Amauta* 27 (November–December 1929): 1–3.

34 The third chapter of Vicky Unruh's *Latin American Vanguards: The Art of Contentious Encounters* (Berkeley: University of California Press, 1994), 125–169, provides a comprehensive look at a number of authors whose work relies on

organicist metaphors, including Gamaliel Churata, *El pez de oro (Retablos del Laykhakuy)*, ed. José Luis Ayala (Puno: Corpuno, 1987).

35 José Carlos Mariátegui, *Siete ensayos de la interpretación de la realidad peruana* (Mexico City: Ediciones Era, 1971), 22.

36 Ibid., 22.

37 Ibid., 219.

38 Ibid.

39 In Julio Ortega's words, "y propuso, en fin, que la poesía es una demanda del porvenir, que se configura en la opción por escribir más allá de los discursos de oficio, desde la intemperie de la crítica .... Desde la tachadura del lenguaje heredado, el poeta adelanta una poética del devenir," *César Vallejo: La escritura del devenir*, 8 (and he proposed, in sum, that poetry is a future demand, that it is configured in the option of writing beyond official discourses, from the outside of criticism. ... From the erasing of inherited language, the poet advances a poetic of becoming).

40 Vallejo, *Poemas en prosa*, ed. Vélez, 25.

41 With respect to *Trilce* as a collection and not just this particular poem, Julio Ortega effectively describes, "*Trilce* es un hueco en el lenguaje, un espacio a deshabitar," "Vallejo: Una poética de la tachadura," *Insula*, 777 (September 2011): 17 (*Trilce* is a hole in language, a space to disinhabit).

42 Jeffrey Jerome Cohen, *Stone: An Ecology of the Inhuman* (Minneapolis: University of Minnesota Press, 2015), 33.

43 Michelle Clayton, "*Trilce*'s Lyric Matters," *Revista de estudios hispánicos* 42, no. 1 (January 2008): 92.

44 Michelle Clayton, *Poetry in Pieces: César Vallejo and Lyric Modernity* (Berkeley: University of California Press, 2011).

45 Vallejo, "Piedra negra sobre una piedra blanca," in *Poemas humanos*, ed. Julio Vélez (Madrid: Cátedra, 1991), 155.

46 Julio Vélez cites Carlos del río León, who wrote that "Vallejo en un paseo y presa de una depresión, encontrándose vestido con un abrigo negro, se sentó sobre una piedra blanca que le recordó un sepulcro. El contraste entre el negro y el blanco le sugirió el título del poema" (quoted in Vallejo, *Poemas en prosa*, ed. Vélez, 155) (Vallejo, on a walk and prisoner of a depression, finding himself dressed in a black overcoat, sat down on a white rock that reminded him of a grave. The contrast between the black and the white suggested the title of the poem to him).

47 César Vallejo, *Obras completas / The Complete Poetry: A Bilingual Edition*, ed. and trans. Clayton Eshleman (Berkeley: University of California Press, 2008), 184.

48 Ibid., 129.

49 Ibid., 127.

50 César Vallejo, *Teatro completo. Piedra cansada*, ed. Enrique Ballón Aguirre (Lima: Pontificia Universidad Católica del Perú, Fondo Editorial, 1979), 2:6.

51 Ibid., 2:9, 18–19.

52 Carolyn Dean describes the "outcrops" of Incan stone work and provides some images of them in her book on stone. "Outcrops" are manipulated stones that demonstrate the architectural techniques of the Incans, but that literally crop up from natural rock. This was a way of building with nature's contours and directly into nature, instead of "on top of it" or "as a replacement for it. See particularly pages 9–10 for a description and images of outcrops in *A Culture of Stone: Inka Perspectives on Rock* (Durham, NC: Duke University Press, 2010).

53 Vallejo, *Piedra cansada*, 2:34.
54 Another famous poem of Vallejo's with stone is "Parado en una piedra," written in Paris. Stephen L. Torres has done a recent reading of the poem via an exploration of the Marxist influence in the same. See "Marxismo y performatividad en 'Parado en una piedra . . .' de César Vallejo: Desempleo, reificación y conciencia de clase," *Letr@s hispanas*, 7 (2010): 147–164.
55 Vallejo, *Obras completas / Complete Poetry*, trans. Eshleman, 138, lines 7–19.
56 Ibid., 139, lines 7–19.
57 von Buelow's article "Vallejo's Venus de Milo and the Ruins of Language" provides an excellent reading of *Trilce* "XXXVI," in dialogue with Walter Benjamin's theorization of symbol and allegory, "Vallejo's poetry . . . affects a critical decomposition of what might be called 'the aesthetics of the symbol,'" 42.
58 Franco, *César Vallejo*, 90.
59 von Buelow, "Vallejo's Venus de Milo and the Ruins of Language,"45.
60 Vallejo, *Trilce* "XVI," in *Obras completas / Complete Poetry*, trans. Eshleman, 196, line 2.
61 Ibid.
62 Vallejo, *Trilce* "VI," in *Obras completas / Complete Poetry*, trans. Eshleman, 176, lines 1–2.
63 Ibid.
64 Clayton, "*Trilce*'s Lyric Matters," 92.
65 Vallejo, *Trilce* "XLIX," in *Obras completas / Complete Poetry*, trans. Eshleman, 264.
66 Ibid.
67 Ibid.
68 Ibid.
69 The poet voice invokes "Madre!" and "mamá" in the poem directly. Ortega cites Ferrari in the former's essential annotated *Trilce*, "Nos volvemos (in the poem) a enfrentar aquí con esa perplejidad dolorosa ante el vacío que ha dejado la ausencia de la madre," cf. in Vellejo, *Trilce*, ed. Ortega (1991), 131 (We find ourselves confronting again that painful perplexity before the void that the absence of his mother has left).
70 Vallejo, *Trilce* "XXIII," in *Obras completas / Complete Poetry*, trans. Eshleman, 210–211.
71 Ibid.
72 "An idea opposed to another idea is always the same idea, albeit affected by the negative sign. The more you oppose one another, the more you remain in the same framework of thought," in Michael Serres and Bruno Latour, *Conversations on Science, Culture, and Time*, trans. Roxanne Lapidus (Ann Arbor: University of Michigan Press, 2011), 81.
73 Emilio Adolfo Westphalen observed with respect to Vallejo's use of paradox, "No sé si se trata en verdad de una equiparidad de los contrarios o más bien de la cancelación de dos inexactitudes. Esta tendencia de Vallejo es muy antigua," *La poesía, los poemas, los poetas* (Mexico City: Universidad Iberoamericana, 1995), 33 (I don't know if this demonstrates an equalizing of opposites or more like a cancellation of inexactitudes. This tendency in Vallejo is very old).
74 Patrick J. Duffey, "El arte humanizado y la crítica cinematográfica de Jaime Torres Bodet y César Vallejo," *Anales de la literatura hispanoamericana* 32 (2003): 48.
75 Julio Ortega, *César Vallejo: la escritura del devenir*, 19.

76 Vallejo, "Voy a hablar de la esperanza," *Poemas en prosa,* ed. Julio Vélez (Madrid: Cátedra, 1991), 99.

77 The full quote from William Rowe is about the three levels at which he interprets Vallejo's suffering, "El tratamiento que hace Vallejo del dolor, reúne tres niveles: el dolor inagotable mestizo, el dolor cósmico de la tradición nativa y la moderna visión de futuro que abolirá el sufrimiento innecesario. En esta intersección, cuya complejidad es la historia del Perú, Vallejo agrega un elemento nuevo: un dolor cósmico cuyo efecto resiste cualquier localización y cuya causa no puede ser identificada," *Hacia una poética radical: Ensayos de hermenéutica cultural* (México DF: Fondo de Cultura Económica, 2014), 173 (The treatment that Vallejo makes of suffering brings together three levels: the inexhaustible suffering of the mestizo, the cosmic suffering of the native traditions, and a modern vision of the future that will abolish unnecessary suffering. In this intersection, whose complexities are the history of Peru, Vallejo adds another element: a cosmic suffering whose effect resists any localization and whose cause cannot be identified).

78 Vallejo, "Los nueve monstruos" *Poemas humanos*, ed. Julio Vélez (Madrid: Cátedra, 1991), 145.

79 Cohen, *Stone*, 20.

80 Ignacio López-Calvo, "El fluir de conciencia en César Vallejo," *Confluencia* 14, no. 1 (Fall 1998): 83.

81 Judith Butler, *Undoing Gender* (New York: Routledge, 2004), 12.

82 Gilles Deleuze and Félix Guattari, *A Thousand Plateaus: Capitalism and Schizophrenia*, trans. Brian Massumi (Minneapolis: University of Minnesota Press, 1987), 238.

83 Vallejo, "Existe un mutilado," *Poemas en prosa*, ed. Julio Vélez (Madrid: Cátedra, 1991), 104.

84 Ibid., 106.

85 Ibid., 105.

86 Ibid., 104.

87 Ibid., 105.

88 Vallejo, "Cesa el anhelo," in *Poemas en prosa*, ed. Julio Vélez (Madrid: Cátedra, 1991), 107.

89 The idea of the crowd as "ethical witness" may be likened to Clayton's reading of the "ethics of the fragment" in Vallejo as, "not a celebration of the fragment on avant-garde terms, but a recognition of its centrality to modes of modern subjectivity and collectivism," Clayton, *Poetry in Pieces*, 3.

90 Vallejo, "Cesa el anhelo," *Poemas en prosa*, ed. Vélez (1991), 107.

91 Ibid. 107.

92 The Spanish Civil War years (July 17, 1936–April 1, 1939) resulted, conservatively, in around 150,000 deaths.

93 Vallejo, *España, aparta de mí este cáliz*, ed. Veléz (1991), 261.

94 Deleuze and Guattari, *Thousand Plateaus*, 25.

95 Julio Ortega, *La teoría poética de César Vallejo* (Providence, RI: Del Sol, 1983), 273.

96 Antonio Cornejo Polar, *Escribir en el aire: Ensayos sobre la heterogeneidad socio-cultural en las literaturas andinas* (Lima: Editorial Horizonte, 1994), 223.

97 Vallejo, *Obras completas / Complete Poetry*, trans. Eshleman, 604.

98 Ibid., 605.

99 Michelle Clayton reads the last line of *Trilce* "II," "¿Qué se llama cuanto heriza nos?" to originate from the verb *herir*, to hurt. The addition of the *h* is also a

complication of the human/animal divide, in Michelle Clayton, "'Animalestar': Animal Affections in Vallejo's Poetry," in *Politics, Poetics, Affect: Re-visioning Cesar Vallejo*, ed. Stephen M. Hart (Cambridge: Cambridge Scholars Publishing, 2013), 118.

100 Georgette moved Vallejo's remains to Montparnasse in 1970, a promise she had made to him before he died. See Stephen M. Hart, *César Vallejo: A Literary Biography* (London: Tamesis, 2013), 270.

Chapter 2 Alejandra Dorado's Installation Art: Material Transmutations in Contemporary Cochabamba

1 Cochabamba, Bolivia is in a valley in the Andes mountain range and has a population of approximately three million people (according to the 2012 census). Quechua is spoken by approximately 800,000 people in the Cochabamba Department.

2 As Benjamin Kohl and Rosalind Bresnahan explain, "Until 2000, Bolivia was best known for holding the record number of governments for any modern country," Kohl and Bresnahan, "Introduction: Bolivia under Morales: Consolidating Power, Initiating Decolonization," *Latin American Perspectives* 37, no. 3 (May 2010): 6.

3 The 2008 documentary *BlueGold: World Water Wars* elaborates on Olivera's role in the water wars in Cochabamba. He also was a protest leader during the gas wars in La Paz/El Alto in 2003. Maude Barlow, Sam Bozzo, and Tony Clarke, *Blue-Gold*, dir. Sam Bozzo (Irvine, CA: Purple Turtle Films).

4 William Assies, "David versus Goliath in Cochabamba: Water Rights, Neoliberalism, and the Revival of Social Protest in Bolivia," *Latin American Perspectives* 30, no. 3 (May 2003): 14.

5 Ibid., 31.

6 The new Constitution went into effect in 2009, and its relevancy is discussed at greater length in the conclusion to this book.

7 Rosi Braidotti, "The Critical Posthumanities; Or, Is Medianatures to Naturecultures as *Zoë* Is to *Bios*?" *Cultural Politics* 12, no. 3 (November 2016): 381.

8 Claire Colebrook, "Queer Vitalism," *New Formations* 68 (Spring 2009): 77.

9 Ibid.

10 *martirio* first opened at Museo de Arte Contemporáneo (MAC) in Santiago, Chile, in November 2005. In 2006, Alejandra Dorado also installed *martirio* in Santa Cruz, Bolivia, at the Manzana I art space, prior to its third installation, the one I discuss in the chapter, in Cochabamba.

11 Simón Patiño (1862–1947) was a famous tin magnate and nicknamed "The Andean Rockefeller." His mother was from Cochabamba, and he was the illegitimate son of Eugenio Iturri, from the Basque region. After making his tin fortune in Bolivia, buying up multiple companies, he moved permanently abroad in the 1920s but remained Bolivia's "most powerful capitalist" until his death. See Herbert S. Klein, *A Concise History of Bolivia* (Cambridge: Cambridge University Press, 2003), 149.

12 Magda Portal, "Frente a la Vida," in *Obra poética completa*, ed. Daniel Reedy (Lima: Fondo de Cultura Económica. 2010), 93–95, lines 45–47.

13 The space varies, quite obviously, depending on the different galleries and museums. On some occasions, Dorado had only one room within which to work; on others, she had multiple rooms.

14 Alejandra Dorado estimates that she took over one hundred photos to arrive at the forty used in the installation (personal interview with author, Cochabamba, Bolivia, 2009).

15 *Polleras* are the thick velvet or brocade skirts that the female Aymara population around La Paz and the Quechua populations concentrated around Cochabamba and Sucre wear. They are also worn throughout the Andes.

16 Deborah Poole, *Vision, Race, and Modernity: A Visual Economy of the Andean Image World* (Princeton, NJ: Princeton University Press, 1997), 9–10.

17 Alejandra Dorado, *martirio: Text and Installation* (Cochabamba, Bolivia: Centro Cultural Simón Patiño, 2006), 3.

18 F. R. Ankersmit elaborates on this concept of political power as a fundamentally aesthetic project in *Aesthetic Politics: Political Philosophy Beyond Fact and Value* (Stanford, CA: Stanford University Press, 1996).

19 Franz Kafka, "In the Penal Colony," in *The Complete Stories*, ed. Nahum N. Glatzer, trans. Edwin Muir (New York: Penguin Random House, Schocken Kafka Library, 1995), 165–192.

20 This essay has never been published in English. It is available in its original French as an introduction to Jean-Pierre Brisset's book and has been translated to Spanish and published by Arena Publishers in Spain, under the same title. See Michel Foucault, *Siete sentencias sobre el séptimo ángel*, trans. Isidro (Herrera. Madrid: Arena libros, 1999); first published as "Sept propos sur le septième ange," in Jean-Pierre Brisset, *La grammaire logique* (Paris: Brisset, 1883).

21 Dorado, *martirio* exhibit catalog, 6. I have not translated the quotation because the anagrammatic games within it and the exhibit are created in Spanish; emphasis in the original.

22 Sigmund Freud, "The Interpretation of Dreams," in *The Standard Edition of the Complete Psychological Works of Sigmund Freud: Early Psycho-Analytic Publications. 1900–1901: The Interpretation of Dreams (Second Part) and On Dreams*, ed. and trans. James Strachey et al. (London: Vintage, 2001), 5:525.

23 The circular organization of the space contests a linear history. Instead, it emphasizes textual accretions or layers, as the exhibit is transformed each time it is installed.

24 *martirio* exhibit catalog.

25 Jacques Derrida, *Of Grammatology*, trans. Gayatri Chakravorty Spivak (Baltimore: Johns Hopkins University Press, 2016), 109.

26 Andrea Bachner, "Anagrams in Psychoanalysis: Retroping Concepts by Sigmund Freud, Jacques Lacan, and Jean-Francois Lyotard," *Comparative Literature Studies* 40, no. 1 (2003): 6.

27 I am using the term "semiosis" in the way that Walter Mignolo defines it in *The Darker Side of the Renaissance* (Ann Arbor: University of Michigan Press, 1995). He distinguishes between colonial discourse and colonial semiosis. Semiosis accounts for interactions "between writing systems," such as picto-ideographic writing or *quipus* as well as more traditionally "written" texts (ibid., 7–8). I conceive the visual pictures of Dorado's exhibit as a component to semiotic exchange.

28 Jane Bennett, "Encounters with an Art Thing," *Evental Aesthetics* 3, no. 3 (2015): 95–96.

29 Rosi Braidotti, *Transpositions: On Nomadic Ethics* (Cambridge: Polity Press, 2012), 4.

30 Diane H. Coole and Samantha Frost, "Introduction," in *New Materialisms: Ontology, Agency, and Politics*, ed. Coole and Frost (Durham, NC: Duke University Press, 2013), 17.

31 Donna Haraway, "A Cyborg Manifesto: Science, Technology, and Socialist-Feminism in the Late Twentieth Century," in *Simians, Cyborgs and Women: The Reinvention of Nature* (New York: Routledge, 1991), 149–181.

32 Silvia Rivera Cusicanqui, "La noción de "derecho" o las paradojas de la modernidad postcolonial: indígenas y mujeres en Bolivia," *Revista aportes andinos* 11 (2004): 2.

33 As Dorado relates the evolution of this exhibit she explains that: "leí un artículo muy interesante sobre el caso de una mujer indígena que mató a su marido en defensa propia, el abogado que escribía esto decía que la mujer tenía todas las que perder porque era mujer, indígena y vivía en concubinato . . . esto me pareció muy triste e importante para hacer algo, entonces comencé a preguntar si alguien conocía una mujer que haya matado a su marido" (I read a really interesting article about an indigenous woman that killed her husband in self-defense; the lawyer that wrote about this said that the woman had everything to lose because she was indigenous and basically lived as a concubine . . . this seemed incredibly sad and important to do something about, so I began to ask if anyone knew this woman that had killed her husband) (Alejandra Dorado, personal email, July 27, 2014).

34 Tara Daly, written interview with Alejandra Dorado, e-mail message, July 27, 2014.

35 Ibid.

36 Dorado, *Castigadores domésticos moderados*, exhibit catalog.

37 See Michel Foucault, *Discipline and Punish: The Birth of the Prison*, trans. Alan Sheridan, 2nd ed. (New York: Vintage Books, 1995). For a discussion on scopic regimes, there is a large body of literature written. For instance, see David Michael Levin's *The Opening of Vision: Nihilism and the Postmodern Situation* (New York: Routledge, 1988), where he links human suffering to particular modes of seeing. Also, Poole's work in Peru in *Vision, Race, and Modernity* traces the visual economies that contributed to the letter class's perception of indigenous peoples, especially as the images circulated between Peru and France.

38 María Lugones, "Heterosexualism and the Colonial/Modern Gender System," *Hypatia* 22, no. 1 (2007): 186.

39 Natasha Lennard and Cary Wolfe, "Is Humanism Really Humane?" *New York Times*, January 9, 2017, https://www.nytimes.com/2017/01/09/opinion/is-humanism-really-humane.html (accessed March 26, 2018).

40 The unsettling images of the stitched wounds also recall an image that appears various times in Argentinian writer and Dorado influencer, Alejandra Pizarnik's *La condesa sangrienta*. This gothic horror story retells the life of Erzébet Bathory, a countess from seventeenth-century Hungary whose exotic sexual appetites caused her to prey on young girls, purportedly killing 650 of them over the course of her life. Before she would kill them, she tortured them extensively and "si la condesa se fatigaba de oír los gritos les cosían la boca," Pizarnik, *Obras completas*, ed. Cristina Piña (Buenos Aires: Corregidor, 1993), 285 (if the countess got tired of hearing the screams of the girls, their mouths were sewn shut).

41 The violence to which I refer is not exclusive to heteronormative relationships.

42 Wilma Peréz, "La mujer boliviana enfrenta 16 tipos de situaciones de violencia,"*La Razón*, November 24, 2013, http://www.la-razon.com/index.php?_url=/sociedad

/mujer-boliviana enfrenta-situaciones-violencia_0_1948605213.html (accessed July 29, 2014).

43 Here, I am referring to Aristophanes' speech in Plato's "The Symposium," where he describes that originally every man and woman were part of one whole person: the two halves were either both male, both female, or male and female. Ever since then, each person seeks his or her other half, according to his or her original "whole." See K. J. Dover, "Aristophanes' Speech in Plato's Symposium," *Journal of Hellenic Studies* 86 (November 1966): 41–50.

44 Braidotti, "Interview with Rosi Braidotti," in *New Materialisms: Interviews and Cartographies*, ed. Graham Harman and Bruno Latour (Ann Arbor: University of Michigan Library, Open Humanities Press, 2012), 19–37.

45 Redacción Central, "1.500 personas en Bolivia se declaran no heterosexuales," *Los Tiempos*, July 20, 2011, http://www.lostiempos.com/actualidad/local/20110720/1500-personas-bolivia-se-declaran-no-heterosexuales (accessed March 13, 2018).

46 http://www.paginasiete.bo/gente/2016/12/18/importancia-llevar-apellido-galan-120781.html (accessed March 31, 2018).

47 The Chilean writer Diamela Eltit observes with respect to this point, "la estructura de este particular tipo de familia, creada por el grupo, resulta una plataforma extraordinariamente propositiva por su amplitud y elasticidad. Se trata de una poderosa iniciativa de asociación que junto con mostrar su deseo—perturbar los límites de las categorías culturales—presenta un modelo metodológico de acción política," Eltit, "La Familia Galán," in *Cruce de lenguas: Sexualidades, diversidad y ciudadanía*, ed. Raquel Olea and Kathya Araujo (Santiago: LOM Ediciones, 2007), 124 (the structure of this particular type of family, created by the group, results in an extraordinarily critical and creative platform due to its breadth and elasticity. We're talking about a powerful initiative based on association that together with demonstrating its desires—to agitate the limits of cultural categories—presents a methodological model for political action).

48 The original manuscript by Santacruz Pachacuti, *Relación de anigüedades deste reyno del Peru; estudio etnohistórico lingüístico de Pierre Duviols y César Itier* (c. 1613), is in *La Biblioteca Nacional* in Madrid.

49 Michael J. Horswell, *Decolonizing the Sodomite: Queer Tropes of Sexuality in Colonial Andean Culture* (Austin: University of Texas Press, 2005), 1.

50 The space represents Viracocha, the creator God, but we see in the drawing that this creative force rests between the male and female halves of the schemata. Horswell interprets the Viracocha as an androgynous creator god. He goes on to explain how the drawing relates to third-gender subjectivity, due to its complementary structure, and the way that the androgynous nature of Viracocha is represented in the egglike figure that also has a parallel correspondence in the Huarochirí manuscript as well (Horswell, *Decolonizing the Sodomite*, 55).

51 Braidotti, "The Critical Posthumanities," 383.

52 Braidotti, *Transpositions: On Nomadic Ethics* (Cambridge: Polity Press, 2006), 35.

53 Lennard and Wolfe, "Is Humanism Really Humane?"

54 Coole and Frost, "Introduction," 20.

55 Alejandra Alarcón is another Bolivian artist whose watercolor paintings also address the relationship between humans and animals in intriguing ways: http://www.alejandra-alarcon.com/ (accessed March 14, 2018).

56 Rosi Braidotti, "Animals, Anomalies, and Inorganic Others," *PMLA* 124, no. 2 (2009): 527.

57 Luis Tapia, *La invención del núcleo común* (La Paz, Bolivia: Universidad Mayor de San Andrés, 2006), 49.

Chapter 3 José María Arguedas's 1960s: The Air as Space of Material Encounters

1 Carlos Cueto Fernandini was the ex-rector of the University of San Marcos, where José María Arguedas worked for many years; John V. Murra, a renowned Romanian but U.S.-based anthropologist who Arguedas admired and with whom he corresponded by letter and met with in person for almost a decade.

2 José María Arguedas "Llamado a algunos Doctores," in Quechua the text reads, "reqsiykanakusunchik; yaqa kikin wayrallatam samanchik," *El Comercio*, July 3, 1966, 23.

3 "Viability" has a direct connection to the concept of "precarity," which means to have a life in danger of being out of one's control because of the institutions by which one is made a subject. A "viable" life is not in danger. Judith Butler elaborates both terms in the book *Precarious Life: The Power of Mourning and Violence* (London: Verso, 2003).

4 I must clarify that this is changing. As urban pollution grows worse by the minute, more than one company has come up with the idea of buying air. Take this one example from Edmonton, Canada: Jennifer Pak, "Chinese Buy Up Bottles of Fresh Air from Canada," *Telegraph*, December 15, 2015, https://www.telegraph.co.uk/news/worldnews/asia/china/12051354/Chinese-buy-up-bottles-of-fresh-air-from-Canada.html (accessed March 1, 2018).

5 With the phrase "set them aflight" I refer to the work of Gilles Deleuze and Félix Guattari, particularly in *Anti-Oedipus* and *A Thousand Plateaus* where they articulate their concept of deterritorialization.

6 I am using the possessive "their" to refer to multiple identities in one person and that stands for the principle of inclusivity and plurality that Arguedas supported.

7 See José María Arguedas, *El sexto* (1961) (Madrid: Drácena, 2016); *Katatay y otros poemas* (1972) in *Obras completas vol. 5.* (Lima: Editorial Horizonte, 1983); and *El zorro de arriba y el zorro de abajo* (1971), ed. Eve-Marie Fell, Edición Crítica (Paris: ALLCA XX, 1996).

8 Antonio Cornejo Polar describes his approximation to the Andean subject as an effort to overcome a romantic version of the same: "It interests me to reflect a moment about how and why the search for an identity, that tends to be associated with the construction of images from solid and coherent spaces, capable of threading together vast social networks of legitimacy and belonging, gave way to the uneasy lament or anxious celebration of our diverse and conflictive configuration," Cornejo Polar, *Escribir en el aire: Ensayos sobre la heterogeneidad socio-cultural en las literaturas andinas* (Lima: Editorial Horizonte, 1994), 13.

9 Antonio Cornejo Polar, *Los universos narrativos de José María Arguedas* (Buenos Aires: Editorial Losada, 1974), 14–15.

10 Arguedas, *Zorros*, 7.

11 Rubén Bareiro Saguier refers to the "marea humana" (human dizzying) that increases from *Los ríos profundos* up until *Los zorros*: "El proceso de declinación frustrante culmina en *El zorro de arriba y el zorro de abajo*, en Chimbote, ese símbolo premonitorio de la devastación, del desmantelamiento . . . donde el tiempo pierde su norte, en que la lengua se babeliza, extravía el sentido esencial de la comunicación," Bareiro Saguier, "José María Arguedas o la palabra herida," in

El zorro de arriba y el zorro de abajo, ed. Eve-Marie Fell, Edición Crítica (Paris: ALLCA XX, 1996), xviii (The process of frustrating decline culminates in *The Fox From Up Above and the Fox From Down Below*, in Chimbote, that premonitory symbol of devastation, of a dismantling . . . where time loses its north, in which language becomes babble, the essential sense of communication is lost).

12 Anne Lambright, *Creating the Hybrid Intellectual: Subject, Space, and the Feminine in the Narrative of José María Arguedas* (Lewisburg, PA: Bucknell University Press, 2007), 189.

13 In one of their more decisive and politics-shifting moves on May 15, 1935, an APRA militant killed the editor of *El Comercio*, Antonio Miró Quesada de la Guerra, and his wife.

14 José Alberto Portugal, *Las novelas de José María Arguedas: Una incursión en lo inarticulado* (Lima: Fondo Editorial Peruano, 2007), 265.

15 Referencing the delay in publication, Ciro A. Sandoval asks, "Por ejemplo, ¿por qué es *El Sexto* una de las novelas que tiene el período más largo de gestación dentro de la producción de Arguedas?" Sandoval, "Vuelta a *El Sexto* de José María Arguedas," in *José María Arguedas: hacia una poética migrante* (Pittsburgh, PA: University of Pittsburgh Press, 2006), 259 (For instance, why is *El Sexto* one of the novels that has the longest period of gestation within the Arguedian corpus?).

16 José María Arguedas, *Las cartas de Arguedas*, ed. John V. Murra and Mercedes López-Baralt (Lima: Pontificia Universidad Católica del Perú, Fondo Editorial, 1996), 43.

17 As Antonio Cornejo Polar summarizes, "en el primer piso están los criminales más peligrosos y los vagos; en el segundo, los delincuentes no avezados; en el tercero, los presos políticos. Entre un piso y otro no hay comunicación y cuando se produce, muy excepcionalmente, genera una cadena de repercusiones trágicas." (Cornejo Polar, *Universos narrativos*, 151) (on the first floor are the most dangerous criminals and the lost causes; on the second, the new delinquents, on the third, the political prisoners. Between one floor and the other, there is no communication and when it is produced, very exceptionally, it generates a chain of tragic repercussions).

18 José María Arguedas and Alfonso Calderón, "Interview: Conversando con Arguedas," *Portal*, 21–22.

19 Arguedas, *Sexto*, 13.

20 For an elaborated discussion on the affective exchange in Arguedas, Sara Castro-Klarén's article "Like a Pig When He's Thinkin'," in *The Fox From Up Above and the Fox From Down Below*, ed. José María Arguedas et al. (Pittsburgh: University of Pittsburgh Press, 2000), 307–323, was field-shifting due to the ways it opened up a field of thinking on the affective relations between species in Arguedas's *El zorro de arriba y el zorro de abajo*.

21 Arguedas, *Sexto*, 49.

22 Ibid., 97.

23 At the end of the novel in the "¿Último diario?" José María Arguedas writes, "¡Cuántos hervores han quedado enterrados!" (How many boilings have remained unearthed!), using the word *hervores* to refer to the infinite number of tales he could have told in the book. He also refers to "la última línea de los *Hervores*" (the last line of the Boilings) in his letter dated August 29, 1969, to Señor Don Gonzalo Losada. In this last case, he uses *Hervores* as a title for *El zorro de arriba y el zorro*

de abajo. Los zorros, ed. Eve Marie-Fell, Edición Crítica (Paris: ALLCA XX, 1996), 251.

24 Arguedas, *Sexto*, 47.

25 Ibid.

26 Arguedas, *Cartas de Arguedas*, ed. Murra and López-Baralt, 51.

27 Ibid., 104.

28 Ibid., 114.

29 Cornejo-Polar, *Universos narrativos*, 151.

30 In Michel Foucault's opinion, the prison is only an additional extension of the mechanisms of discipline that already exist in society: "Prison continues, on those who are entrusted to it, a work begun elsewhere, which the whole of society pursues on each individual through innumerable mechanisms of discipline," Foucault, *Discipline and Punish: The Birth of the Prison*, trans. Alan Sheridan, 2nd ed. (New York: Vintage Books, 1995), 302.

31 Sara Castro-Klarén, "Posting Letters: Writing in the Andes and the Paradoxes of the Postcolonial Debate," in *Coloniality at Large: Latin America and the Postcolonial Debate*, ed. Mabel Moraña et al. (Durham, NC: Duke University Press, 2008), 136.

32 José María Arguedas, "No soy un aculturado," in *El zorro de arriba y el zorro de abajo*, ed. Eve-Marie Fell, Edición Crítica (Paris: ALLCA XX, 1996), 256–258.

33 Priscilla Archibald, *Imagining Modernity in the Andes* (Lewisburg, PA: Bucknell University Press, 2011). I refer particularly to the chapter "Science in the Andes" in which Archibald discusses the history of the Cornell-Peru project, "Vicos," in detail; this was a project that was largely guided by the principles of rational modernization. As Archibald describes it, "Using methods of applied anthropology, which included not just observation but also intervention, the anthropologists intended to liberate workers [of the Vicos Hacienda] from their habitual servitude and raise them to a state of productive self-sufficiency" (ibid., 83). In Arguedas's letters to John V. Murra, there is also a good deal of information about the Vicos project. See Arguedas, *Cartas de Arguedas*, ed. Murra and López-Baralt, 27.

34 Editor Alberto Escobar, "Introducción," in *Mesa redonda sobre Todas las sangres: 23 de junio de 1965* (Lima: Instituto de Estudios Peruanos, 1965), 2.

35 While there had been interruptions in the flow of letters before for a few months or so, never were they so long as this break, which was almost a full year.

36 As told later in a letter to Dr. Hoffman included in Arguedas's letters to John V. Murra and Lola Hoffman, in *Cartas de Arguedas*, ed. Murra and López-Baralt, 98.

37 Unfortunately, the July 17, 1966, Sunday supplement "Dominical," to *El Comercio* is missing from the Biblioteca Nacional de Perú, and so I could not see the original printed Quechua version. The Spanish version is cited in note 1, found in *El Comercio*, July 3, 1966, 23. However, John V. Murra and López Baralt include the Quechua and Spanish versions in the volume of letters, *Cartas de Arguedas*, ed. Murra and López-Baralt (Lima, Peru: Pontificia Universidad Católica del Perú, 1996).

38 José María Arguedas, *Obras completas* (Lima: Editorial Horizonte, 1983), 5:253.

39 Alberto Escobar, *Arguedas, o, la utopía de la lengua* (Lima: Instituto de Estudios, 1984), 10.

40 Arguedas, *Obras completas*, 5:257.

41 Ibid.

42 Ibid.

43 Jesús Lara, *La literatura de los quechuas* (Cochabamba: Editorial Canelas, 1961), 23.
44 Arguedas, *Obras completas*, 5:225.
45 Ibid., 5:227.
46 Ibid.
47 Ibid.
48 Arguedas, *Zorros*, ed. Fell, 403.
49 Ibid., 403–404.
50 Cornejo Polar, *Universos narrativos*, 188.
51 Martin Lienhard, "La andinización del vanguardismo urbano" (in Arguedas, *Zorros*, ed. Fell, 327). Later in the same article Lienhard reiterates the ending that is not really an ending, "el *relato,* finalmente, termina en el *¿Último diario?* de Arguedas, conclusión inconclusa del libro y apertura hacia algo nuevo: la utopia" (the story, finally, ends in Arguedas's "Last Diary?," the inconclusive conclusion to the book and the aperture to something new: utopia), ibid., 331.
52 Arguedas, "Carta de José María Arguedas a Gonzalo Losada," in *Zorros*, ed. Fell, 250.
53 Cornejo Polar, *Universos narrativos*, 233.
54 Arguedas, *Zorros*, ed. Fell, 79.
55 Ibid., 176.
56 Ibid.
57 Ibid.
58 Ibid., 177.
59 Gordon Brotherston, *The Emergence of the Latin American Novel* (Cambridge: Cambridge University Press, 1979), 102.
60 Arguedas, *Zorros*, ed. Fell, 249.
61 Rubén Bareiro Saguier makes a link as well to "la palabra viva que había escuchado desde mi infancia, en guaraní" (the living word that I had listened to since my infancy, in guaraní), drawing in not just the Quechua cosmovision but other indigenous viewpoints to the Arguedian experience. Bareiro Saguier, "José María Arguedas o la palabra herida," in *El zorro de arriba y el zorro de abajo*, ed. Eve-Marie Fell, Edición Crítica (Paris: ALLCA XX, 1996), xv.
62 Arguedas, *Zorros*, ed. Fell, 10.
63 Jorge Marcone, "Latin American Literature at the Rise of Environmentalism: Urban Ecological Thinking in José María Arguedas's *The Foxes*," *Comparative Literature Studies* 50, no. 1 (November 2013): 66.
64 Ariel Dorfman, "Arguedas y la epopeya americana," in *Recopilación de textos sobre José María Arguedas*, ed. Juan Larco (La Habana: Centro de Investigaciones Literarias, Casa de las Americas, 1976), 19.
65 Letter to John Murra November 12, 1961, in *Cartas de Arguedas*, ed. Murra and López-Baralt (Lima, Peru: Pontificia Universidad Católica del Perú, 1996), 66.
66 José María Arguedas, *Diamantes y pedernales* (1954) (Lima: Editorial Horizonte, 2011), 100.
67 Ibid.
68 Ibid., 103.
69 Ibid.
70 Ibid., 106.
71 Ibid., 107.
72 Ibid.

73 Spanish–Quechua Dictionary, *Diccionario Qheshwa-Castellano/Castellano-Qheshwa*, ed. Jesús Lara, Quinta Edición (Cochabamba, Bolivia: Los amigos del libro, 1971), 283.

74 Churata, *El pez de oro*, 55.

Chapter 4 Mujeres Creando Comunidad: Communitarian Feminisms from the Bolivian Soil

1 I do not wish to imply that by entering her house I somehow "saw things from her eyes." I am expressing that my embodied experience of being there gave me insight into the necessity of holding difference and similarity at once.

2 As an example of this, Julieta Paredes writes in one of her poems from the 1990s, "Se me perdió una poesía" (One of my poems got away from me) but that in the end, when she went to look for it, all she found was "dos manitas gorditas picaras / niñas pelando una mandarina," Paredes, "Poem 4," in *Con un montón de palabras* (A pile of words) (La Paz, Bolivia: Ediciones Mujeres Creando, 1997) (two adorable, mischievous buddies / girls peeling a mandarin). Also included in this collection is the poem "Las lavanderas" (The washer women), from the section, "Del mismo barro" (Of the same mud), which turns into poetry the simple daily action of women washing clothes in the river.

3 Julieta Paredes, "Cuerpos que gritan y los oídos sordos del rey" (unpublished manuscript, 2003), n.p. The "misma mierda," is a way of turning the abject back on the elites, instead of the reverse. When Javier Sanjinés speaks of "lo grotesco social" (the social grotesque) in Bolivia, he analyzes the grotesque and its role in the decolonization of the symbolic order. Sanjinés C., *Literatura contemporánea y grotesco social en Bolivia* (La Paz, Bolivia: Instituto Latinoamericano de Investigaciones Sociales, 1992), 29. In this sense, by redeploying "lo grotesco," Paredes, too, mobilizes "lo grotesco" as something already contained within the elite class. She also parodies their knowledge production and implicitly acknowledges other modes of knowing in the world.

4 The content of her talk was based on an unpublished manuscript titled, "Cuerpos que gritan y los oídos sordos del rey" (2003).

5 In this same way, it is difficult, as I will elaborate, to classify Paredes's and Mujeres Creando's "performances." "Su *performance*, entonces, es al mismo tiempo una forma de acción social, un tipo de pedagogía popular y una manera de hacer arte," John Beverley, "Prefacio" (Preface), in *No pudieron con nosotras: El desafío del feminismo autónomo de "Mujeres Creando,"* ed. Elizabeth Monasterios (Pittsburgh: University of Pittsburgh Press; La Paz: Plural editores, 2006), 13 (Their *performance*, then, is at the same time a form of social activism, a type of popular pedagogy, and a manner of making art). Paredes would deny that it is "art," in order to resist the institutionalization of the work.

6 Mujeres Creando's work has been extensive, so it is difficult to summarize the plethora of projects, both written and performed, that members have undertaken. I use these three genres not as exclusive categories, but as a means of organizing their body of work.

7 As intercultural philosopher Josef Estermann has observed, "El sujeto andino en general es un sujeto colectivo o comunitario; en lo específico, lo mismo también vale para la filosofía," *Filosofía andina: Estudio intercultural de la sabiduría autóctona andina* (Quito, Ecuador: Abya Yala, 1998), 74 (The Andean subject, in

general, is a collective or communitarian subject; in its specific form, the same is also relevant in philosophy). Paredes's most recent work assumes this vantage point: that the community is the central actor in the construction of society.

8 Julieta Paredes, *Hilando fino: Desde el feminismo comunitario* (La Paz, Bolivia: CEDEC, 2008), 35.

9 Noting this same prepositional predicament, Elizabeth Monasterios writes about the challenges that *Mujeres Creando* posed to other Bolivian feminists and academics at large: "Por principio ético, había que renunciar a la práctica del conocimiento representativo y más que escribir *sobre Mujeres Creando* atreverse a escribir *con Mujeres Creando*; desde sus provocaciones y no *a propósito* de ellas," Monasterios, "Introducción," in *No pudieron con nostotras: El desafío del feminismo autónomo de Mujeres Creando* (Pittsburgh and La Paz, Bolivia: Plural editores, 2006), 11 (As an ethical principal, we had to renounce the practice of representative knowledge and more than write *about Mujeres Creando,* dare to write *with Mujeres Creando*; from their provocations and not on behalf of them).

10 Patricio Guerrero Arias, "Heartening the Sense of Dominant Epistemologies from Insurgent Forms of Wisdom, in Order to Build New Meanings of Existence," *Calle 14* 4, no. 5 (2010): 83.

11 It is important to understand that Mujeres Creando, now led by María Galindo and Julieta Ojeda, is distinct from Paredes's group, Mujeres Creando Comunidad. The split is explained in some detail later in the chapter.

12 Unlike some of the avant-garde figures of Peru who were forced into exile or else would have been imprisoned, Paredes and Galindo actively chose exile as a positive alternative to living with the fear of personal threats in Bolivia.

13 Mujeres Creando, *La virgen de los deseos* (Buenos Aires: Tinta Limón, 2005), 36.

14 *Porque la memoria no es puro cuento*, ed. Mujeres Creando (La Paz, Bolivia: Mujeres Creando, 2002), 8.

15 Julieta Paredes and María Galindo, with Mónica Mendoza, *¿Y si fuésemos una espejo de la otra? Por un feminismo no racista* (La Paz, Bolivia: Talleres ediciones gráficas, 1992).

16 Mujeres Creando, *Virgen de los deseos*, 41.

17 Writes Helen Álvarez, "Con el nacimiento de Mujeres Creando, surgió otra necesidad: tener un espacio propio . . . como resultado de un intenso trabajo, en julio de 1992 abrió sus puertas el Centro Cultural Feminista, 'Café Carcajada.' El azoro de la sociedad paceña no se dejó esperar, la cultura urbana no entendía el concepto de un espacio de mujeres, incluso intentaron identificarlo con un burdel," Álvarez, "El camino de Mujeres Creando: Una sucesión de estridencias," in *Porque la memoria no es puro cuento*, ed. Mujeres Creando, 12 (With the birth of Mujeres Creando, another necessity emerged: to have our own space . . . as a result of intense work, in July 1992, the Feminist Cultural Center "Cackling Café" opened. The shock in La Paz was not anticipated, the urban culture didn't understand the concept of a space for women, they even attempted to label it a whorehouse).

18 *No pudieron con nosotras*, ed. Elizabeth Monasterios (La Paz, Bolivia: Plural, 2006).

19 For instance, Bartolina Sisa was executed alongside her husband, Túpac Katari, a peasant leader and direct descendant of the Incans, on September 5, 1782. Despite her belief in the rights of the indigenous *ayllus* to political and territorial sovereignty, her body was transformed into a public spectacle, as has been recorded through the written and oral traces of these events. First, an official decree stipulated that she be

paraded around the Plaza Murillo and hanged at the gallows. Second, she was to be tortured before her death as gaping spectators observed. The plaza holds the memory of her flagellation and her rape, before she was dragged through La Paz.

20 Ralph Waldo Emerson, "Gifts," in *The Logic of the Gift: Toward an Ethic of Generosity*, ed. Alan D. Schrift (New York: Routledge, 1997), 25.

21 C. A. Gregory, *Gifts and Commodities*, cited in ibid., 2.

22 Ibid., 26.

23 Mujeres Creando.

24 Estermann, *Filosofía andina*, 132.

25 Ketal Hipermercado, whose slogan is "Tú lo vales" ("You deserve it") is the largest supermarket chain in Bolivia, with eight different outlets. They have now expanded to Chile. "KETAL nació en el año 1986, y en el 2008, luego de lograr la representación de la firma nacional CASA IDEAS, abrió la tienda de decoración KETAL HOGAR. Fue también parte de la creación del primer Mega Center en Bolivia, donde construyó el que se considera el más grande supermercado en La Paz, con más de 8.000 metros cuadrados y una inversión total de cinco millones de dólares," "Supermercado boliviano Ketal ingresará a Chile," Santa Cruz, *El Día*, November 4, 2010, http://www.eldia.com.bo/index.php?cat=1&pla=3&id_articulo =45288 (accessed August 25, 2013) (KETAL opened in 1986, and in 2008, after gaining representation by the national firm "House of Ideas," they opened the decorative store "Ketal Home." This was also part of the creation of the first Mega Center in Bolivia, where they constructed what is considered to be the largest supermarket in La Paz, more than eight thousand square meters, with an investment of five million dollars).

26 For instance, one older woman says with a sigh, "Ya he comprado. No puedo comprar todos los días" (*Mujeres Creando Colección de videos:* Acción 4. La Paz, Bolivia, 1998) (I've already bought one. I cannot buy one every day). Another one says, "No tengo nada de monedas para darte" (Ibid.) (I don't have any change to give you), even though neither one was ever asked for money.

27 Paredes, *Hilando fino*, 39.

28 The Mattel Company produced the first Barbie in 1959.

29 For criticism of Barbie, see Marlys Pearson and Paul R. Mullins, "Domesticating Barbie: An Archaeology of Barbie Material Culture and Domestic Ideology," *International Journal of Historical Archaeology* 3, no. 4 (December 1999): 225–259, which presents a balanced view of the reductionist "symbolism" of Barbie in U.S. culture. Also the more recent, "We're Not Barbie Dolls: Tweens Transform a Feminine Icon," by Louise Collins et al., *Feminist Formations* 24, no. 1 (2012): 102–126; or "La Princesa Plástica: Hegemonic and Oppositional Representations of Latinidad in Hispanic Barbie," by Karen Goldman, in *From Bananas to Buttocks: The Latina Body in Popular Film and Culture,* ed. Myra Mendible (Austin: University of Texas Press, 2007), 263–278, provide newer critiques of Barbie, and of shortcomings of Hispanic Barbie in a U.S. cultural context.

30 Guy Debord, *The Society of the Spectacle*, trans. Donald Nicholson-Smith (New York: Zone Books, 1995), 29.

31 Ibid., 24.

32 Schiwy Freya, "Decolonization and the Question of Subjectivity," *Cultural Studies* 21, nos. 2–3 (March 2007): 271.

33 Ángel Rama, *La ciudad letrada*, prologue by Hugo Achugar (Montevideo, Uruguay: ARCA Press. 1998), 52.

34 *Porque la memoria no es puro cuento*, ed. Mujeres Creando, 205.
35 Gamaliel Churata, *El pez de oro* (*Retablos del Laykhakuy*), ed. José Luis Ayala (Puno, Peru: Corporación de formento y promoción social y económica de Puno, 1987), 1:93.
36 Mujeres Creando, *Grafiteadas*, 48; Sor Juana Inés de la Cruz, "Hombres necios" in *Las obras completas* (Mexico City, Mexico: Editorial Porrúa, 1997), 109.
37 Mujeres Creando also cites Alfonsina Storni and additional poems by Sor Juana Inés de la Cruz.
38 Carrie Noland, *Agency and Embodiment: Performing Gestures/Producing Culture* (Cambridge, MA: Harvard University Press, 2009), 1.
39 Mujeres Creando, *Virgen de los deseos*, 78
40 The book carries the same title, *Ninguna mujer nace para puta*, by María Galindo and Sonia Sánchez, and was published in 2007 by Argentinian press, la vaca: http://www.mujerescreando.org/pag/calles/2007argentina/prostituyentes2007.htm (accessed March 29, 2018).
41 Rosi Braidotti, *Transpositions: On Nomadic Ethics* (Cambridge: Polity Press, 2012), 3.
42 See Elizabeth Monasterios's chapter "Los desafíos del feminismo autónomo en sociedades que arrastran pasados coloniales" (The challenges of autonomous feminism in societies defined by colonial pasts), in her edited book *No pudieron con nosotras* for a more elaborate explanation (153–172).
43 Julieta Paredes, *Con un montón de palabras* (La Paz, Bolivia: Ediciones Mujeres Creando, 2000), 1.
44 Paredes, *Con un montón de palabras*, 2.
45 Ibid., 43.
46 Julieta Paredes, *Hilando fino: Perspectives from Communitarian Feminism*, trans. Margaret Cerullo and Antonia Carcelén (La Paz, Bolivia: Comunidad Mujeres Creando Comunidad, 2015).
47 Paredes, *Hilando fino*, 13.
48 Ibid., 32.
49 Ibid., 34.
50 Silvia Rivera Cusicanqui, "Chhixinakax utxiwa. Una reflexión sobre prácticas y discursos descolonizadores," in *Modernidad y pensamiento descolonizador: Memoria del Seminario Internacional*, comp. Mario Yapu (La Paz, Bolivia: Universidad para la Investigación Estratégica en Bolivia (U-PIEB), 2006), 12.
51 Ibid., 3.
52 Translations of these terms are imperfect, but in general, reflect indigenous cosmovisions that espouse living in harmony with nature and with each other.
53 Estermann, *Pachasofía*, 97–98.
54 Javier Medina, *Suma Qamaña: por una convivialidad postindustrial* (La Paz, Bolivia: Garza Azul Editores, 2006), 79.
55 Irene Silverblatt's book *Sun, Moon, and Witches: Gender Ideologies and Class in Colonial* (Princeton, NJ: Princeton University Press, 1987) traces the "interplay between political hierarchy and gender, as first the Incas and then the Spanish consolidated their rule" (ibid., xix). Gender systems were at work already within the Incan Empire, and they had implications on the class structure as well, as she argues through her engagement with a range of colonial sources.
56 Paredes, *Hilando Fino*, 34.
57 Ibid., 28.

58 Ibid., 38.

59 Ibid., 38.

60 Ibid., 48.

61 Ibid., 13–14.

62 Ibid., 9.

63 The expression "q'amaña," with or without the apostrophe, loosely translates as "vivir" or "viviendo," and therefore, with "suma," "the good life/living a good life." For a synthesis of the ways in which "suma qamaña" has been used in the new constitution in Bolivia see *Transiciones hacia el vivir bien o la construcción de un nuevo proyecto político en el estado plurinacional boliviano*, ed. Katu Arkonada (La Paz: Bolivia, December 2012). While Paredes uses an apostrophe, as in suma q'amaña, it is the same Spanish translation, "vivir bien."

64 Paredes, *Hilando fino*, trans. Cerullo and Carcelén, as cited by Paredes, 43.

65 Ibid., 18.

66 Ibid., 12.

67 Paredes, *Con un montón de palabras*, 86.

Chapter 5 Magda Portal's Bare Life in the Sea

1 Magda Portal, *Obra poética completa*, ed. Daniel R. Reedy (Lima: Fondo de Cultura Económica, 2010); "Canto a Lima," in *Obras completas*, 363, lines 1–3.

2 Today, the Rímac River in Peru is the largest potable water source for Lima and Callao.

3 Rosi Braidotti, *Transpositions: On Nomadic Ethics* (Cambridge: Polity Press, 2012), 37.

4 The decentering of *Anthropos* challenges therefore the separation of *bios*, life as the prerogative of humans, from *zoë*, the life of animals and nonhuman entities, writes Rosi Braidotti, "The Critical Posthumanities; Or, Is Medianatures to Naturecultures as *Zoë* Is to *Bios*?" *Cultural Politics* 12, no. 3 (November 2016): 381. Portal is relevant to this conversation because the subject up until her era had been underwritten by exclusions: of the female, as well as the indigenous. I agree, as Myriam Gonzales Smith asserts, that Magda Portal "se considera enfáticamente feminista," Gonzales Smith, *Poética e ideología en Magda Portal: Otras dimensiones de la vanguardia en Latinoamérica* (Lima: IEP, Instituto de Estudios Peruanos, 2007), 17 (is considered emphatically feminist) but by a feminism that comes from having always been surrounded by men.

5 In her book *José Carlos Mariátegui's Unfinished Revolution: Politics, Poetics, and Change in 1920s Peru* (Lewisburg, PA: Bucknell University Press, 2014), Melisa Moore notes, "Arguably then female subjects across class and ethnic divides enjoyed greater social and sexual mobility, within and between public and private spheres during the *oncenio*, than did their predecessors" (ibid., 166). This is certainly true, and at the same time, this mobility does not mean that their feminist contribution was the only contribution of their poetry.

6 See Vicky Unruh's chapter "Ad-Libs by the Women of Amauta: Magda Portal and María Wiesse," in *Performing Women and Modern Literary Culture in Latin America: Intervening Acts* (Austin: University of Texas Press, 2006), 165–194.

7 To clarify, deemed subversive by the Leguía government, Magda Portal and many of the *Amauta* collaborators were exiled in 1927 (Gonzales-Smith, *Poética e ideología en Magda Portal*, 74).

8 The white male body ostensibly "does not matter," because it is the material norm from which other bodies differ, making its own materiality negligible.

9 In her essential biography of Portal, Kathleen Weaver speaks about the tension between life and death in Portal's poetry as well as the tension "between wanting to reveal and the same time wanting to destroy her writing." The desire to be legibly seen and to remain under the radar or to keep writing to oneself, is metaphoric of the bios/zoë distinction, Weaver, *Peruvian Rebel: The World of Magda Portal, with a Selection of her Poems* (University Park: Pennsylvania State University Press, 2009), 9.

10 I am indebted to Jorge Coronado's work in *The Andes Imagined: Indigenismo, Society, and Modernity* (Pittsburgh: University of Pittsburgh Press, 2009), as a work that helped me think through the ways in which Portal also participated in a local modernity in and around Lima that both did and did not represent her "interior life" based on the decisions she made around what she would share and how others, like José Carlos Mariátegui, chose to portray and frame her. The idealized version of the *indio* that Coronado takes up, particularly in chapter 4 of his book, is resonant with the idealized version of Portal that Mariátegui depicts, as I discuss in this chapter.

11 Rosi Braidotti, "Critical Posthumanities," 232. As an example of this phenomenon, Portal is interested in Flora Tristán, nineteenth-century traveler and feminist icon *avant la letter.* She is no longer a breathing political subject, and yet, she is a network of ideas, of publications, of work, as is Magda Portal, now.

12 Mauricio Duarte's chapter on Portal in *Contra narrativas del paisaje*: *Magda Portal, Pedro Nel Gómez, Fernando Vallejo y Blancha Wiethuchter* (Madrid: Pliegos D.L., 2013) makes the point, as well, that landscape in Portal's work, especially in the "journal of four names," *Trampolín-Hangar-Rascacielos-Timonel* (1924–1925), was transformed from static genre produced by the cultura criolla to a renovated form that reflected a neo-Andean version. This version broke with artistic convention to fragment the landscape into its raw material form as "nature" (111–113).

13 Here I am referring to the expansive work of Eduardo Viveiros de Castro and his development and revision of anthropology not as the study of "culture" but rather as the study of ontologies, based on his work in the Brazilian Amazon. This is elaborated upon in the conclusion.

14 I refer readers to Kathleen Weaver's and Daniel R. Reedy's books.

15 Kathleen Weaver, *Peruvian Rebel: The World of Magda Portal, with a Selection of her Poems* (University Park: Pennsylvania State University Press, 2009), 54.

16 Mirko Lauer, *La polémica del vanguardismo 1916–1928* (Lima: Fondo Editorial de la Universidad Nacional Mayor de San Marcos, 2001), vii.

17 *Mujeres de Amauta*, ed. Sara B. Guardia and Angela Ramos (Caracas, Venezuela: Fundación Biblioteca Ayacucho. 2014), xvi.

18 The avant-gardes, at least in principle, were about new origins. At times, Portal would seem to eradicate the need for genealogical origins in her poetry. However, Weaver is also right to observe that "the early loss of her father may also have predisposed her to attach herself to powerful men, to whom she could look as mentors in the battle for social reform (Weaver, *Peruvian Rebel*, 5).

19 Daniel R. Reedy, *Magda Portal, La pasionaria peruana: biografía intelectual* (Lima: Ediciones Flora Tristán, 2000), 1.

20 Peter F. Klarén, *Modernization, Dislocation, and Aprismo: Origins of the Peruvian Aprista Party, 1870–1932* (Austin: University of Texas Press, 1973), xvii.

21 Weaver, *Peruvian Rebel*, 9–10.

22 Two additional international events influenced the political climate of Peru: the Mexican Revolution, and the University Reform Movement in Argentina. Víctor Raúl Haya de la Torre founded APRA in 1924 while he was in exile in Mexico as "a Latin American alternative to the international communism supported by the Comintern in the Soviet Union," Iñigo García-Bryce, "Revolucionaria peregrina: Magda Portal, el exilio y el APRA como partido continental, 1926–1945," 68, http://www.udesa.edu.ar/files (accessed June 24, 2014). Haya de la Torre (1895, born in Trujillo like Vallejo) was one of Portal's primary interlocutors and collaborators, and a dominating force in early twentieth-century Peruvian politics. He was responsible for leading the general strike of 1918–1919, when workers demanded an eight-hour workday. In order to rally support for the party, Haya de la Torre primarily garnered allegiance from labor unions, the middle class, and peasants against Leguía's conservative regime. When he returned to Lima in 1931 he announced his candidacy for president of the Republic under the APRA party ticket, with his now famous line, "solo el Aprismo podrá salvarnos" (only el Aprismo will save us). As Klarén notes, "To thousands of Peruvians in 1931 that emotion-packed phrase touched a vital cord" (*Modernization*, xi).

23 Reedy, *Magda Portal, La pasionaria peruana*, 2.

24 Ibid., 3.

25 Magda Portal, "Andamios de vida," ed. José Carlos Mariátegui, *Amauta* 5 (1927): 12.

26 José Carlos Mariátegui's most well-known essay, arguably, bears this title "El problema del indio," and is included in *Siete ensayos sobre la interpretación de Perú* (1928). For Mariátegui, the redistribution of land is the first step in securing a more just future for the indigenous populations of Peru.

27 David Nugent, *Locating Capitalism in Time and Space: Global Restructurings, Politics, and Identity* (Stanford, CA: Stanford University Press, 2002), 150.

28 Gonzales-Smith, *Poética e ideología Ideología en Magda Portal*, 33.

29 She is not the only one to describe her art as an organ; this was a tendency of the era.

30 Portal, "Andamios de vida," 12.

31 The citations come from *Amauta*, Portal, "Andamios de la vida," 12; as a side note, Mirko Lauer signals the shared "fonofobia," as he calls it, that Portal and Vallejo experienced (Lauer, *La polémica del vanguardismo 1916–1928*, 15).

32 Portal, "Andamios de vida," 12.

33 Ibid.

34 Toward the end of 1927, Portal was deported to Cuba after President Leguía declared that the Amauta group was subversive and Communist. She later was deported to Mexico, where she reconnected with Haya de la Torre (Gonzales Smith, *Poética e ideología en Magda Portal*, 74).

35 Magda Portal, *El nuevo poema i su orientación económica* (Mexico City: Ediciones APRA, 1928), 24.

36 Ibid., 26.

37 Portal's break with the APRA party is documented most explicitly in her novel *La Trampa* (Lima: Editorial Poma, 1982), which criticizes the ways in which she interpreted the hypocrisy of Haya del Torre.

38 Magda Portal, "Mensaje," in *Obra poética completa*, ed. Daniel R. Reedy (Lima: Fondo de Cultura Económica, 2010), 260, lines 5–8.

39 Portal is not the only one to use the metaphor of art as another form of life. Mariátegui as well describes, "Lo que existe en mí ahora, existía embrionariamente y larvadamente cuando yo tenía veinte años y escribía disparates de los cuales no sé por qué la gente se acuerda todavía" (*Mujeres de Amauta*, ed. Guardia and Ramos, viii) (What exists with me now, existed before embryonically and larvally when I was twenty and I wrote random pieces, pieces that I don't know why people still remember).

40 Mariátegui, *Siete ensayos*, 294.

41 Weaver, *Peruvian Rebel*, xiiv.

42 Horacio Legrás, *Literature and Subjection: The Economy of Writing and Marginality in Latin America* (Pittsburgh: University of Pittsburgh Press, 2008), 19.

43 Ibid., 18–19.

44 Mihai Grünfeld, "Voces femeninas de la vanguardia: El compromiso de Magda Portal," *Revista de crítica literaria latinoamericana* 26, no. 51 (2000): 72.

45 Magda Portal, "Identidad," in *Obra poética completa*, ed. Daniel R. Reedy (Lima: Fondo de Cultura Económica. 2010), 212, lines 1–3.

46 See Moore's book, *The Unfinished Revolution*, for the most comprehensive elaboration of the relationship between Mariátegui and Portal.

47 Mariátegui, *Siete ensayos*, 294.

48 Ibid., 297.

49 Magda Portal writes, "Como un homenaje a la amistad que me unió con José Carlos Mariátegui en mis años juvéniles y que duró hasta la muerte del ilustre ideólogo, quiero perpetuar aquí la nota publicada en su libro *Siete ensayos de la realidad peruana*," Portal, *Constancia del ser* (Lima: Taller Gráfica Villanueva, 1965), 9 (As homage to the friendship that united me with José Carlos Mariátegui in my younger years and that lasted until this illustrious ideologue's death, I want to revisit here the section published in his book *Seven essays on Peru's reality*). She adds that "Nada podría ser más auspicioso para este libro . . . que el juicio de este maestro" (ibid.) (Nothing could be more auspicious for this book . . . than the opinion of this master).

50 Mariátegui, *Siete ensayos*, 297.

51 Ibid., 294–295.

52 Vicky Unruh, *Latin American Vanguards: The Art of Contentious Encounters* (Berkeley: University of California Press, 1994), 130.

53 Gonzales-Smith, *Poética e ideología en Magda Portal*, 103.

54 Magda Portal, "Un pálido reflejo," in *Obra poética completa*, ed. Daniel Reedy (Lima: Fondo de Cultura Económica), 125–126.

55 Ibid.

56 Frantz Fanon, *Black Skin, White Masks*, trans. Richard Philcox (New York: Grove Press, 2008), 109.

57 Ibid., 112.

58 Giorgio Agamben, "To Whom Is Poetry Addressed?" trans. Daniel Heller-Roazen, *New Observations* 130 (2014): 11.

59 Julio Ortega, *César Vallejo: La escritura del devenir* (Lima: Taurus, 2014), 29.

60 Diana Fuss, *Dying Modern: A Meditation on Elegy* (London and Durham, NC: Duke University Press, 2013), 55.

61 Unruh recuperates the female voices of the Latin American avant-gardes in her book *Performing Women*, 2006. Her chapter on Magda Portal and María Wiesse unearths two of the more present but marginalized female voices included in José Carlos Mariátegui's journal *Amauta* (1926–1930).

62 I cite 1985 because the last poem in Portal's collection, *Obra poética completa*, is dated accordingly.

63 Agamben, "To Whom Is Poetry Addressed?" 11.

64 Túpac Amaru was forced to watch the execution of his comrades and family members, including his wife and key confidante, Micaela Bastidas, whose tongue was cut out before she was strangled. Executioners then tortured José Gabriel at length and tied him to four horses to be quartered. When his limbs did not separate from his torso he was beheaded. The arms, legs, and heads of José Gabriel and Micaela were displayed throughout the viceroyalty. See Charles F. Walker, *The Túpac Amaru Rebellion* (Cambridge, MA: Belknap Harvard, 2016), for a comprehensive account of this moment in Andean history.

65 Magda Portal, "Palabras a Micaela Bastidas," in *Obras poéticas completas*, 289, lines 14–16.

66 Eva María Valero Juan summarizes Portal's interest in Micaela Bastidas: "Ésta fue la primera gran heroina de la libertad que, con esta rebelión, trató no sólo de liberar a su pueblo de la explotación, sino también de restablecer la tradición indígena—de herencia prehispánica—de participación de la mujer en la vida social y política," Valero Juan, "De Micaela Bastidas a Magda Portal: Recuperaciones críticoliterarias de las Independistas de Perú," *América sin nombre* 13–14 (2009): 66 (She [Bastidas] was the first great heroine of freedom that, with this rebellion, tried not only to free the people from exploitation but to also reestablish the indigenous tradition—of prehispanic inheritance—of female participation in social and political life).

67 Portal, "Palabras a Micaela Bastidas," in *Obras poéticas completas*, 291, lines 52–54.

68 Ibid., 289, lines 20–21.

69 Ibid., 291, lines 77–78.

70 Ibid., 291, lines 85–90.

71 Portal, "Imprecación," in *Obras poéticas completas*, 282.

72 Agamben, "To Whom Is Poetry Addressed?" 8.

73 The title of Portal's book is taken up later by Román Hernández Matos's biography on Micaela Bastidas titled, *Micaela Bastidas, precursora* (1981). Portal's book on Tristán was first published in 1945 and republished in 1983 in honor of International Women's Day.

74 Portal, *Flora Tristán*, 9.

75 Ibid., 13.

76 Etymology Dictionary, https://www.etymonline.com/word/hymn (accessed March 30, 2018).

77 Portal, "Himno a Flora Tristán," in *Obras poética completa*, 387–388.

78 Ibid., 387–388.

79 Ibid., 387.

80 Diana Fuss, *Dying Modern*, 78.

81 Ibid., 1.

82 Ibid., 78.

83 Portal; all previous quotes from *Obra poética completa*, 84.

84 Ibid.

85 Florencia Ferreiro de Cassone writes, "El haber nacido en Barranco produjo en Portal un amor y una constante preocupación por el mar, la cual se refleja en su obra poética, revelando un concepto de autoidentidad simbiótica entre ella y el mar," Ferreiro de Cassone, "Magda Portal: Una voz femenina en el aprismo,"

Cuadernos Americanos 128 (2009): 26 (Having been born in el Barranco led to a constant love and worry for the sea, which is reflected in her poetry, revealing a conception of self-identity based on the symbiotic relationship between her and the sea).

86 Portal, "Elegías trémulas," in *Obra poética completa*, 55.

87 Portal, "Clamor," in *Obra poética completa*, 154–155.

88 Portal, "Poema 17," in *Obra poética completa*, 113.

89 Rosi Braidotti, *Transpositions*, 41.

90 Portal, "Las palabras oscuras," in *Obra poética completa*, 271.

91 Ibid.

92 Portal, "Dudas," in *Obra poética completa*, 316–317.

93 Portal, "Clamor," in *Obra poética completa*, 155–156.

94 Portal, "Caminar,"in *Obra poética completa*, 342–343.

95 García-Bryce "Revolucionaria peregrina," 1.

96 In his book *Contra narrativas del paisaje,* Mauricio Duarte makes the argument that the landscape in South America becomes denaturalized and activated at different historical moments (in his analysis, the 1920s and the 1980s) as a tool for animating political action and revolution. In Duarte's interpretation, Portal presents us with a visceral landscape that prompts readers to configure our own interpretation of how the landscape abandons the sublime and comes to be charged with political and revolutionary weight. In her work, particularly in the "magazine of four names," *THRT: Trampolín, Hangar, Rascacielos*, and *Timonel* (1929), Duarte argues that Portal, "exhibe y explota una poesía sustentada en un paisaje que fluye desde el subsuelo para convocar la acción política y que incomoda el carácter contemplativo y pasivo de sus conterráneos," Duarte, *Contra narrativas del paisaje: Magda Portal, Pedro Nel Gómez, Fernando Vallejo y Blanca Wiethuchter* (Madrid: Pliegos, 2013), 29 (exhibits and exploits a poetry sustained in the landscape that flows from below the soil to convoke political action that discomforts the contemplative and passive character of her co-inhabitants).

97 Gustavo Valcárcel, "Magda Portal, la poeta de los pobres ha muerto," *República*, July 12, 1989, 8.

98 In contrast, in *El Comercio* on July 14, 1989, there was only a tiny blurb in the obituaries section that read: "DEFUNCION: El Instituto Nacional de Cultura cumple con el penoso deber de participar el sensible fallecimiento de la ilustre escritora nacional: MAGDA PORTAL, acaecido en la ciudad de Lima el día 11 de julio del año en curso" (DEATH: The National Institute of Culture is pained to share the news of the death of the illustrious national writer: MAGDA PORTAL, who passed away in Lima July 11th of this year), 9.

99 Portal, "Génesis de la Vida," in *Obra poética completa*, 119.

100 Emanuele Coccia, "Speaking Breathing," trans. Claudia Chierichini, *New Observations* 130 (2014): 17.

101 César Vallejo, *Trilce* "LXIX," in *Obras completas / The Complete Poetry: A Bilingual Edition*, trans. Clayton Eshleman (Berkeley: University of California Press, 2008), 306, lines 1–2.

Conclusion

1 Michelle Clayton, *Poetry in Pieces: César Vallejo and Lyric Modernity* (Berkeley: University of California Press, 2011), 15.

2 Political Database of the America (PDBA), Edmund A. Walsh School of Foreign Service, Georgetown University, http://pdba.georgetown.edu/Constitutions/constudies.html (accessed March 12, 2018).

3 Constitución Política del Estado Plurinacional de Bolivia, http://www.harmonywithnatureun.org/content/documents/159Bolivia%20Consitucion.pdf (accessed March 12, 2018).

4 Eduardo Gudynas, "Los progresismos sudamericanos: Ideas y prácticas, avances y límites," in *Rescatar la esperanza: Más allá del neoliberalismo y el progresimo* (Barcelona: EntrePueblos, 2016), 36.

5 Ibid.

6 Ibid.

7 Rosi Braidotti, "The Critical Posthumanities; Or, Is Medianatures to Naturecultures as *Zoë* Is to *Bios*?" *Cultural Politics* 12, no. 3 (November 2016): 381.

8 See Eduardo Viveiros de Castro, "Cosmological Deixis and Amerindian Perspectivism," *Journal of the Royal Anthropological Institute* 4 (September 1998): 469–488 for a comprehensive discussion on perspectivism within the Amazon region of Brazil.

9 Jorge Marcone, "Latin American Literature at the Rise of Environmentalism: Urban Ecological Thinking in José María Arguedas's *The Foxes*," *Comparative Literature Studies* 50, no. 1 (November 2013): 68.

10 Colectivo Bufeo, Exhibit catalog, "Del tiempo en el que humanos y animales todavía no se distinguían" (Lima, Peru, 2017). This exhibit ran from January 21 to March 26, 2017. The collective's public Facebook page with many examples of their art is found here: https://www.facebook.com/Bufeoarte (accessed April 1, 2018).

Bibliography

Agamben, Giorgio. *The Coming Community*. Translated by Michael Hardt. Minneapolis: University of Minnesota, 1993.

———. *Homo sacer: Sovereign Power and Bare Life*. Translated by Daniel Heller-Roazen. Stanford, CA: Stanford University Press, 1995.

———. "To Whom Is Poetry Addressed?" Translated by Daniel Heller-Roazen. *New Observations* 130 (2014): 11.

Ahmed, Sara. "Orientations Matter." In *New Materialisms: Ontology, Agency, and Politics*, edited by Diana H. Coole and Samantha Frost, 234–357. Durham, NC: Duke University Press, 2010.

———. *Queer Phenomenology: Orientations, Objects, Others*. Durham, NC: Duke University Press, 2006.

Alaimo, Stacy. "Sustainable This, Sustainable That: New Materialisms, Posthumanism, and Unknown Futures." *PMLA* 127, no. 3 (May 2012): 558–564.

Albornoz, Pedro. "Castigadores domésticos moderados." In *Catálogo: Castigadores domésticos moderados*, edited by Alejandra Dorado, 2–3. Cochabamba, Bolivia: 2008.

Alva Castro, Luis, ed. *Antenor Orrego: la unidad continental y los orígenes de la modernidad en el Perú*. Lima: Fondo Editorial del Congreso del Perú, 2009.

Álvarez, Helen. "El camino de Mujeres Creando: Una sucesión de estridencias." In *Porque la memoria no es puro cuento*, edited by Mujeres Creando, 7–12. La Paz, Bolivia: Mujeres Creando, 2002.

Andradi, Esther, and Ana María Portugal. "Magda Portal, escritora y política." In *Ser mujer en el Perú*, edited by Esther Andradi and Ana María Portugal, 209–232. Lima: Mujer y Autonomía, 1978.

Ankersmit, F. R. (Franklin Rudolf). *Aesthetic Politics: Political Philosophy beyond Fact and Value*. Stanford, CA: Stanford University Press, 1996.

Archibald, Priscilla. *Imagining Modernity in the Andes*. Lewisburg, PA: Bucknell University Press, 2011.

Arguedas, Alcides. *Pueblo enfermo* (1909). Chile: Ediciones Ercilla, 1937.

Arguedas, José María. *Diamantes y pedernales* (1954). Lima: Editorial Horizonte, 2011.

———. *El Sexto* (1961). Madrid: Drácena, 2016.

———. *El zorro de arriba y el zorro de abajo* (1971). Edited by Eve-Marie Fell. Edición Crítica. Paris: ALLCA XX, 1996.

———. *Katatay, Temblar*. Edited by Sybila A. Arguedas. Lima: I. N. C, 1972.

———. *Las cartas de Arguedas*. Edited by John V. Murra and Mercedes López-Baralt. Lima: Pontificia Universidad Católica del Perú, Fondo Editorial, 1996.

———. "Llamado a algunos doctores." *El Comercio*, Sección "Dominical," July 10, 1966.

———. *Los ríos profundos*. Edited by Ricardo González Vigil. 2nd ed. Madrid: Catedra, 1998.

———. "No soy un aculturado." In *El zorro de arriba y el zorro de abajo*, edited by Eve-Marie Fell, 256–258. Edición Crítica. Paris: ALLCA XX, 1996.

———. *Obras completas*. Vol 5. Lima, Editorial horizonte, 1983.

Arkonada, Katu, ed. *Transiciones hacia el vivir bien o la construcción de un nuevo proyecto político en el estado plurinacional boliviano*. La Paz, Bolivia: Icaria Editorial, December 2012.

Arrington, Melvin S., Jr. "Magda Portal, Vanguard Critic." In *Reinterpreting the Spanish American Essay: Women Writers of the 19th and 20th Centuries*, edited by Doris Meyer, 148–156. Austin: University of Texas Press, 1995.

Asamblea constituyente de Bolivia. *Constitución del estado plurinacional de Bolivia*. El Alto, Bolivia. 2009. http://www.justicia.gob.bo/index.php/normas/doc_download/35-nueva-constitucion-politica-del-estado (accessed August 12, 2014).

Assies, Willem. "David versus Goliath in Cochabamba: Water Rights, Neoliberalism, and the Revival of Social Protest in Bolivia." *Latin American Perspectives* 30, no. 3 (May 2003): 14–36.

Bachner, Andrea. "Anagrams in Psychoanalysis: Retroping Concepts by Sigmund Freud, Jacques Lacan, and Jean-Francois Lyotard." *Comparative Literature Studies* 40, no. 1 (2003): 1–25.

Badiou, Alain. *The Age of the Poets: And Other Writings on Twentieth-Century Poetry and Prose*. Edited and translated by Bruno Bosteels. New York: Verso, 2014.

Bareiro Saguier, Rubén. "José María Arguedas o la palabra herida." In *El zorro de arriba y el zorro de abajo*, edited by Eve-Marie Fell, xv–xx. Edición Crítica. Paris: ALLCA XX, 1996.

Barlow, Maude, Sam Bozzo, and Tony Clarke. *BlueGold World Water Wars*. Directed by Sam Bozzo. Irvine, CA: Purple Turtle Films, 2008.

Bastien, Joseph. *Qollahuaya Rituals: An Ethnographic Account of the Symbolic Relations of Man and Land in an Andean Village*. Ithaca, NY: Cornell University Press, 1973.

Bendayán, Christian. "Del tiempo en que humanos y animales todavía no se distinguían." Catalogue. Lima, Bufeo Art Collective, 2017.

Bennett, Jane. "Encounters with an Art Thing." *Evental Aesthetics* 3, no. 3 (2015): 91–110. http://eventalaesthetics.net/vital-materialism-vol-3-no-3-2015/jane-bennett-encounters-with-an-art-thing/ (accessed July 4, 2016).

———. *Vibrant Matter: A Political Ecology of Things*. Durham, NC: Duke University Press, 2010.

Bergson, Henri. *The Creative Mind*. Translated by Mabelle L. Andison. New York: Philosophical Library, 1946.

———. *Matter and Memory*. Translated by Nancy Margaret Paul and W. Scott Palmer. New York: Zone Books, 1988.

Bermúdez Gallegos, Marta. "Magda Portal: Eterna rebelde." In *Las desobedientes:*

Mujeres de Nuestra América, edited by Betty Osorio and María Mercedes Jaramillo, 288–308. Bogotá, Colombia: Panamericana, 1997.

Beverley, John. *Latinamericanism after 9/11*. Durham, NC: Duke University Press, 2011.

———. "Prefacio." In *No pudieron con nosotras: El desafío del feminismo autónomo de "Mujeres Creando,"* edited by Elizabeth Monasterios P., 11–16. Pittsburgh: University of Pittsburgh; La Paz: Plural editores, 2006.

Braidotti, Rosi. "Animals, Anomalies, and Inorganic Others." *PMLA* 124, no. 2 (2009): 526–532.

———. "The Critical Posthumanities; Or, Is Medianatures to Naturecultures as *Zoë* Is to *Bios*?" *Cultural Politics* 12, no. 3 (November 2016): 380–390.

———. "Interview with Rosi Braidotti." In *New Materialisms: Interviews and Cartographies*, edited by Graham Harman and Bruno Latour, 19–32. Ann Arbor: University of Michigan Library, Open Humanities Press, 2012.

———. *Transpositions: On Nomadic Ethics*. Cambridge: Polity Press, 2012.

Brotherston, Gordon. *The Emergence of the Latin American Novel*. Cambridge: Cambridge University Press, 1979.

Bueno, Raúl. *Antonio Cornejo Polar y los avatares de la cultura latinoamericana*. Lima: Fondo Editorial, Universidad Nacional Mayor de San Marcos, 2004.

Bufeo (Art Collective). "Del tiempo en el que los humanos y los animales no se distinguían." Poster to promote exhibit, Lima, Peru, 2017.

Bürger, Peter. "Avant-Garde and Neo-Avant-Garde: An Attempt to Answer Certain Critics of *Theory of the Avant-Garde*." Translated by Bettina Brandt and Daniel Purdy. *New Literary History* 41, no. 4 (Autumn 2010): 695–715.

———. *Theory of the Avant-Garde*. Translated by Michael Shaw. Foreword by Jochen Schulte-Sasse. Minneapolis: University of Minnesota Press, 1984.

Bush, Matthew, and Luis Hernán Castañeda, "Introducción: Un asombro renovado." In *Un asombro renovado: Vanguardias contemporáneas en América Latina*, edited by Matthew Bush and Luis Hernán Castañeda, 9–17. Madrid: Iberoamericana; Frankfurt am Main: Vervuert, 2017.

———. *Un asombro renovado: Vanguardias contemporáneas en América Latina*. Madrid: Iberoamericana; Frankfurt am Main: Vervuert, 2017.

Bustamante, Cecilia. "Intelectuales peruanas de la generación de José Carlos Mariátegui." *NS, NorthSouth* 7, no. 13 (1982): 111–126.

Butler, Judith. *Precarious Life: The Powers of Mourning and Violence*. London: Verso, 2003.

———. *Undoing Gender*. New York: Routledge, 2004.

Carpentier, Alejo. *Los pasos perdidos*. La Habana: Consejo nacional de cultura, 1953.

Castro-Gómez, Santiago. "(Post)Coloniality for Dummies: Latin American Perspectives on Modernity, Coloniality, and the Geopolitics of Knowledge." In *Coloniality at Large: Latin America and the Postcolonial Debate*, edited by Mabel Moraña, Enrique Dussel, and Carlos A. Jáuregui, 259–285. Durham, NC: Duke University Press, 2008.

Castro-Klarén, Sara. *El mundo mágico de José María Arguedas*. Lima: Instituto de Estudios peruanos. 1973.

———. "Like a Pig When He's Thinkin'." In *The Fox from Up Above and the Fox from Down Below*, edited by José María Arguedas, Frances H. Barraclough, and Julio Ortega, 307–323. Pittsburgh: University of Pittsburgh Press, 2000.

———. "Posting Letters: Writing in the Andes and the Paradoxes of the Postcolonial

Debate." In *Coloniality at Large: Latin America and the Postcolonial Debate*, edited by Mabel Moraña, Enrique Dussel, and Carlos A. Jáuregui, 130–157. Durham, NC: Duke University Press, 2008.

Cerna-Bazán, José. *Sujeto a cambio: De las relaciones del texto y la sociedad en la escritura de César Vallejo (1914–1930)*. Lima: Latinoamericana editores, 1995.

Certeau, Michel de. *The Writing of History*. Translated by Tom Conley. New York: Columbia University Press, 1988.

Chang-Rodríguez, Eugenio. *Antenor Orrego: Modernidad y culturas americanas*. Lima: Fondo Editorial del Congreso de Perú, 2004.

———"Sobre la angustia y las alteraciones linguisticas en Cesar Vallejo." *Revista de Crítica Literaria Latinoamericana* 3, no. 5 (1977): 49–55.

Churata, Gamaliel. *El pez de oro (Retablos del Laykhakuy)*. Edited by José Luis Ayala. 2 vols. Puno, Peru: Corporación de formento y promoción social y económica de Puno, 1987.

Clayton, Michelle. "'Animalestar': Animal Affections in Vallejo's Poetry." In *Politics, Poetics, Affect: Re-visioning Cesar Vallejo*, edited by Stephen M. Hart, 117–133. Cambridge: Cambridge Scholars Publishing, 2013.

———. *Poetry in Pieces: César Vallejo and Lyric Modernity*. Berkeley: University of California Press, 2011.

———. "*Trilce*'s Lyric Matters." *Revista de Estudios Hispánicos* 42, no. 1 (January 2008): 83–108.

Coccia, Emanuele. "Speaking Breathing." Translated by Claudia Chierichini. *New Observations* 130 (2014): 16–17.

Cohen, Jeffrey Jerome. *Stone: An Ecology of the Inhuman*. Minneapolis: University of Minnesota Press, 2016.

Colebrook, Claire. "Queer Vitalism." *New Formations* 68 (Spring 2009): 77–92.

Collins, Louise, et al. "We're not Barbie Dolls: Tweens Transform a Feminine Icon." *Feminist Formations* 24, no. 1 (2012): 102–126.

Colomer, Josep Maria. "Taming the Tiger: Voting Rights and Political Instability in Latin America." *Latin American Politics & Society* 46, no. 2 (Summer 2004): 29–58.

Constitución del Ecuador. 2008. http://www.asambleanacional.gov.ec/documentos/constitucion_de_bolsillo.pdf (accessed August 3, 2017).

Constitución Política del Estado Plurinacional de Bolivia. 2009. http://www.ftierra.org/index.php/generales/14-constitucion-politica-del-estado (accessed March 24, 2018).

Coole, Diana H., and Samantha Frost, eds. *New Materialisms: Ontology, Agency, and Politics*. Durham, NC: Duke University Press, 2013.

Cornejo Polar, Antonio. *Escribir en el aire: Ensayos sobre la heterogeneidad socio-cultural en las literaturas andinas*. Lima: Editorial Horizonte, 1994.

———. *Los universos narrativos de José María Arguedas*. Buenos Aires: Editorial Losada, 1974.

———. *Writing in the Air: Heterogeneity and the Persistence of Oral Tradition in Andean Literatures*. Translated by Lynda J. Jentsch. Durham, NC: Duke University Press, 2013.

Coronado, Jorge. *The Andes Imagined: Indigenismo, Society, and Modernity*. Pittsburgh: University of Pittsburgh Press, 2009.

Coyne, André. "Los nueve monstruos." In *Aproximaciones a César Vallejo*, edited by Ángel Flores, vol. 2, 305–312. New York: Las Américas, 1971.

Dean, Carolyn. *A Culture of Stone: Inka Perspectives on Rock*. Durham, NC: Duke University Press, 2010.

Debord, Guy. *The Society of the Spectacle*. Translated by Donald Nicholson-Smith. New York: Zone Books, 1995.

De Grandis, Rita. "Neo-Postcolonial Condition of the Work of Art in Latin America: Evidence from Peruvian Ethnoliterature." In *José María Arguedas: Reconsiderations for Latin American Cultural Studies*, edited by Ciro A. Sandoval and Sandra M. Boschetto-Sandoval, 53–69. Athens: Ohio University Center for International Studies, 1998.

de la Cadena, Marisol. *Earth Beings: Ecologies of Practice across Andean Worlds*. Durham, NC: Duke University Press, 2015.

———. "Indigenous Cosmopolitics in the Andes: Conceptual Reflection beyond 'Politics.'" *Cultural Anthropology* 25, no. 2 (2010): 334–370.

de la Cruz, Sor Juana Inés. *The Answer/La Respuesta*. Edited by Electa Arenal and Amanda Powell. 2nd ed. New York: Feminist Press at CUNY, 2009.

———. *Obras completas*. Prologue by Francisco Monterde. Mexico City, Mexico: Editorial Porrúa, 1997.

DeLanda, Manuel. "Interview with Rick Dolphijn and Iris van der Tuin." In *New Materialisms: Interviews and Cartographies*, edited by Graham Harman and Bruno Latour, 38–47. Ann Arbor: University of Michigan Library, Open Humanities Press, 2012. http://hdl.handle.net/2027/spo.11515701.0001.001 (accessed March 24, 2018).

Deleuze, Gilles. *Difference and Repetition*. Translated by Paul Patton. New York: Columbia University Press, 1994.

Deleuze, Gilles, and Félix Guattari. *A Thousand Plateaus: Capitalism and Schizophrenia*. Translated and foreword by Brian Massumi. Minneapolis: University of Minnesota Press, 1987.

Derrida, Jacques. *Of Grammatology*. Translated by Gayatri Chakravorty Spivak. Baltimore: Johns Hopkins University Press, 2016.

Dorado, Alejandra. *Martirio: Text and Installation*. Cochabamba, Bolivia: Centro Cultural Simón Patiño, 2006.

———. Interview with Tara Daly. Recorded. Cochabamba, Bolivia, June 15, 2008.

———. Written Interview. Email message to Tara Daly, July 29, 2014.

Dorfman, Ariel. "Arguedas y la epopeya americana." In *Recopilación de textos sobre José María Arguedas*, edited by Juan Larco, 320–329. La Habana: Centro de Investigaciones Literarias, Casa de las Americas, 1976.

Dover, K. J. "Aristophanes' Speech in Plato's Symposium." *Journal of Hellenic Studies* 86 (November 1966): 41–50.

Duarte, Mauricio. *Contra narrativas del paisaje: Magda Portal, Pedro Nel Gómez, Fernando Vallejo y Blanca Wiethuchter*. Madrid: Pliegos, 2013.

Duchesne Winter, Juan. *Comunismo literario y teorías deseantes*. La Paz, Bolivia: Plural Editores; Pittsburgh, PA: University of Pittsburgh, 2009.

Duffey, J. Patrick. "El arte humanizado y la crítica cinematográfica de Jaime Torres Bodet y César Vallejo." *Anales de la literatura hispanoamericana* 32 (2003): 37–52. http://revistas.ucm.es/index.php/ALHI/article/view/ALHI0303110037A (accessed September 28, 2018).

Dunkerley, James. *Bolivia: Revolution and the Power of History in the Present*. London: Institute for the Study of the Americas, 2007.

El Día. "Supermercado boliviano Ketal ingresará a Chile." Santa Cruz, November 4,

2010. http://www.eldia.com.bo/index.php?cat=1&pla=3&id_articulo=45288 (accessed August 25, 2013).

Eltit, Diamela. "La familia Galán." In *Cruce de lenguas: Sexualidades, diversidad y ciudadanía*, edited by Raquel Olea and Kathya Araujo, 121–143. Santiago: LOM Ediciones, 2007.

Emerson, Ralph Waldo. "Gifts." In *The Logic of the Gift: Toward an Ethic of Generosity*, edited by Alan D. Schrift, 25–27. New York: Routledge, 1997.

Escobar, Alberto. *Arguedas, o, la utopía de la lengua*. Lima: Instituto de Estudios, 1984.

———. "Introducción." In *Mesa redonda sobre Todas las sangres: 23 de junio de 1965*, 1–12. Lima: Instituto de Estudios Peruanos, 1965.

Escudero, Gonzalo. "Introducción: *Hélice*." In *Vanguardia latinoamericana*. Tomo IV, *Historia, crítica y documentos*, edited by Klaus Müller-Bergh and Gilberto Mendonça Teles, 351–352. Madrid: Iberoamericana, 2000.

Espejo Asturrizaga, Juan. *Cesar Vallejo: Itinerario de un hombre*. Lima: Seglusa, 1989.

Estermann, Josef. *Filosofía andina: Estudio intercultural de la sabiduría autóctona andina*. Quito, Ecuador: Abya Yala, 1998.

———. *Si el sur fuera el norte: chakanas interculturales entre Andes y Occidente*. Quito, Ecuador: Ediciones Abya-Yala, 2008.

Fanon, Frantz. *Black Skin, White Masks*. Translated by Richard Philcox. New York: Grove Press, 2008.

Feldman, Irina Alexandra. *Rethinking Community from Peru: The Political Philosophy of José María Arguedas*. Pittsburgh: University of Pittsburgh Press, 2014.

Ferreiro de Cassone, Florencia. "Magda Portal: una voz femenina en el aprismo." *Cuadernos Americanos* 128 (2009): 23–37.

Forgues, Roland. *José María Arguedas: del pensamiento dialéctico al pensamiento trágico. Historia de una utopía*. Lima: Ed. Horizonte, 1989.

Foucault, Michel. *Discipline and Punish: The Birth of the Prison*. Translated by Alan Sheridan. 2nd ed. New York: Vintage Books, 1995.

———. *Siete sentencias sobre el séptimo ángel*. Translation by Isidro Herrera. Madrid: Arena libros, 1999. First published as "Siete sentencias sobre el séptimo angel," in Jean-Pierre Brisset, *La grammaire logique*. Paris: Brisset, 1883.

Franco, Jean. *César Vallejo: The Dialectics of Poetry and Silence*. Cambridge: Cambridge University Press, 1976.

———. "Vallejo and the Crisis of the Thirties." *Hispania* 72, no. 1 (1989): 42–48.

Freud, Sigmund. *The Standard Edition of the Complete Psychological Works of Sigmund Freud: Early Psycho-Analytic Publications*. Vol. 5, *1900–1901: The Interpretation of Dreams (Second Part) and On Dreams*. Edited and translated by James Strachey, Anna Freud, Alix Strachey, and Alan Tyson. London: Vintage, 2001.

Fuss, Diana. *Dying Modern: A Meditation on Elegy*. London and Durham, NC: Duke University Press, 2013.

Gala, Candelas. *Poetry, Physics, and Painting in Twentieth-Century Spain*. New York: Palgrave, 2011.

Galeano, Eduardo. *Las venas abiertas de América Latina*. Revised ed. México DF: Siglo XXI, 2004.

Galindo, María. "Las exiliadas del neoliberalismo." http://www.mujerescreando.org (accessed September 30, 2018).

———. "Mujeres Creando: Evo Morales y la descolonización fálica del Estado Boliviano. http://www.mujeresenred.net (accessed September 30, 2018).

Galindo, María, and Sonia Sánchez. *Ninguna mujer nace para puta*. 2007. http://www.mujerescreando.org/pag/calles/2007argentina/prostituyentes2007.htm (accessed March 29, 2018).

García-Bryce, Iñigo. "Revolucionaria peregrina: Magda Portal, el exilio y el APRA como partido continental, 1926–1945." http://www.udesa.edu.ar/files (accessed June 24, 2014).

———. "Transnational Activist: Magda Portal and the American Popular Revolutionary Alliance (APRA), 1926–1950." *Americas* 70, no. 4 (April 2014): 667–706.

García Linera, Alvaro. "Bolivia Enshrines Natural World's Rights with Equal Status for Mother Earth." *Guardian*, April 10, 2011. https://www.theguardian.com/environment/2011/apr/10/bolivia-enshrines-natural-worlds-rights (accessed March 12, 2018).

García-Pabón, Leonardo. "Sensibilidades callejeras: El trabajo estético y político de Mujeres Creando." *Revista de crítica literaria latinoamericana* 1, no. 1 (Winter 2003): 29–58.

Gaztambide-Fernández, Rubén. "Decolonial Options and Artista/AestheSis Entanglements: An Interview with Walter Mignolo." *Decolonization: Indigeneity, Education + Society* 3, no. 1 (2014): 196–212.

Goldman, Karen. "La Princesa Plástica: Hegemonic and Oppositional Representations of Latinidad in Hispanic Barbie." In *From Bananas to Buttocks: The Latina Body in Popular Film and Culture*, edited by Myra Mendible, 263–278. Austin: University of Texas Press, 2007.

Goldstein, Daniel M. *The Spectacular City: Violence and Performance in Urban Bolivia*. Durham, NC: Duke University Press, 2004.

Gonzales Smith, Myriam. *Poética e ideología en Magda Portal: Otras dimensiones de la Vanguardia en Latinoamérica*. Lima: IEP, Instituto de Estudios Peruanos, 2007.

Grünfeld, Mihai. "Voces femeninas de la Vanguardia: El compromiso de Magda Portal." *Revista de crítica literaria latinoamericana* 26, no. 51 (2000): 67–82.

Guardia, Sara B., and Angela Ramos, eds. *Mujeres de Amauta*. Caracas, Venezuela: Fundación Biblioteca Ayacucho, 2014.

Gudynas, Eduardo. "Los progresismos sudamericanos: Ideas y practices, avances y límites." In *Rescatar la esperanza: Más allá del neoliberalismo y el progresimo*, 26–61. Barcelona: EntrePueblos, 2016.

Gudynas, Eduardo, and Oliver Balch. "Buen vivir: The Social Philosophy Inspiring Movements in South America." February 4, 2013. https://www.theguardian.com/sustainable-business/blog/buen-vivir-philosophy-south-america-eduardo-gudynas (accessed July 4, 2017).

Guerrero Arias, Patricio. *Corazonar: Una antropología comprometida con la vida: Miradas "Otras" desde Abya-Yala para la decolonización del poder, el saber y el ser*. Quito, Ecuador: Ediciones Abya-Yala, Universidad Politécnica Salesiana, 2010.

———. "Heartening the Sense of Dominant Epistemologies from Insurgent Forms of Wisdom, in Order to Build New Meanings of Existence." *Calle 14* 4, no. 5 (2010): 80–94.

Haraway, Donna. *The Companion Species Manifesto: Dogs, People, and Significant Otherness*. Chicago: Prickly Paradigm Press, 2003.

Harding, James Martin. *The Ghosts of the Avant-Garde(s): Exorcising Experimental Theater and Performance*. Ann Arbor: University of Michigan Press, 2013.

Hart, Stephen M. *César Vallejo: A Literary Biography*. London: Tamesis, 2013.

———. "César Vallejo y sus espejismos." *Romance Quarterly* 49, no. 2 (Spring 2002): 111–118.

———. Prologue. In *Politics, Poetics, Affect: Re-visioning Cesar Vallejo*, edited by Stephen M. Hart, x–xiii. Cambridge: Cambridge Scholars, 2013.

Hernández Matos, Román. *Micaela Bastidas, la precursora*. Lima: E. Carpesa, 1981.

Horswell, Michael J. *Decolonizing the Sodomite: Queer Tropes of Sexuality in Colonial Andean Culture*. Austin: University of Texas Press, 2005.

Huamán, Miguel Angel. "Una visión andina del 'Descubrimiento.'" *Literaturas Andinas* 3, nos. 5–6 (1991): 23–44.

Huidobro, Vicente. "Arte poética." In *Las vanguardias latinoamericanas: Textos programáticos y críticos*, edited by Jorge Schwartz, 100–101. Mexico City: Fondo Cultural Económico de México, 2002.

Irigaray, Luce. "Women on the Market." In *The Logic of the Gift: Toward and Ethic of Generosity*, edited by Alan D. Schrift, 174–189. New York, London: Routledge, 1997.

Jay, Martin. "Scopic Regimes of Modernity." In *Vision and Visuality*, by Hal Foster, 3–23. Seattle: Bay Press, 1988.

Kafka, Franz. "In the Penal Colony." In *The Complete Stories*, edited by Nahum N. Glatzer, translated by Edwin Muir, 165–192. New York: Penguin Random House, Schocken Kafka Library, 1995.

Klarén, Peter F. *Modernization, Dislocation, and Aprismo: Origins of the Peruvian Aprista Party, 1870-1932*. Austin: University of Texas Press, 1973.

Klein, Herbert S. *A Concise History of Bolivia*. Cambridge: Cambridge University Press, 2003.

Kohl, Benjamin, and Rosalind Bresnahan. "Introduction: Bolivia under Morales: Consolidating Power, Initiating Decolonization." *Latin American Perspectives* 37, no. 3 (May 2010): 5–17.

Lambright, Anne. *Creating the Hybrid Intellectual: Subject, Space, and the Feminine in the Narrative of José María Arguedas*. Lewisburg, PA: Bucknell University Press, 2007.

Lara, Jesús, ed. *Diccionario Qheshwa-Castellano/Castellano-Qheshwa*. Quinta Edición. Cochabamba, Bolivia: Los amigos del libro, 1971.

———. *La literatura de los quechuas*. Cochabamba, Bolivia: Editorial Canelas, 1960.

Lauer, Mirko. *Antologia poesía vanguardista peruana, 1916–1930*. Lima: El Virrey, 2001.

———. *La polémica del vanguardismo 1916–1928*. Lima: Fondo Editorial de la Universidad Nacional Mayor de San Marcos, 2001.

Legrás, Horacio. *Literature and Subjection: The Economy of Writing and Marginality in Latin America*. Pittsburgh: University of Pittsburgh Press, 2008.

Lennard, Natasha, and Cary Wolfe. "Is Humanism Really Humane?" *New York Times*, January 9, 2017. https://www.nytimes.com/2017/01/09/opinion/is-humanism-really-humane.html (accessed March 26, 2018).

Levin, David Michael. *The Opening of Vision: Nihilism and the Postmodern Situation*. New York: Routledge, 1988.

Lienhard, Martín. "La 'andinización' del vanguardismo urbano." In *El zorro de arriba y el zorro de abajo*, edited by Eve-Marie Fell, 321–332. 2nd ed, Edición Crítica. Paris: ALLCA XX, 1996.

López-Calvo, Ignacio. "El fluir de conciencia en César Vallejo." *Confluencia* 14, no. 1 (Fall 1998): 82–86.

Lorde, Audre. *Sister Outsider: Essays and Speeches*. Berkeley, CA: Crossing Press, 2007.

Los Tiempos, gen. ed. "Bolivia: Violencia contra mujeres, el más alto de la región." *Los Tiempos*. November 23, 2013. http://www.lostiempos.com/actualidad/nacional/20131123/bolivia-violencia-contra-mujeres-mas-alto-region (accessed July 23, 2014).

Lugones, María. "Heterosexualism and the Colonial/Modern Gender System." *Hypatia* 22, no. 1 (2007): 186–209.

———. "Toward a Decolonial Feminism." *Hypatia* 25, no. 4 (2010): 742–759.

Maldonado-Torres, Nelson. "Césaire's Gift and the Decolonial Turn." *Radical Philosophy Review* 9, no. 2 (2006): 111–138.

Marcone, Jorge. "Latin American Literature at the Rise of Environmentalism: Urban Ecological Thinking in José María Arguedas's *The Foxes*." *Comparative Literature Studies* 50, no. 1 (November 2013): 64–86.

Mariátegui, José Carlos. "Presentación de *Amauta*." Edited by José Carlos Mariátegui, Ricardo Martinez de Torre, and Alberto Tauro. *Amauta* 1, no 1. (1926): 1.

———. *7 [i.e. Siete] ensayos de interpretación de la realidad peruana*. Havana: Casa de las Américas, 1969.

———. *Siete ensayos de la interpretación de la realidad peruana*. Mexico City: Ediciones Era, 1971.

Mauro, Evan. "The Death and Life of the Avant-Garde: Or, Modernism and Biopolitics." *Mediations* 26, nos. 1–2 (Fall 2012–Spring 2013): 119–142. http://www.mediationsjournal.org/articles/the-death-and-life-of-the-avant-garde (accessed July 2016).

Mauss, Marcel. *The Gift: The Form and Reason for Exchange in Archaic Societies*. New York and London: W. W. Norton, 2000.

Medina, Javier. "Acerca del Suma Qamaña." In *Vivir bien: ¿Paradigma no capitalista?*, edited by Ivonne Farah H. and Luciano Vasapollo, 39–64. La Paz, Bolivia: CIDEM-UMSA, 2011.

———. *Suma Qamaña: Por una convivialidad postindustrial*. La Paz, Bolivia: Garza Azul Editores, 2006.

Mignolo, Walter. *The Darker Side of the Renaissance: Literacy, Territoriality, and Colonization*. Ann Arbor: University of Michigan Press, 1995.

Miller, Nicola. "To Interpret the World or to Change It: César Vallejo and the Role of the Intellectual." *Romance Quarterly* 49, no. 3 (Summer 2002): 174–191.

Monasterios Pérez, Elizabeth. "Introducción." In *No pudieron con nostotras: El desafío del feminismo autónomo de Mujeres Creando*, 17–26. Pittsburgh and La Paz, Bolivia: Plural editores, 2006.

———. "Poéticas del conflicto andino." *Revista Iberoamericana* 73, no. 220 (2007): 541–561.

———. *Vanguardia plebeya del Titikaka: Gamaliel Churata y otras beligerancias estéticas en los Andes*. La Paz, Bolivia: Editorial Plural, 2015.

Moore, Melisa. *José Carlos Mariátegui's Unfinished Revolution: Politics, Poetics, and Change in 1920s Peru*. Lewisburg, PA: Bucknell University Press, 2014.

———. "Politics, Poetics and Female Presence in the Avant-Garde in Peru." *Journal of Iberian and Latin American Studies* 12, no. 1 (2006): 1–14.

Moran, Dominic. "'The Word and the Herd': Poeticizing the Animal and Animalizing the Poetic in César Vallejo." *Romance Quarterly* 49, no. 3 (Summer 2002): 162–173.

Moraña, Mabel. *Churata postcolonial*. Lima: Latinoamericana Editores, 2015.

———. "La cuestión del humanismo: puntos ciegos y líneas de fuga." *Inscripciones críticas* (2014): 183–212.

Moreiras, Alberto. "The End of Magical Realism: José María Arguedas's Passionate Signifier." In *The Exhaustion of Difference: The Politics of Latin American Cultural*

Studies, edited by Alberto Moreiras, 184–207. Durham, NC: Duke University Press, 2001.

Mujeres Creando (Bolivia). *La virgen de los deseos*. Buenos Aires: Tinta Limón, 2005.

———. ed. *Porque la memoria no es puro cuento*. La Paz, Bolivia: Mujeres Creando, 2002.

Mullarkey, John. *Bergson and Philosophy*. Notre Dame, IN: University of Notre Dame Press, 2000.

———. "Life, Movement, and the Theory of the Event." *Theory, Culture, & Society* 24, no. 6 (2007): 53–70.

Muñoz, José Esteban. *Cruising Utopia: The Then and There of Queer Futurity*. London and New York: New York University Press, 2009.

Noland, Carrie. *Agency and Embodiment: Performing Gestures/Producing Culture*. Cambridge, MA: Harvard University Press, 2009.

Norton, Kim M. "A Brief History of Prosthetics." *Amputee Coalition* 17, no. 7 (2007): 1–11, https://www.amputee-coalition.org/resources/a-brief-history-of-prosthetics/ (March 25, 2018).

Nugent, David. *Locating Capitalism in Time and Space: Global Restructurings, Politics, and Identity*. Stanford, CA: Stanford University Press, 2002.

Orrego, Antenor. *Mi encuentro con César Vallejo*. Bogotá, Colombia: Tercer Mundo Editores, 1989.

———. "Palabras prologales." In *Trilce*, by César Vallejo. Lima: Talleres Tipográficos de la Penitenciaría, 1922.

———. *Pueblo Continente: Ensayos para una interpretación de la América Latina*. Santiago: Ediciones Ercilla, 1939.

———. "¿Qué es una filosofía?" *Amauta* 27 (November–December 1929): 1–3.

Ortega, Julio. *César Vallejo: La escritura del devenir*. Lima: Taurus, 2014.

———. "Introducción." In *Trilce*, by César Vallejo, 1–17. Madrid: Cátedra, 1991.

———. *La teoría poética de César Vallejo*. Providence, RI: Del Sol, 1986.

———. "Vallejo: Una poética de la tachadura." *Ínsula* 777 (September 2011): 16–19.

Ortega y Gasset, José. *La deshumanizacón del arte y otros ensayos de estética*. Madrid: Revista de Occidente en Alianza Editorial, 2006.

Pachacuti, Santacruz. *Relación de anigüedades deste reyno del Peru; estudio etnohistórico lingüístico* (c. 1613). Edited by Pierre Duviols and César Itier. Lima: Institut francais d'études andines, 2014. http://books.openedition.org/ifea/2333 (accessed April 1, 2018).

Pak, Jennifer. "Chinese Buy Up Bottles of Fresh Air from Canada." *Telegraph*, December 15, 2015. https://www.telegraph.co.uk/news/worldnews/asia/china/12051354/Chinese-buy-up-bottles-of-fresh-air-from-Canada.html (accessed March 1, 2018).

Paredes, Julieta. *Con un montón de palabras*. La Paz, Bolivia: Ediciones Mujeres Creando, 2000.

———. *Hilando fino: Desde el feminismo comunitario*. La Paz, Bolivia: CEDEC, 2008.

———. *Hilando fino: Perspectives from Communitarian Feminism*. Translated by Margaret Cerullo and Antonia Carcelén. La Paz, Bolivia: Comunidad Mujeres Creando Comunidad, 2015.

———. "Mirando el signo." In *Memoria: Diálogos sobre escritura y mujeres*. La Paz, Bolivia: 2008.

———. "Nuestro nombre está prohibido." *La razón*, July 14, 2013. La Paz: Bolivia. http://www.la-razon.com/opinion/columnistas/nombre-prohibido_0_1869413062.html (March 25, 2018).

———. "Para que el sol vuelva a calentar." In *No pudieron con nosotras*, edited by Elizabeth Monasterios, 61–96. La Paz, Bolivia: Plural, 2006.

Pearson, Marlys, and Paul R. Mullins. "Domesticating Barbie: An Archaeology of Barbie Material Culture and Domestic Ideology." *International Journal of Historical Archaeology* 3, no. 4 (December 1999): 225–259.

Peralta, Alejandro. *Ande; El Kollao.* Edited by Luis F. Chueca and Domingo Patigoso. Lima: Pontificia Universidad Católica del Perú, 2006.

Peralta, Antero. "El uno y vario del arte vanguardista." *Chirapu*, Arequipa 1, no. 2 (1928): 2.

Pérez, Wilma. "La mujer boliviana enfrenta 16 tipos de situaciones de violencia." *La Razón*. November 24, 2013. http://www.la-razon.com/index.php?_url=/sociedad/mujer-boliviana enfrenta-situaciones-violencia_0_1948605213.html (accessed July 29, 2014).

Pizarnik, Alejandra. *Obras completas*. Edited by Cristina Piña. Buenos Aires: Corregidor, 1993.

Poggioli, Renato. *The Theory of the Avant-Garde.* Translated by Gerald Fitzgerald. Cambridge, MA: Harvard University Press, 1968.

Political Database of the Americas (PDBA). Edmund A. Walsh School of Foreign Service, Georgetown University. http:/pdba.georgetown.edu/Constitutions/constudies.html (accessed March 12, 2018).

Pollock, Griselda. "Moments and Temporalities of the Avant-Garde 'in, of, and from the feminine.'" *New Literary History* 41, no. 4 (Autumn 2010): 795–820.

Poole, Deborah. *Vision, Race, and Modernity: A Visual Economy of the Andean Image World.* Princeton, NJ: Princeton University Press, 1997.

Portal, Magda. "Andamios de vida." Edited by José Carlos Mariátegui. *Amauta* 5 (1927): 12.

———. *Constancia del ser.* Lima: Taller Gráfica Villanueva, 1965.

———. *Costa sur.* Santiago, Chile: Imprenta Nueva, 1945.

———. *El Aprismo y la mujer.* Lima: Editorial cooperativa aprista "Atahualpa," 1933.

———. *El nuevo poema i su orientación hacia una estética económica.* Mexico City: Ediciones APRA, 1928.

———. *Flora Tristán, Precursora.* Lima: Editorial La Equidad, 1983.

———. *La Trampa.* Lima: Editorial Poma, 1982.

———. "Nicolás Guillén, Poeta de Cuba." *Cuadernos americanos* 197 (1974): 234–244.

———. *Obra poética completa.* Edited and Introduction by Daniel R. Reedy. Lima: Fondo de Cultura Económica, 2010.

———. "Réplica." Edited by José Carlos Mariátegui. *Amauta* 7 (1927): 80–81.

Portugal, José Alberto. *Las novelas de José María Arguedas: Una incursión en lo inarticulado.* Lima: Fondo Editorial Peruano, 2007.

Prada, Ana Rebeca. "La marca de Mujeres Creando en la piel de la urbe paceña: Trabajo en curso a partir de diversas voces y criterios." In *No pudieron con nostotras*, edited by Elizabeth Monasterios, 97–131. La Paz, Bolivia: Plural, 2006.

Preciado, Beatriz. "Cuerpo impropio. Guía de modelos somatopolíticos y de sus posibles usos desviados. November 2–4, 2011. http://ayp.unia.es/index.php?option=com_content&task=view&id=678&Itemid=93 (accessed July 27, 2014).

———. Interview "Pienso, luego existo." Madrid: TVE. August 12, 2013. http://www.rtve.es/alacarta/videos/pienso-luego-existo/pienso-luego-existo-beatriz-preciado/1986547/ (accessed April 1, 2018).

———. *Manifiesto contrasexual.* Translated by Julio Díaz and Carolina Meloni. Barcelona: Anagrama, 2002, 2011.

Premat, Julio. "Los relatos de la vanguardia o el retorno de lo nuevo." *Cuadernos de literatura* 17, no. 34 (July–December 2013): 47–64.

———. "Los tiempos insólitos de Mario Bellatin: Notas sobre *El Gran vidrio* y las radicalidades actuales." In *Un asombro renovado: Vanguardias contemporáneas en América Latina*, edited by Matthew Bush and Luis Hernán Castañeda, 149–172. Madrid: Iberoamericana; Frankfurt am Main: Vervuert, 2017.

Prieto, Julio. *La escritura errante: Ilegibilidad y políticas del estilo en Latinoamérica.* Madrid: Iberoamericana, 2016.

Quijano, Aníbal. "Colonialidad del poder, eurocentrismo y América Latina." In *La colonialidad del saber: Eurocentrismo y ciencias sociales. perspectivas latinoamericanas*, edited by Edgardo Lander, 201–246. Buenos Aires: CLACSO, Consejo Latinoamericano de Ciencias Sociales, 2001.

———. "Coloniality and Modernity/Rationality." *Cultural Studies* 21, nos. 2–3 (Spring 2007): 168–178.

———. "Coloniality of Power, Eurocentrism, and Latin America." *Nepantla: Views from South* 1, no. 3 (2000): 533–580.

Rada, Rodrigo. *Arteria: Arte de performance en las calles del centro de la ciudad de La Paz.* October 22, 2010. http://cimientosperformance.blogspot.com/2010/10/5.html?q=arteria (accessed July 27, 2014).

Rama, Ángel. *La ciudad letrada.* Prologue by Hugo Achugar. Montevideo, Uruguay: ARCA Press. 1998.

———. *Transculturación narrativa en América Latina.* México DF: Siglo Veintiuno Editores, 1982.

Ramos, Juan G. "Disruptive Capital in Andean/World Literature: A Decolonial Reading of Enrique Gil Gilbert's *Nuestro Pan*." In *Decolonial Approaches to Latin American Literatures and Cultures*, edited by Juan G. Ramos and Tara Daly, 141–160. New York: Palgrave Macmillan, 2016.

Rancière, Jacques. *The Politics of Aesthetics: The Distribution of the Sensible.* London: Continuum, 2004.

Redacción Central, "1.500 personas en Bolivia se declaran no heterosexuales." *Los Tiempos.* July 20, 2011. http://www.lostiempos.com/actualidad/local/20110720/1500-personas-bolivia-se-declaran-no-heterosexuales (accessed March 13, 2018).

Reedy, Daniel R. "Magda Portal." In *Spanish American Women Writers: A Bio-Bibliographical Source Book*, edited by Diane E. Marting, 483–492. New York: Greenwood Press, 1990.

———. *Magda Portal, la pasionaria peruana: Biografía intelectual.* Lima: Ediciones Flora Tristán, 2000.

Rivera Cusicanqui, Silvia. "Chhixinakax utwixa. Una reflexión sobre prácticas y discursos descolonizadores." In *Modernidad y pensamiento descolonizador: Memoria del Seminario Internacional*, compiled by Mario Yapu, 3–16. La Paz, Bolivia: Universidad para la Investigación Estratégica en Bolivia (U-PIEB), 2006.

———. "La noción de "derecho" o las paradojas de la modernidad postcolonial: Indígenas y mujeres en Bolivia." *Revista aportes andinos* 11 (2004): 1–15.

Rochabrún S., Guillermo. "El Árbol, el injerto, el nudo: Entrevista a Guillermo Rochabrún." In *¿He vivido en vano?* La mesa redonda sobre *Todas las sangres*, edited by Guillermo Rochabrún, 118–127. Lima: IEP Fondo Editorial de la Pontificia Universidad Católica del Perú, 2011.

———. *¿He vivido en vano? La mesa redonda sobre Todas las sangres.* Lima: IEP Fondo Editorial de la Pontificia Universidad Católica del Perú, 2011.

Rojas Benavente, Lady. "Magda Portal Moreno en el debate de los géneros 1920 a 1930." In *La mujer en la literatura del mundo hispánico*, edited by Juana Alcira Arancibia, Rosa Tezanos-Pinto, 95–104. Westminster, CA: Instituto Literario y Cultural Hispánico, 2009.

Rosenberg, Fernando J. *The Avant-Garde and Geopolitics in Latin America.* Pittsburgh, PA: University of Pittsburgh Press, 2006.

Rowe, William. *Ensayos vallejianos.* Lima: Latinoamericana editores, 2006.

———. *Hacia una poética radical: Ensayos de hermenéutica cultural.* México DF: Fondo de Cultura Económica, 2014.

———. *Mito e ideología en la obra de José María Arguedas.* Lima: Instituto nacional de cultura, 1979.

Sandoval, Ciro A. "*El Sexto* de José María Arguedas: Espacio entrópico de hervores metatestimoniales." *Revista Iberomericana* 63, no. 181 (October–December 1997): 697–709.

———. "Vuelta a *El Sexto* de José María Arguedas." In *José María Arguedas: Hacia una poética migrante*, 247–266. Pittsburgh, PA: University of Pittsburgh Press, 2006.

Sanjinés C., Javier. *Embers of the Past: Essays in Times of Decolonization.* Durham, NC: Duke University Press, 2013.

———. *Literatura contemporánea y grotesco social en Bolivia.* La Paz, Bolivia: Instituto Latinoamericano de Investigaciones Sociales, 1992.

———. *Mestizaje Upside-Down: Aesthetic Politics in Modern Bolivia.* Pittsburgh, PA: University of Pittsburgh Press, 2004.

Schavelzon, Salvador. *Plurinacionalidad y Vivir Bien/Buen Vivir: Dos conceptos leídos desde Bolivia y Ecuador post-constituyentes.* Quito, Ecuador: Abya-Yala; Buenos Aires: CLACSO: 2015.

Schiwy, Freya. "Decolonization and the Question of Subjectivity." *Cultural Studies* 21, nos. 2–3 (March 2007): 271–294.

Schrift, Alan D., ed. *The Logic of the Gift: Toward an Ethic of Generosity.* New York: Routledge, 1997.

Serres, Michel, and Bruno Latour. *Conversations on Science, Culture, and Time.* Translated by Roxanne Lapidus. Ann Arbor: University of Michigan Press, 2011.

Silverblatt, Irene. *Moon, Sun, and Witches: Gender Ideologies and Class in Inca and Colonial Peru.* Princeton, NJ: Princeton University Press, 1987.

Spivak, Gayatri. "Can the Subaltern Speak?" In *Marxism and the Interpretation of Culture*, edited by Cary Nelson and Lawrence Grossberg, 271–313. Urbana: University of Illinois Press, 1988.

Suleiman, Susan Rubin. *Subversive Intent: Gender, Politics and the Avant-Garde.* Cambridge, MA: Harvard University Press, 2012.

Tapia, Luis. *La invención del núcleo común.* La Paz, Bolivia: Muela del diablo, 2006.

———. *La transformación pluralista del estado*, by Alvaro García Linera, Luis Tapia Mealla, Raúl Prada Alcoreza. La Paz: Muela del Diablo, 2007.

Tarica, Estelle. *Intimate Indigenismo: The Inner Life of Mestizo Nationalism.* Minneapolis: University of Minnesota Press, 2008.

Temperman, Jeroen. *State–Religion Relationships and Human Rights Law: Towards a Right to Religiously Neutral Governance.* Leiden, Netherlands: Brill, 2010.

Torres, Stephen. "Marxismo y performatividad en 'Parado en una piedra . . .' de César Vallejo: Desempleo, reificación y conciencia de clase." *Letr@s hispanas* 7 (2010): 147–164.

Unruh, Vicky. *Latin American Vanguards: The Art of Contentious Encounters.* Berkeley: University of California Press, 1994.

———. *Performing Women and Modern Literary Culture in Latin America: Intervening Acts.* Austin: University of Texas Press, 2006.

Valcárcel, Gustavo. "Magda Portal, la poeta de los pobres ha muerto." *República*, July 12, 1989, 8.

Valero Juan, Eva María. "De Micaela Bastidas a Magda Portal: Recuperaciones críticoliterarias de las Independistas de Perú." *América sin nombre* 13–14 (2009): 64–72.

Vallega, Alejandro A. "Displacements–Beyond the Coloniality of Images." *Research in Phenomenology* 41 (2011): 206–227.

Vallejo, César. *Artículos y crónicas completos.* Edited by Febres S. Lerner and Jorge Puccinelli. 2 vols. Lima: Pontificia Universidad Católica del Perú, 2002.

———. *Ensayos y reportajes completos.* Edited by Manuel Miguel de Priego. Lima: Pontificia Universidad Católica del Perú, 2002.

———. *Obras completas / The Complete Poetry: A Bilingual Edition.* Translation, introduction, and notes by Clayton Eshleman. Berkeley: University of California Press, 2008.

———. *Poemas en prosa; Poemas humanos; Esapña, aparta de mí este cáliz.* Edited by Julio Veléz. Madrid: Cátedra, 1991.

———. *Teatro completo.* Vol. 2, *Piedra cansada.* Edited by Enrique Ballón Aguirre. Lima: Pontificia Universidad Católica del Perú, Fondo Editorial, 1979.

———. *Trilce.* Edited by Julio Ortega. Madrid: Cátedra, 1991.

Viezzer, Moema. *Si me permiten hablar: Testimonio de Domitila, una mujer de las minas de Bolivia.* Mexico City: Siglo veintiuno editores, 1977.

Viveiros de Castro, Eduardo. "Cosmological Deixis and Amerindian Perspectivism." *Journal of the Royal Anthropological Institute* 4, no. 3 (September 1998): 469–488.

von Buelow, Christiane. "Vallejo's Venus de Milo and the Ruins of Language." *PMLA* 104, no. 1 (January 1989): 41–52.

Walker, Charles F. *The Túpac Amaru Rebellion.* Cambridge, MA: Belknap Harvard, 2016.

Weaver, Kathleen. *Peruvian Rebel: The World of Magda Portal, with a Selection of her Poems.* University Park: Pennsylvania State University Press, 2009.

Westphalen, Emilio Adolfo. *La poesía, los poemas, los poetas.* Mexico City: Universidad Iberoamericana, 1995.

———. "La sustancia de la vida y la obra literaria." *Recopilación de textos sobre José María Arguedas* (1976): 349–352.

Wolfe, Cary. *What Is Posthumanism?* Minneapolis: University of Minnesota Press, 2010.

Yúdice, George. "Rethinking the Theory of the Avant-Garde from the Periphery." In *Modernism and Its Margins: Reinscribing Cultural Modernity from Spain and Latin America*, edited by Anthony L. Geist and José B. Monleón, 52–81. New York and London: Taylor and Francis, 1999.

Zulén, Pedro. *La filosofía de lo inexpresable: Bosquejo de una interpretación y una crítica de la filosofía de Bergson.* Lima: Talleres tipográficos de Sanmarti y Cia, 1920.

Index

About the Author

TARA DALY is an assistant professor of Spanish at Marquette University, and the coeditor of *Decolonial Approaches to Latin American Literatures and Cultures*.